SAVANNAH
DUELS AND DUELLISTS

1733-1877

BY

Thomas Gamble

Reprinted 1997

The Oglethorpe Press, Inc.
326 Bull Street
Savannah, Georgia
31401

1-891495-01-1

Gamble, Thomas

Savannah Duels and Duellists
1733-1877

1. Duels - Savannah - Georgia - 18th century

2. Duels - Savannah - Georgia - 19th century

3. History - Savannah - Georgia

FOREWORD

We look back on the customs and standards and ideals of the men of former generations with critical eyes, sometimes with amusement twinkling therein, all too frequently with condemnation wrinkled on our faces. The quickly passing years have made it most difficult to put ourselves in their places, to understand their surroundings, the social atmosphere in which they lived, to visualize the spirit of their times. Perhaps it would be better, before we criticise, if in all humility we studied the customs and standards and ideals of to-day, and asked ourselves, what will future generations think and say of them and of us?

It is not necessary to endorse duelling to emphasize that in some of the cardinal elements of high manhood the forefathers of Savannah, who believed in and fought duels, do not suffer by comparison with their progeny of the present. They need no apologist. They were made virile—and sometimes bitter—men, by the severe trials and tribulations they unflinchingly faced and overcame. They had strong virtues, and what to us may seem equally pronounced weaknesses. They transmitted to their posterity the best of their traits, and the sterling character of many later Georgians may be traced to the qualities inherited from these men who, sword, or pistol, or rifle, in hand, faced each other complacently on the "Field of Honor."

There is no use in wrapping the notables of early Savannah, shadowy silhouettes though they have become, in what has been so aptly termed "The rosy halo of a vanished past." They were very human, disinclined to veneer their dislikes and hatreds, quick to open the gates for a full flood of vehement passion when their bitterness against others was stirred. Some of them, like Jackson and McIntosh and Charlton and Troup, were almost volcanic in their outbursts, at times almost eager to find or create an occasion to vent their splenetic feelings. If they lived today they would chafe under the more restrained and more orderly procedures of an artificial society further removed from the natural outlets for personal grievances and enmities.

Their calendar of mortal sins was headed by ingratitude and treachery as the basest and least forgivable. Once aroused they seemingly saw little that was good in an opponent. They were the fruit of the period in which they lived, an era of turbulence, of disregard of life, a day when their little world was "Turned upside down," the hours of the travail of a new nation born through force of arms. Savannah and Georgia needed such men as leaders. Conditions demanded them. It was no time for those of sluggish temperament, for the pacifist, for those who shrank from violence and bloodshed. They were the political pioneers of a new commonwealth, and successful pioneers have always been men of their type. They not only wrested the State from the control of the British, but they likewise wrested it from those of a reactionary trend and planted it firmly on the highways of democracy as Georgians know it today.

T. G.

v

CONTENTS

ILLUSTRATIONS

CORRECTIONS AND ADDITIONS

Page 61, line 18, read "Gibbons vs. Ogden," instead of "Ogden vs. Gibbons." This noted case was first incorrectly docketed in 1820 as "Aaron Ogden vs. Thomas Gibbons." Dismissed by the Supreme Court in 1821 because of defective record, it was docketed again in 1822, this time under the corrected title of "Thomas Gibbons vs. Aaron Ogden."

Page 63, line 28, read "Pinkney, of Maryland," instead of "Pinckney, of South Carolina."

Page 195, above sixteenth line from bottom, insert line, "County. Colonels Alston and Hayne, of South Carolina."

Page 132, difficulty between Francis H. Welman and John Moorhead. Welman published a card stating that the senior and junior officers of the military company of which Moorhead was a lieutenant had reflected upon the conduct of Moorhead. David Taylor, Jr., as captain of the company, stated that this was incorrect. Welman charged that when referred to as a "spy and traitor," Lieut. Moorhead had failed to promptly resent the insult. At the request of Lieut. Moorhead, a Board of Commissioned Officers of the Sixteenth Battalion met to "enquire into the charges reflecting on his character as an honorable soldier." The Board reported that "in the most patient, solemn and deliberate manner" it had enquired into the "validity of the charges" and that "nothing can be found derogatory" to Moorhead's "spirit as a soldier," and that "if he had understood the insult in the manner and shape which report afterwards gave to it, he would immediately have acted under the impulse of an honorable resentment." As to Welman, the Board believed it was through error and want of complete information that he was led to the belief that Moorhead was "not influenced by his own sentiments of honor in demanding satisfaction," and "had not acted until urged to do so by others." The members of this early Board were Ralph May, chairman; Sterling Grimes, secretary; Thomas Stewart, David Taylor, John W. Mendenhall, William Magee, Robert J. Houstoun, A. G. Oemler, Charles Machin, Thomas Telfair, William Gaston. It is evident that a challenge passed, not accepted by Welman, and that then Lieut. Moorhead advertised or posted him. Whether a duel was later fought is not ascertainable.

Page 151, referring to Capt. R. P. Johnson, who slew James Wilde in duel, the records of the Adjutant General's office, War Department, Washington, show that Roswell Post Johnson served as first lieutenant and as captain in the 8th U. S. Infantry within the period of the war of 1812, but neither the date of his appointment nor the date of his separation from the service has been found. His name appears upon various records from July 6, 1813, to April 30, 1815, at which latter date he was reported absent with leave at Savannah. In a letter dated Georgetown, June 5, 1815, addressed to the Secretary of War, he states that he was appointed a first lieutenant on March 12, 1812, and expresses a desire to be retained in the peace establishment of the Army. "Heitman's Historical Register and Dictionary of the United States Army, 1789-1903," an unofficial publication entitled to credit, shows "Johnson, Roswell Post, S. C., 1st Lt. 8th Inf. 12 March, 1812; Capt. 13 Feb. 1814; honorably discharged 15 June, 1815."

CHAPTER I.

Duelling in Colonial Days

THE CODE CAME TO GEORGIA WITH THE FIRST SETTLERS
—FATAL MEETINGS TOO COMMON AMONG OGLE-
THORPE'S OFFICERS—OGLETHORPE ASSERTED A
MAN'S RIGHT TO DEFEND HIS HONOR—THE MEMOR-
ABLE DINNER AT OGLETHORPE'S LONDON HOME.

DUELLING came into Georgia with the first settlers
from England as an accepted element of the social
code. Among the army men who soon came to its shores
were unquestionably those who had participated in duels
either as principals or seconds. It was an age when few
questioned the propriety of settling personal affairs of honor
at the point of the sword, or with bullets from a brace of
pistols.

When the first duel occurred in the colony cannot be
definitely stated, but Stephens in his Journal settles beyond
dispute that Georgia was but an infant when recourse was
had to the code with fatal results. In that most interesting of diaries appears this early item:

"Thursday, June 12, 1740. This Day began with the
melancholy News of more Duelling at the Camp in the
South, and the fatal Consequences of it. Ensign Tolson, of
Capt. Norbury's Company, having a Quarrel with Mr. Eyles,
a Surgeon in the Army, they fought; and the latter was
killed on the spot; a Man of very good skill in his Profession,
and well esteemed; Not many Days after Peter Grant, lately
of this Town, and a Freeholder, afterwards made Naval
Officer at Frederica by the General, and since changing to
be a Cadet in the Army; having a Quarrel with one Mr.
Shenton, a Cadet likewise; which Mr. Shenton endeavoured
(as far as he well could) to avoid deciding by the Sword;
but the other admitting of no Terms of Reconciliation, they
fought, and the Aggressor dropt dead.

"These Tidings came by a small Boat on its Way from the Camp to Charles Town. It is not very long since (December, 1739) Ensign Leman, in a Rencounter (with Sutherland, another ensign) being wounded in his leg, and a Mortification ensuing he was forced to suffer an Amputation, and supply its Place with a wooden one. Surely our Enemies will hear this with pleasure."

Peter Grant, one of the earliest freeholders in Savannah, seems to be entitled to the honor of having been the first citizen to be killed in a duel in Georgia.

The possibility of the Spaniards rejoicing over these signs of internal strife could not keep the swords of angry, half-drunken disputants, within their scabbards. Wine and beer were furnished in abundance at the camps and heated brains were quick to resent affronts. A few months later two of the officers at St. Simon's fell out at a dinner party. Attempts to pacify and smooth the ruffled feelings of wounded honor and reconcile them to one another were of no avail. They met and one was slain. This was in May, 1741. Stephens tells of it briefly:

"In the evening arrived the long look'd for Captain Thompson from St. Simon's, who spent an Hour or two with Mr. Jones and me. One Piece of ill News we now learnt, that in a Duel betwixt Captains Norbury and Desbrisay the former was killed on the Spot."

Fortunately a more detailed statement of this affair was published in the South Carolina Gazette, complete files of which are in the keeping of the Charleston Library. In its issue of June 25, 1741, I found this extract from a letter from Frederica, dated May 16, 1741:

"Capt. Richard Norbury, Capt. Albert Desbrisay and several other of General Oglethorpe's officers dined together at St. Simon's Camp on Sunday, the 10th of this month; there arose a Dispute between Capt. Norbury and Capt. Desbrisay; the other Gentlemen interposed and in appearance reconcil'd the two captains and they drank several Glasses of Wine together (after the Dispute in a friendly Way); soon after, the Company broke up, and went different ways; but unfortunately Capt. Norbury and Capt. Desbrisay met, upon which a fresh Dispute arose, they drew their Swords, and before any Body had Time to part them, Capt. Norbury received Three Wounds, one in his Belly, the other two in his Arms; he died on the Spot. Capt. Desbrisay receiv'd Three Wounds, he was run through one Thigh, wounded in the other, and in his left Hand."

Captain Desbrisay was soon after appointed by Oglethorpe to command a privateer. He was a brave officer, figuring in the capture of Fort St. Francis from the Spaniards in 1740. In the retreat of the English from the unfortunate expedition against St. Augustine that year he was one of the officers who headed the little force which drove the Spaniards within their works when they sallied out to attack the retiring English.

More references to this duel are found in the Journal of the Earl of Egmont, under date of June 29, 1741:

"Col. Oglethorpe wrote to the Trustees concerning the Tryal of Capt. Desbrisey for killing Capt. Norbury in duel; that he was brought in Manslaughter, but the widow intended to appeal into England for a new Tryal; whereas all the Colonys try finally in criminal causes."

And under date of October 2, 1741:

"Accts of the Court proceedings relating to Capt. Norbury's being kill'd in a duel by Capt. Desbrisay 11 May, which last was brought in Manslaughter."

From William Bowler, surgeon, who had returned to England, the Earl had the statement that "Capt. Norbury was a quarrelsome, drunken officer". Inasmuch as Oglethorpe had Norbury with him as his aide on a visit of importance to Charleston this statement by Bowler may be assigned to the ill feeling all too early engendered among the colonists and soldiers alike. Georgia, and particularly Savannah, was very far from being the abiding place of the dove of peace and brotherly love at that time. Norbury, though, in 1739, had been required by a Court Martial to beg the pardon of Lt. Col. Cochrane for disrespectful language toward him.

England had laws against duelling, but they were in the main ignored. Army and navy men were especially immune from prosecution.   That Capt. Desbrisay suffered beyond the inconvenience and humiliation of a trial is doubtful.   The colonial records throw no further light on the case but it is reasonable to assume he escaped imprisonment even though the verdict of manslaughter was returned.   The jury's finding may have been the result of a desire to check the too frequent duels at the camps and the consequent antagonisms among the officers at a time when the Spaniards were threatening the very existence of the colony.   There is no evidence that Oglethorpe himself dealt at all harshly with his officers who resorted to the code to settle their difficulties.

Did Oglethorpe ever fight a duel?   There is no record that he did, yet that is not conclusive proof that he did not. His views were pronouncedly in favor of the code.   To Georgians there is no incident in Boswell's life of Dr. Samuel Johnson that is so full of interest in every line and word as that in which the founder of Georgia expressed himself on this subject.   Boswell served the very useful purpose of introducing topics of conversation.   On this memorable occasion he "started the question whether duelling was consistent with moral duty."   This was on Friday, April 10, 1772, when the great lexicographer dined at Oglethorpe's London home with Oliver Goldsmith and Boswell as the other guests.   Oglethorpe was then in his 76th year, but still full of animation.

"The brave old General fired at this," wrote "Bossy," "and said with a lofty air:

" 'Undoubtedly a man has a right to defend his honor.' "

Goldsmith turned to Boswell: "I ask you, sir, what would you do if you were affronted."

"I answered I should think it necessary to fight."

"Why, then," replied Goldsmith, "that solves the question."

Dr. Johnson was accustomed to delving deeper in their topics than that.   At once he began moralizing.

"No, Sir, it does not solve the question," said he.   "It does not follow that what a man should do is, therefore, right."

Boswell wished to "have it settled whether duelling was contrary to the laws of Christianity." "Johnson immediately entered on the subject," says his biographer, "and treated it in a masterly manner; and so far as I have been able to recollect, his thoughts were these:

" 'Sir, as men become in a high degree refined, various causes of offence arise, which are considered to be of such importance that life must be staked to atone for them, though in reality they are not so. A body that has received a very fine polish may be easily hurt. Before men arrive at this artificial refinement, if one tells his neighbor 'he lies,' his neighbor tells him 'he lies'; if one gives his neighbor a blow, his neighbor gives him a blow; but in a state of highly polished society, an affront is held to be a serious injury. It must, therefore, be resented, or rather a duel must be fought upon it; as men have agreed to banish from their society one who puts up with an affront without fighting a duel. Now, Sir, it is never unlawful to fight in self defence. He, then, who fights a duel, does not fight from passion against his antagonist, but out of self defence; to avert the stigma of the world; and to prevent himself from being driven out of society. I could wish there was not that superfluity of refinement; but while such notions prevail no doubt a man may lawfully fight a duel."

And Boswell added as his interpretation of this: "Let it be remembered, that this justification is applicable only to the person who received an affront. All mankind must condemn the aggressor." Fifty years later Boswell's own son and heir, Sir Alexander Boswell, died from a bullet wound received in a duel resulting from "political squibs he had written imputing cowardice to another Scotch gentleman."

General Oglethorpe, sitting back in his easy chair, had no doubt followed with interest the learned doctor's remarks. Perhaps his mind went hastily back through the many years of martial service, from early boyhood to the half-century point of life, for Oglethorpe's active army connection had extended from 1710 to 1746. He recalled the many duels that had come under his own observation, even those which had been fought on St. Simon's Island in that far away

Oglethorpe At the Age of Eighty-eight, the Year Before His Death
"A Man Has the Right to Defend His Honor," Said the
Founder of Georgia to Dr. Samuel Johnson

Georgia, when his own officers had taken each other's lives despite the fewness of their numbers and the nearness of the Spaniards. In those few minutes, while the doctor was rolling out his sentences, many scenes in his eventful life may have flashed from memory's inexhaustible picture gallery, and from among them all he selected one to show how he himself had met an affront that called for a challenge except for the high rank of the aggressor. And to Boswell all Georgians are indebted for that particularly delightful glimpse of the gallant Oglethorpe in this first flush of approaching manhood:

"The General told us that, when he was a very young man, I think only fifteen, serving under Prince Eugene of Savoy, he was sitting in company at table with a Prince of Wirtemberg. The Prince took up a glass of wine and, by a fillip, made some of it fly in Oglethorpe's face.

"Here was a nice dilemma. To have challenged him instantly might have fixed a quarrelsome character upon the young soldier; to have taken no notice of it, might have been considered as cowardice.

"Oglethorpe, therefore, keeping his eye upon the Prince, and smiling all the time, as if he took what his Highness had done in jest, said: 'Mon Prince' (I forget the French words he used, the purpose, however, was) 'That's a good joke; but we do it much better in England'; and threw a whole glass of wine in the Prince's face.

"An old General who sat by, said 'Il a bien fait, mon Prince, vous l'avez commence'; and thus all ended in good humor."

And so the talk about duelling closed and Oglethorpe then told them of the famous siege of Belgrade.

Can any one doubt that Oglethorpe stood ready to give a challenge if, in his opinion, the necessity arose, and that no officer under him felt other than "the right to defend his honor" at the point of the sword? For a hundred years after this little dinner party at the old General's home, Georgians held with Dr. Johnson that "A man may shoot the man who invades his character, as he may shoot him who attempts to break into his house."

What a pity some great painter has not seized upon
that scene for a picture of rare historic and literary interest: The venerable founder of Georgia at his ease, the
"hulky, uncouth" Johnson, greatest of English conversation-
alists, his "deep impressive tones" filling the room, "Jupiter-
like to praise or damn", dogmatic and brilliant; Boswell,
paragon of biographers, whose work is at once "a classic
and a companion", and the smiling Goldsmith, poet, novelist, historian, one of the delightful figures of eighteenth
century English literature, saying so little that one recalls
it was said of him, that he "Wrote like an angel and
talked like poor Poll." No wonder Oglethorpe enjoyed his
old age when he could gather about him companions like
these. All praise be unto Boswell, on the sensitive plates of
whose memory were so deeply impressed the utterances of
this and other occasions, to be later chronicled for the en-
joyment of the world for many generations to come.

Other duels, no doubt, came during the colonial period.
It would have been wondrously strange if it had been other-
wise. But in all the musty pages of the Savannah and
Charleston papers of 1740-1775 I found no allusions to them.
Interesting though the colonial newspapers are, they are
signally deficient in the items one seeks for so diligently.

CHAPTER II.

DUELLING DURING THE REVOLUTIONARY PERIOD.

BUTTON GWINNETT, SIGNER OF THE DECLARATION OF
INDEPENDENCE, KILLED BY GEN. LACHLAN McINTOSH
—DUEL BETWEEN COLONEL BAKER AND MAJOR JONES
STOPPED BY THE PLEAS OF GENERAL SCREVEN—
GENERAL HOWE WINGED GENERAL GADSDEN IN THE
EAR AND DREW A SATIRICAL POEM FROM MAJOR
ANDRE—DUEL WITH SABRES BETWEEN LIEUTENANT-
COLONEL McINTOSH AND CAPTAIN ELHOLM.

DURING the revolutionary war there was the usual quota of duels fought in each of the contending armies. In the British army duelling had long been the customary way of finally settling personal disputes that did not yield readily to the mediation of friends. One might think, though, that men fighting together, as the Americans were, for liberty, endangering their lives from day to day for the freedom of their home land, and whose lives, in the event of failure, were apt to be forfeited with their properties, would have been drawn in such close ties of friendship that personal mortal combat between them would have been entirely out of the question. But the sacred cause in which they fought did not lessen their ambitions, nor check their animosities, and instances of personal ill feeling deepening into hatred cropped out in different sections of the country, with resulting appeals to the code. Georgia was no exception to this.

With the British duels we have little to do. Suffice it to say that the very first meeting of this character in this period, in or near Savannah, was between officers on one of His Majesty's ships. The "Georgia Gazette" of January 24, 1776, gave this scant information about it:

"We are informed that on Thursday morning last a duel was fought with pistols, on the island of Cockspur, between the captain of marines on board the Syren and

General Lachlan McIntosh
Who Killed Button Gwinnett, Signer of the Declaration of Independence, in a Duel

Mr. Pennington, first lieutenant of said ship, when the latter was killed."

Outside of a few copies of the "Royal Georgia Gazette" of 1779 and of 1782, on file in the Congressional Library at Washington, there are no Savannah newspapers available from February 7, 1776, until May 8, 1783, when the publication of the "Georgia Gazette" was resumed and the continuous files are available at the Georgia Historical Society. Much of local historical interest in that thrilling period has undoubtedly been lost through the absence of a weekly chronicler, meagre though the news jottings in that day were. Owing to the prominence of the parties involved, some details are at hand of the first important duel of the Revolution between American officers—the meeting between Button Gwinnett, signer of the Declaration of Independence, and Gen. Lachlan McIntosh, one of Georgia's two brigadiers of the Continental line during the seven years' struggle. Of other hostile meetings of Georgia officers there is an utter absence of information with the exception of three instances told of later, the fatal duel between Col. Jackson and Lieut. Gov. Wells, the adjusted differences between Maj. Jones and Col. Baker, and the sanguinary fight between Col. McIntosh and Capt. Elholm.

The duel between McIntosh and Gwinnett was the closing clash between two determined, impetuous, courageous men, both devoted to republican principles, but each also governed by personal impulses and ambitions and little inclined to mediate personal differences when they assumed the nature of a serious affront. Political jealousies lay at the root of their meeting. Button Gwinnett, a merchant first in Bristol, Eng., then in Charleston, S. C., entered the mercantile life of Savannah in 1765. The commercial developments of the port were so unsatisfying that three years later he purchased part of St. Catherine's Island from the Bosomworths and became a planter there, not far from the thriving community of Sunbury, then the promising commercial rival of Savannah. His decision to cast his fortunes with the colonists seems to have been contemporary with the movement against England. He was a delegate from St. John's parish to the Provincial Congress of 1776,

Grave of General Lachlan McIntosh
In Old Christ Church Burying Ground, Now the Colonial Park

and by it was sent as a delegate to the memorable Congress at Philadelphia, where he supported and signed the Declaration of Independence. The same year he became a member of the Georgia Council of Safety, and the following year helped in the framing and passage of the State Constitution of 1777. Jones says he may be regarded as the parent of that instrument.

When President Archibald Bulloch died Gwinnett was promptly elected by the Council of Safety as his successor as President and Commander-in-Chief of Georgia. In two years he had come from the position of a private planter to the highest command in the new commonwealth. On the day of his election the Executive Council passed an order requesting President Gwinnett to march into Florida "with a competent force of militia and volunteers, erect the American standard, and proclaim protection and security of person and property to all who would take the oath of allegiance." The idea prevailed that the inhabitants of Florida only needed the opportunity to revolt and enter the union of colonies to the north.

Prior to this the General Assembly had created Lachlan McIntosh a brigadier-general, to command three battalions of infantry and a squadron of dragoons to serve in the Continental establishment as a brigade. Gwinnett's aspirations to command this brigade were disappointed and therein lay the seeds of the animosity to McIntosh and the subsequent developments. Anxious for military as well as civic honors, Gwinnett in his office as Commander-in-Chief determined to set aside McIntosh and personally lead the forces against Florida. He called the Executive Council together as a council of war, elaborated his plans, sent Col. Baker and his militia forces by land and Col. Elbert with the Continentals by sea, with a rendezvous on the St. John's river. The expedition was a pitiable and disastrous failure. Historian Jones says: "It was conceived in ambition, planned without due caution, and sadly marred in execution."

To add to Gwinnett's humiliation, when the new Assembly gathered to elect the successor to Bulloch, Gwinnett was defeated and Treutlen was elected. It was no more than human for expressions of gratification at this result

Old Home of General McIntosh, Now 110 East Oglethorpe Ave.,
As It Appeared As Late As 1870, When It Was Remodeled

to be emitted by McIntosh. Nor was it at all unnatural that they should quickly reach the ears of Gwinnett and intensify his wounded pride. When it came to him that McIntosh, in addition, in the presence of members of the Executive Council, had denounced him as a scoundrel, Gwinnett's decision was quickly reached. He challenged Gen. McIntosh to immediate mortal combat. The next morning, May 16, 1777, they met, it is believed on the area now occupied by the children's playground to the south of Colonial cemetery. Four paces, or twelve feet apart, they faced each other. Both men were accustomed to fire arms and at that short distance it is not surprising that both fell at the first exchange of shots. Both men were wounded in the thigh. In the morning of May 19th Gwinnett died, while McIntosh was confined for some time as a result of his wound.

Dr. Lyman Hall, who had signed the Declaration of Independence immediately under the name of Gwinnett, and who had been his close friend and supporter, wrote to Roger Sherman, one of the "Signers" from Connecticut, as follows:

"Here it was (in Assembly) that the Genl. called him (as 'tis said) a Scoundrell and lying Rascal—I confess I did not hear the words, not being so nigh the parties. A Duel was the consequence, in which they were placed at 10 or 12 foot Distance. Discharged their Pistols nearly at the same Time. Each wounded in the Thigh. Mr. Gwinnett's thigh broke so that he fell—on wh'h ('tis said) the Genl. Asked him if he chose to take another shot—was Answered Yes, if they would help him up (or words nearly the same). The seconds interposed.

"Mr. Gwinnett was brought in, the Weather Extremely hot. A Mortification came on—he languish'd from that Morning (Friday) till Monday Morning following & expired.

"O Liberty. Why do you suffer so many of your faithful sons, your warmest Votaries, to fall at your Shrine. Alas, my Friend, my Friend.

"Excuse me, Dr. Sir, the man was VALUABLE, so attached to the Liberty of this State & Continent that his whole Attention, Influence & Interest centered in it, &

seemed riveted to it. He left a Mournful Widow and Daugr.
and I may say the Friends of Liberty on a whole Continent
to deplore his Fall."

Dr. Hall and others brought to the Assembly's attention
the fact that the law officers had taken no cognizance of the
duel. McIntosh then surrendered to the civil authorities,
gave bond, was indicted, tried and acquitted. The feeling
among many Georgians against him was intense, the Gwinnett faction including many men of prominence and their
followers. Joseph Clay, in one of his published letters,
refers to the antagonism that existed. Said he: "General
McIntosh is called to the Northward, which I am very glad
of, both for his own & the State's Sake. 'Twas impossible
for him to have or to give any satisfaction here, prejudice
was so strong against him."

Accepting the advice of friends, Gen. McIntosh secured
a transfer to the North, gave valiant service, and on his
return to the South after nearly two years there, Gen.
Washington wrote of him, in a letter to the Continental
Congress: "General McIntosh's conduct, while he acted
immediately under my observation, was such as to acquire
my esteem and confidence, and I have no reason since to
alter my good opinion of him." Near home he continued
to fight bravely for the cause, was second in command of
the American forces in the attack on Savannah in 1779, was
among the officers taken prisoners by the British when Gen.
Lincoln surrendered at Charleston, on his release made his
home temporarily in Virginia, and returned to Savannah in
1782, dying at his home on old South Broad street on
February 20, 1806. His varied services are too well known
to need reiteration. McIntosh county was named in his
honor, while Gwinnett county perpetuates the memory of
the rival so unfortunately slain in the duel of 1777.

Among other recorded American meetings is one in
which three Georgians of prominence appear—Gen. James
Screven, Col. John Baker and Maj. John Jones, progenitors
of many Georgians of to-day. The last two were the antagonists, while Screven was the successful pacificator by an
appeal to the patriotic ideals of his angered officers. The
affair took place in 1778, near the historic Midway church

in Liberty county, the shrine and Mecca of to-day. The cause of the trouble is given as a misunderstanding of orders, precipitating a personal issue between Baker and Jones.

There were no more sterling or braver officers in the patriot forces than Col. Baker and Maj. Jones. Baker was of the old Calvinistic stock that had come to Georgia from Dorchester, S. C., a lineal descendant of those who had left England to find a religious haven in Massachusetts early in the seventeenth century. In common with the others of the Midway settlement, he was fervent in antagonism to British domination after the issue was joined between the colonies and the mother country. When the Provincial Congress met at Tondee's tavern on July 4, 1775, he was among those representing St. John's parish, and was among the first to take up arms. As Captain of the St. John's Riflemen, organized by him—the Midway settlement then being in the parish of that name—he participated in the attack on the British ships in the Savannah river in March, 1776. Shortly after, with a band of volunteers he is found attacking the notorious Florida Rangers on the St. Mary's river, and in May, 1777, led the militia volunteers in the unfortunate movement into Florida that eventuated in the duel between Gwinnett and McIntosh. In November, 1778, he met the British and Indians invading Liberty from the south and was wounded in the skirmish at Bulltown swamp. In 1779 he attacked and dispersed the Georgia Royalists under Capt. Goldsmith near Sunbury. In 1781 he gathered together the militia of South Georgia and took part in the siege and capture of Augusta.

These are some of the incidents in the stirring life led by Baker during the revolutionary period. Defeat never discouraged him nor dampened his ardor. His name was naturally in the list of those proscribed by Governor Wright's Assembly of 1780. The legislature named Baker county in his memory in 1825.

Major John Jones was no less ardent in the American cause. After serving in the army in minor positions he is found as aide to Brigadier-General Elbert in 1778. When the American and French forces laid siege to Savannah he

was aide to Gen. Lachlan McIntosh and was the bearer under
flag of the letter to the British General Prevost, requesting
that the women and children be permitted to leave the city.
In the fateful attack on October 9, 1779, he sealed his devotion to his country with his life. He was, says Jones, "Literally cut in twain by a cannon shot while within a few
paces of the embrasure from which the piece was discharged." In 1839 the City Council of Savannah, then
laying out a new street, ordered that it should be named
Jones, as the "Georgian" stated, "in compliment to the
brave father of Col. Joseph Jones, of Liberty county, who
fell within one hundred yards of the spot patriotically dedicated to his name while fighting for the liberties of his
country. Thus has posterity been grateful to one of its
deliverers of this hemisphere from foreign thraldom."

Such was the calibre of the patriots who, with bitterness of heart, met prepared to slay one another in personal
combat while the enemy were gathering their forces to
take Savannah. The two officers had doubtless known each
other for years prior to the uprising of the colonies in the
close intimacy that marked the early families of their section. Serious must have been the misunderstanding that
forced them to the code duello. The meeting is stated to
have been in a grove near Midway church, the two mounted
on horses. Just as they prepared for action Gen. James
Screven came in post haste upon the scene. His appeal to
their patriotism was too strong to be resisted. There was
the common enemy of their homes and liberties to be met.
Why slay each other in fratricidal strife when their common country demanded their blood sacrifices, if any were
to be made? "If you cannot extend to each other the hand
of confidence and friendship, for your country's sake do
not destroy each other's lives." Reconciliation was effected
and the two returned to camp to resume their duties. Soon
after, on November 22, 1778, Gen. Screven was mortally
wounded in the skirmish near Midway. The next year
Jones was killed. Baker survived to enter Savannah after
its evacuation by the British, to resume his home life in
Liberty, to fight against the Indians under Gen. James Jackson, and passed away in 1792.

Doubtless there were other duels between Georgia officers that were bloodless, or prospective affairs of honor that were adjusted without stationing the disputants on the field of honor. The custom and the spirit of the times could hardly have made it otherwise.

Out of the unsuccessful defence of Savannah against the British in December, 1778, grew a duel between General Howe, commanding the American forces at that time, and Gen. Christopher Gadsden, of South Carolina, that is not without its amusing features and has a local connection, inasmuch as it developed solely from severe strictures on Howe's failure to hold Savannah against the enemy. Howe's "supineness," as Col. Henry Lee called it, brought a published letter from Gen. Gadsden, analyzing and condemning Howe's whole course unmercifully. Howe was then with his forces in South Carolina and demanded an apology. Neither retraction nor apology was forthcoming, and a challenge passed. When they met a ball from Howe's pistol grazed Gadsden's ear, Gadsden firing in the air. Blood had been drawn, honor was satisfied, a perfunctory entente cordiale was established. The accounts of the duel drew an amusing satirical poem from Maj. John Andre, then in New York. The last five stanzas are worth repeating:

> H. missed his mark but not his aim,
>   The shot was well directed;
> It saved them both from hurt and shame,
>   What more could be expected?
>
> Then G., to show he meant no harm,
>   But hated jars and jangles,
> His pistol fired across his arm,
>   From H. almost at angles.
>
> H. now was called upon by G.
>   To fire another shot, Sir;
> He smiled, and after that, quoth he.
>   No, truly, I cannot, Sir.

Such honor did they both display,
They highly were commended;
And thus in short this gallant fray
Without mischance was ended.

No fresh dispute, we may suppose,
Will e'er by them be started;
And now the chiefs, no longer foes,
Shook hands, and so they parted.

Many another meeting is not inaptly described in Andre's facetious lines.

Most romantic of the duels of the revolutionary period, though, was that between John McIntosh, then a lieutenant-colonel, and Captain Elholm, in which both were disabled.

McIntosh was the nephew of Gen. Lachlan McIntosh. He was as gallant an officer as ever wore the patriot uniform.

Elholm was a Pole who held a commission as captain in Lee's Legion. He had likewise given demonstrations of his bravery.

While the American forces were in South Carolina, Elholm was accused of oppressive conduct to some of the inhabitants. When McIntosh protested a quarrel ensued and the outcome was an appeal to their swords under the code.

The quarrel between the officers had occurred in the neighborhood of the home of Miss Sarah Swinton, to whom McIntosh was engaged. The men were equal in physical strength, in their prowess as swordsmen, and their difficulty had awakened such bitterness of feeling that the approaching duel was looked upon as almost assured of fatal results.

Georgians are indebted to Rev. George White for the story of this meeting. It is told in his "Historical Collections."

"As the parties were moving on to the place of combat Miss Swinton requested to see for an instant her intended consort. The friends of the colonel hesitated, fearing the consequences of an interview at such a moment, which he had not the heart to decline, though he had one for a different and desperate encounter.

"He called on her, and was met with a serious firmness, and after a little conversation she observed: 'If you are, then, inviolably pledged to meet this man, and feel that your honor is dearer than life, what shall I do?'

"Seeing that his cravat was but loosely bound about his neck, she continued: 'Yes, but let me adjust your cravat'. And having with scrupulous care, as she thought, protected the most vulnerable and exposed part, after a few brief words, feeling the softer susceptibilities of her nature beginning to prevail, she hastily gave him her hand and fled to her room, to conceal there her agitation and the anguish of a devoted heart.

"The hostile parties met under a large oak, the ground about which was soon cleared of every obstacle that might impede the movements of the combatants.

"At the word 'Ready', they drew, and, advancing with sharp and glittering swords, commenced the battle in good earnest, with firm hearts and sturdy arms. In a little time the right arm of Captain Elholm was nearly severed from his body and fell powerless by his side.

"Here it might be supposed that the contest would cease; not so; there was but a temporary pause, for he was a proud, fearless soldier, expert with his weapon, and naturally left-handed. His sword was dexterously transferred to his left hand, which he used with great effect; and the blows came so awkwardly that they were not easily parried by his right-handed antagonist. Both were in a few minutes disabled in such a manner that the friends present felt it proper to interfere, and end this bloody conflict.

"They carried to their graves the scars, and deeply furrowed cheeks, as evidences of a once terrible struggle. Miss Swinton was not long in suspense. The combatants were soon taken from the field, disfigured by many deep and dangerous sabre wounds, of which, however, in due time, they both recovered; and the colonel often remarked that he was more indebted to the tender attentions of Miss Swinton for his restoration to health than to the management or skill of his surgeon."

Soon after his recovery they were married. Eight years after the war they removed to Florida. Hardly had he succeeded in establishing a home on the St. John's river when, on a visit to St. Augustine, he was treacherously seized and imprisoned, accused of designs against the Spanish government, and later thrown into Moro Castle at Havana. After nearly a year's imprisonment he was released through the efforts of President Washington and others. In 1799 his wife, who had long been blind, died on St. Simon's Island.

When the second war came with Great Britain John McIntosh was called into his country's service again, this time as a general to command three regiments of infantry and a battalion of artillery for the protection of Savannah and the seaboard. When the British threatened the Gulf country General McIntosh with his gallant Georgians, including many Savannahians, marched a thousand miles through the wilderness to the defence of Mobile. On their return in June, 1815, Mayor Thomas U. P. Charlton wrote to him:

"You had devoted the vigor of manhood in combatting for the liberty and independence of your country, and when that liberty was again menaced by the same foe, an advanced period of life did not prevent you from again unsheathing the sword of seventy-six in defence of the same righteous cause. This consistent patriotism and bravery of conduct exhibits the true features of a character in which love of country and freedom predominates over every other consideration."

The Savannah City Council also adopted resolutions of thanks and he retired to private life again, followed by the plaudits of Georgians. When he died in 1826 the editor of the "Georgian" wrote:

"Noble soul! How the spirit of Washington will greet thee."

Too little is known by the present generation of this heroic Georgian. Savannah might well revive through its school histories the memory of him and many other patriots and men of public service whose lives have been so closely identified with it.

CHAPTER III.

THE COTTINEAUS, FATHER AND SON.

CAPT. DENIS L. COTTINEAU COMMANDED THE PALLAS IN
JOHN PAUL JONES' GREAT FIGHT WITH THE SERAPIS
AND FOUGHT A DUEL AS AN OUTCOME OF THE
TREACHERY OF CAPT. LANDAIS—LIES BURIED IN THE
OLD COLONIAL CEMETERY—HIS SON SLAIN IN A DUEL
AT HAVANA BY A SAVANNAH OFFICER HE SOUGHT
TO BEFRIEND—THE STORY OF CATHOLIC ARISTO-
CRATS WHO SOUGHT SAVANNAH AS A REFUGE FROM
THE STORM OF REVOLUTION.

BUTTON GWINNETT, it is generally and reasonably believed, lies in the present Colonial Park, the old burying ground of Christ church. There was no other burial
place in Savannah at the time of the duel with McIntosh,
and it is extremely improbable that the body would have
been removed from the city for interment. Wherever his
ashes may rest in the old cemetery they are not far distant
from those of another revolutionary character, associated
with John Paul Jones in his greatest of naval combats and
victories, and whose body, when it was laid away in Savannah's parish burying ground, was scarred with a wound
received in a duel with one whose name is now chiefly remembered for an act of the basest treachery and a general
misconduct and insubordination that present day alienists
attribute to a neurotic mentality approaching insanity.

On the Abercorn street side of Colonial Park, beneath
the shadow of trees and bushes, but a few feet from the
sidewalk where hundreds pass daily, almost directly east of
McDonough street crossing, is the tombstone that tells. in
brief the story of Captain Cottineau, commander of the
Pallas at the battle between the Bon Homme Richard and
the Serapis, which immortalized Jones.

No flag of our country or of France ever flutters above
the grave to draw attention to the inadequate inscription
on the stone. No patriotic celebration ever finds a wreath

Captain Denis Cottineau
From the Collection of St. Memin's Works at the Corcoran Gallery of Art, Washington, D. C.

of laurel placed upon it. Citizens and strangers alike ignore
its presence. The story of the Frenchman who stood true
to the American in the hour of his most desperate conflict is
seldom, if ever, recalled by Savannahians.

The wording on the stone, roughened by the weather of
a hundred years, is sadly worn and needs rechiseling that
it may be preserved for future generations less indifferent
to the glorious romances of Savannah. Here it is:

Sacred
to the memory of
Denis L. Cottineau de
Kerloguen
Native of Nantes (France)
Formerly a Lieut. in his late Most
Christian Majesty's Navy. Knight
of the Royal Military Order
of St. Louis. Capt. Commanding a
Ship of War of the United States
During their Revolution, and
a member of the Cincinnati
Society.
Obit. Nov. 29th 1808. Aged 63 years.

The story of the great naval fight off Flamborough
Head, on the eastern coast of England, in which, for the
first and only time in the annals of the British navy, a British ship of war struck her colors to a weaker and sinking
enemy, should not require repeating. Yet it is so thrilling,
and the man who lies in this almost forgotten grave played
his part so well, that one feels tempted to sketch it in out-
line, told though it has been a hundred times.

The British were on the lookout for Jones—and they
found him. Prior to this he had left his indelible mark,
made himself dreaded and hated by the British merchant
marine, and respected as a fearless fighter by British naval
men. In 1778 his capture of the Drake, of superior build
and armament to his own vessel, the Ranger, showed more
than ever the superior skill and the mettle of the intrepid
Scotch-American sailor.

In August, 1779, with his flagship, the old, slow-sailing,
almost rotten, converted merchantman, Bon Homme Richard, with an armament of 42 guns, largely old and condemned French cannon, some of which burst at the first
discharge in the engagement, he left L'Orient on his most
famous cruise. In company with him sailed Capt. Cottineau,

in the Pallas, a former merchant ship, with 32 guns; the
Alliance, Capt. Landais, described as "the best ship in the
American navy", also with 32 guns, and the smaller Vengeance.   A cutter and two privateers which accompanied
them soon deserted and the Vengeance played no part in
the final battle.

The purpose of the little squadron was to harrass the
Scotch and English coasts, to take Leith and levy tribute
thereon, to demoralize the British shipping, to gather in
rich prizes, and to give the Admiralty further evidence of
Jones' fighting prowess, if fate should bring him into contact with the English war vessels.   He failed in none of
these things except as to Leith, and unfavorable winds and
consequent delays saved that town from a heavy toll.

On the Bon Homme Richard had been gathered as mot-
ley a crew as ever sailed.   Portuguese, Malays, Swedes,
French, and a number of English prisoners, made up three-
fourths of it, leavened by eight officers and seventy men of
American stock.   Such was the martial spirit and unrivalled
powers of leadership of Jones that the heterogenous mass,
discordant and half-rebellious, was controlled and welded
into a wonderful fighting unit when the final issue came.
As Capt. Pearson testified at his court-martial, "The Bon
Homme Richard was dominated by a commanding will of
the most unalterable resolution."

Of far greater drawback than the miscellaneous crew
was the captain of the Alliance.   Landais, although it was
not known when he was placed in command, was a cashiered
officer of the French navy, unstable in every way.   Jealousy
forbade any of the French officers serving under the unrestrained authority of an officer of a yet unrecognized nation.
The French Minister of Marine had handicapped Jones with
instructions that left the commanders of the other vessels
largely independent of his orders.   It was theirs to do or
not to do, as they might see fit.   And for that very reason
the greater honor is due to Cottineau.

More than a month passed, with numerous evidences
of insulting insubordination and treachery on the part of
Landais, with an occasional departure of the Alliance from
the squadron with an utter contempt of the authority of

Jones. Then came the day of days, the meeting, when evening's dusk was coming on, with the fleet of Baltic merchantmen escorted by the Serapis and the Countess of Scarborough. The Serapis was new, strongly constructed, carrying fifty of the best guns of English make, a crew of 320 English sailors of the finest type, and was commanded by Pearson, one of the most courageous and most skilful of the English captains. Her companion vessel was smaller but powerful.

The story will thrill the world as long as acts of supreme heroism are admired and held worthy of emulation. The Bon Homme Richard was literally shot to pieces, sinking under the feet of what was left of her crew, her guns mainly silenced, the English prisoners from captured vessels escaping on deck were forced to man the pumps, the dead and the dying were counted by the scores, the upper deck was ready to collapse, the entire vessel a mere shattered hulk at the mercy of wind and wave—but above and beyond all stood out the coolness and unshaken determination of Jones. His matchless maneuvres finally locked the two vessels together.

Then came the desperate attempts from each vessel to board, the almost cessation of fighting to partially quell the flames that promised to destroy both vessels, the final rally of the Bon Homme Richard's forces, with Jones cheering them on as they fought the British hand to hand—and then the unexpected, the sudden advent of the Alliance and the firing of her broadsides into the Bon Homme Richard. It was only the superhuman valor of Jones that resisted the urgings to strike his colors. Then came the final surrender of the Serapis, Capt. Pearson himself hauling down his flag.

It is no wonder artists and sea historians have loved to dwell upon it. As an English writer has said: "It was Jones and Jones alone, rather than the Bon Homme Richard, who beat Pearson to a standstill."

And while the Serapis and the Bon Homme Richard fought out their duel of the sea, where was Cottineau?

Unlike Landais, he had stood true to his promise: "I will stand by you in any event," he had told Jones.

Grave of Captain Denis Cottineau
In Colonial Park, Formerly Christ Church Burying Ground

Engaging the Countess of Scarborough, after an hour's hard fighting, he had captured the smaller of the British vessels, and stood ready to go to the aid of Jones when Landais came up with the Alliance and sailed around the Pallas and her prize. When called by Cottineau to take charge of the prize and permit him to help the Bon Homme Richard in her unequal contest, Landais withdrew and a few minutes after had dastardly poured his shot into the American vessel.

Fortunate it was that Cottineau was not of the low calibre of Landais. The additional guns of the Countess of Scarborough, if left to herself, would have consigned the Bon Homme Richard and her valiant commander and crew to an ocean grave.

Cottineau, to his eternal credit, had refused to be misled by his jealous and unbalanced countryman and justified the faith that Jones had in him when he said: "I only wish that another man like you were in command of the Alliance."

For his part in the engagement Cottineau was praised by Jones and by Benjamin Franklin, the latter representing the United States in France, and his own government later decorated him with the Cross of Saint Louis.

Thirty hours after the battle the Bon Homme Richard went down. No one has ever told of her plunge beneath the Atlantic more graphically than John Paul Jones himself:

"No one was now left aboard the Richard but our dead. She sank peacefully in about forty fathoms. Our torn and tattered flag was left flying when we abandoned her. As she plunged down to the head at the last, her taffrail momentarily rose in the air, so the very last vestige mortal eyes ever saw of the Bon Homme Richard was the defiant waving of her unconquered and unstricken flag. And as I had given them the good old ship for their sepulchre, I now bequeathed to my immortal dead the flag they had so desperately defended, for their winding sheet."

The flag that thus went down above the heroic dead was the first banner with the stars and stripes that Europe ever saw—a flag with one star for Georgia in the thirteen stars of its constellation. It had floated over the Ranger when she received the salute of the French war ships at Brest, the first national salute to the American flag from a foreign fleet, and it had been the first stars and stripes to which a British ship had struck her colors.

Out of the battle off Flamborough Head grew the duel between Cottineau and Landais.

Cottineau openly supported Jones in his accusations against Landais, who then challenged him to a duel with swords, in the use of which the former captain of the Alliance was an expert.

The duel was fought on an island in the Texel and Cottineau was dangerously wounded in the right side.

Emboldened by this, Landais then challenged Jones, who accepted and specified pistols. Knowing the expertness of John Paul Jones with that weapon, Landais refused to meet him on the ground that pistols were not a French weapon of honor, and quickly left Amsterdam to avoid being forced to a meeting.

Of Cottineau's further connection with the French navy little has been ascertained. In 1790 he was confirmed as captain of an armed ship for the campaign against England. His name disappeared from the list of the French Marine two years later. During that period, though, he had evidently been upon the retired list, as in 1790 he was living in St. Domingo as a coffee planter, with his wife, nee Mmlle. Lucie Mocquet de Montalet, sister of the Marquis Jean Berard Mocquet de Montalet, later of Sapelo Island and Savannah, and of William Polycarp Montalet, the early owner of the Hermitage plantation. On St. Domingo Island were born the Cottineaus' two children, Achilles and Denis. These boys later became students at St. Mary's Academy, Baltimore.

When the blacks under Toussaint l'Ouverture rebelled and began the massacre of the French in the island the Cottineaus fled to Pennsylvania and became part of the picturesque colony established at Azilium on the Susquehanna. With them was Rev. Antoine Carles, former Canon of Guernsey, kinsman of Madame Cottineau. In 1803 they migrated to Savannah, where Father Carles became the second permanent pastor of the Church of St. John the Baptist. His name is found occasionally in the old records and newspapers. He and Madame Cottineau also conducted a school where the sons and daughters of prominent Savannahians were instructed in "French and Good Manners."

In this city, twenty-nine years after he captured the Countess of Scarborough, Cottineau passed away. In the mortuary reports at the City Hall there is found this brief allusion:

"Denis Nichs. Cottineau, 63 years, native of France. Gentleman. From consumption. Died Nov. 29, 1808. Buried Nov. 30. Was afflicted three years. He died and was buried from the house of the Roman Catholic priest, Mr. Carles, on Broughton street."

The local newspapers made no mention of his death.

John Paul Jones, who died in Paris, now lies in a magnificent tomb at the naval academy at Annapolis, an ever-living reminder to the cadets of the memorable reply he sent back to Pearson from the bullet-showered deck of his sinking ship when that officer, thinking Jones was surrendering, hailed him:

"Have you struck?"

And across the few feet of intervening space, under the ensign of the new-born nation, came back the words that will never be forgotten:

"I have just begun to fight."

Landais lived on for many years in New York, ignored. A monument at St. Patrick's cathedral is his memento.

Cottineau's grave in Savannah is visible to all and recognized by few. Yet that little, venerable, blackened stone, which awakens so meagre an interest, connects Savannah with the greatest of the naval battles of the American struggle for freedom.

Four years after Capt. Cottineau's death his son, Achilles, aged 22 years, was buried with him, a victim of the fever.

H.	Kn.	Fa.	Course.	Winds.	L.W.	REMARKS.
1						
2						
3						
4						
5						
6						
7						
8						
9						
10						
11						
12						
1						
11						
12						

The other of the Cottineau sons, Denis, reared in Savannah, obeying the traditions of his father, followed the sea.

He became an officer in the American navy, fought a duel as his father had done, fell in the combat, and lies in an unknown grave in a foreign land.

The story of his death is a tragedy tinged with the flavor of quixotic friendship, the story of an ardent spirit eager to assist a Savannah comrade of boyhood days, of a brave young life sacrificed to no purpose.

In 1819 Cottineau was a midshipman on the U. S. corvette John Adams, of 24 guns, Capt. Alexander S. Wadsworth, cruising in West India waters. This vessel was built from the subscriptions of the citizens of Charleston when war threatened with France in 1799. On the ship with him was another Savannah boy, Midshipman Pierson. The ties of former association in their old home town probably drew them together more closely than would otherwise have been the case.

Pierson gave some offence that put him in coventry with the other officers of the John Adams. What the error was that consigned him to the harsh treatment of exclusion from the pale of the officers' society is not known.

To be in coventry meant to be treated with the coldest courtesy so far as the official life of the vessel went, to be ignored whenever his path crossed another officer's path beyond the line of strict duty. It was a contempt that was all the more odious and hateful because of its studied, frigid official politeness, its positive refusal to give occasion for active offence. It was marked by the cessation of all comradeship. It was harder to encounter than open insult because it was a perpetual covert insult that could not be challenged. It was the boycott of the navy, unendurable to the man condemned to the small quarters of a ship of that day and sufficient to break the spirit and drive from the service any one who encountered it.

To be in coventry meant that no officer in the service considered the victim a gentleman. No other officer would be the subject of a challenge.

To see another Savannahian in this frightful plight touched the sympathies of Cottineau. Perhaps he felt that the offense was being punished beyond justification. The desire to help the unfortunate midshipman came upon him.

On deck one night, as they drew near Havana, he ventured to broach the subject.

They were on watch duty. As they approached one another Cottineau said to his brother officer:

"Pierson, you are in a bad fix."

The midshipman did not need to be told that. In his heart he may have resented his attention being called to the fact.

"What can I do?" was his reply.

"Call one of the officers out," was Cottineau's advice.

Pierson would have been eager to accept the advice if it had been feasible. Too well he knew the cartel would have been returned to him unanswered.

"To meet me would break the coventry," he is reported to have said. "No one would meet me."

Cottineau was keenly touched. Perhaps as boys they had played together in the squares of the old home town. The impulses of youth are impetuous and thoughtless. His heart dominated his brain. Cottineau hesitated no longer:

"Challenge me," he cried. "I will meet you. That will break the ban."

A few days later the John Adams lay in the harbor of Havana. The challenge had been passed and had been accepted.

From the Navy Department at Washington I secured a photograph of the page of the log of the John Adams on which the officer of the day, in the perfunctory way in which a log is kept, told of the meeting and its fatal result. It is reproduced herewith.

There are three little items interspersed with the notes as to the weather conditions and the usual routine of the boat:

"Saturday, April 3, 1819. At 3 P. M. a duel took place between Midshipman Cottineau and Midshipman Pierson in which the former was killed."

"From 4 to 6 * * * * Carpenters employed in making a Coffin."

"Sunday, April 4. At ½ past 9, the funeral of Midshipman Cottineau."

Pistols were used and at the first fire Cottineau fell dead. The bullet from the weapon of the man he had sought to befriend had found a lodgment in his heart.

It may be that Pierson did not intend to slay Cottineau. It seems incredible that he should have done so. It is a hundred years and more ago and he left no defence of himself when many years later he died in Savannah. But he was more than ever an ostracised man. He was driven from the navy by a sentiment that was far more irresistible than the original coventry that poor Cottineau had endeavored to break.

Mr. Charles Spalding Wylly, of Brunswick, in his delightful little volume, "The Seed That Was Sown," recalls that in his faraway youth he saw Pierson in the Pulaski House bar, "a supernumerary in life."

In a letter from Havana, dated April 14, 1819, from the "Savannah Republican's" correspondent there, appeared this item:

"Two midshipmen on the John Adams fought a duel on the 3d inst., one of whom was killed the first fire".

Madame Cottineau doubtless read this without the slightest realization of what it meant to her.

That was the sole reference to the affair in the local papers, or the papers elsewhere.

Soon after they laid away the midshipman in the cemetery at Havana the last link that connected the Cottineau family with Savannah was severed.

When the Bourbons came back to the throne Father Carles returned to France. Other aristocrats who had made Savannah their home followed. A number, though, died here in absolute poverty. Some time after 1825 Madame Cottineau likewise went back to her native land and resumed her position in the court circle of that period. There is no more interesting chapter in all the romance of old Savannah than the stories of these noble French emigres. Fortunately Rev. Joseph D. Mitchell, recently Vicar-General of the Diocese of Savannah, is preserving them from oblivion by his researches and writings.

Back in the old yet new France, never to be the same after the touch of Napoleon, Madame Cottineau lingered a few years, and the Abbe Carles continued his holy offices until 1834. On Easter Sunday of that year he fell dead soon after officiating at the altar in the cathedral of Bordeaux.

When the news of his death reached Savannah a requiem mass in his memory drew many old friends and acquaintances of its former rector to the Church of St. John the Baptist.

The memories of the family in Savannah gradually faded out with the generation that had known them.

CHAPTER IV.

JAMES JACKSON, CHIEF OF SAVANNAH DUELLISTS.

IN HIS FIRST AFFAIR LIEUT. GOV. WELLS WAS SLAIN—
STABBED IN AN ASSAULT BY WATKINS, ONLY TO
LATER RECEIVE A BULLET FROM HIM IN A DUEL—EX-
CHANGED SHOTS WITH EX-MAYOR GIBBONS IN DUEL
GROWING OUT OF THE JACKSON-WAYNE CONTESTED
ELECTION—THE GREAT ANTAGONIST OF SENATOR
GUNN IN THE YAZOO LAND GRANT AGITATION—RE-
FUSED CHALLENGE FROM JACOB WALDBURGER.

FOLLOWING the McIntosh-Gwinnett duel came the duel
in which Lieutenant Governor George Wells was killed.
This introduces us to one of the most vibrant personalities
in the early political history of Georgia, James Jackson, revolutionary hero, organizer and leader of the Jeffersonian
party in this state, United States Senator, nullifier of the
sale of the vast western empire of Georgia to the speculating land companies—a truly notable man whose life is an
inspiration in sterling patriotism and unselfish devotion to
the public weal, one of that exceptional type whose careers
and characters should be more impressed upon the receptive
minds of the children of to-day.

Valiantly Jackson had fought for the liberties of his
adopted country. He had only come to Georgia from England in 1772, a mere stripling of fifteen years. Early identi-
fying himself with the patriot forces, he threw himself into
the war with all the zeal and recklessness of one whose life
counted for naught compared with the cause. His bravery
in various encounters with the British, from old Midway
church to Cowpens, won for him promotion. In 1780, when
the difficulty came with Wells, he had the rank of major and
was held in high esteem for unfailing courage and exceptional ability.

Wells had not been quite as prompt as the less mature
Jackson in espousing the severance of the ties which bound
the colony to England. He was a planter of some promi-

James Jackson, Savannah's Most Noted Duellist
Revolutionary Hero, United States Senator, Governor of Georgia, and
Successful Antagonist of the Yazoo Land Grants

nence, near the old town of Queensborough, in what is now Jefferson county. When the patriots assembled at Tondee's tavern put forth their ringing resolutions of August 10, 1774, many of the residents of St. George's Parish adopted counter resolutions of protest, and condemned the Savannah action as "reflecting improperly upon the King and Parliament". Heading the list of signers was the name of George Wells. Like many others, North and South, who were subsequently ardent patriots, the hope was still entertained that a satisfactory peaceful solution would be found and open rebellion avoided.

The next year, though, St. George's was represented at the Provincial Congress assembled at Savannah, but Wells was not among its delegates. Comparatively little of his career is now ascertainable but presumably he identified himself with the American cause at an early stage and became a leading factor in his parish in promoting the struggle for independence. In June, 1776, he was appointed by the Council of Safety a Justice of the Peace for St. Paul's Parish. Soon after a bench warrant was issued against him for some unknown cause. After the failure of the siege and attack on Savannah in 1779 many patriots refugeed to the vicinity of Augusta. The actions of the old Executive Council were resented. Divisions had unfortunately too often marked the patriots in Georgia. Wells apparently had personal grievances as the basis for his bitterness. Elected Colonel of the Lower Battalion of the Augusta District in June, 1779, complaints were soon made about his conduct. The original protest was sent to him that he might make a reply. He refused to return it and in August the old Executive Council declared that he "had thereby in a great measure acknowledged the heinous charges set forth against him", and ordered that "he no longer be recognized as colonel". In November George Walton, Richard Howley, George Wells and others set up a deliberative body which they called the General Assembly, with William Glascock as president. Walton was elected Governor and Wells one of the new Executive Council. The next year Howley succeeded Walton as Governor and Wells was made president of the Executive Council, and on Howley's departure to take his seat in the Continental Congress Wells and three others, Stephens says, "were announced as fully competent for the transaction of all public business".

This was in February, 1780. The next month came the meeting with Jackson in which Wells met his death. It was a period when the patriot cause was at its lowest ebb in Georgia. As has been pointed out, "Unseemly dissensions had arisen among leading citizens and the land was a prey alike to external and internal foes". The cause of the irreconcilable clash between Wells and Jackson has never been clearly defined. The challenge evidently passed from Jackson and grew out of arbitrary methods of Wells as acting governor—probably an instance of a too aspiring and domineering nature unwisely entrusted with an uncertain executive authority. Jackson described himself in later years as of fiery disposition, and Wells is depicted as "governed by jealousy, inordinate ambition, and a desire for power and place". Jones says of him and his associate leaders that they were "jealous of the honors accorded to others who like themselves were engaged in a lethal struggle for independence". "In the agonies of extreme peril human nature could not forget its passion, or subdue its petty animosities".

Where they met is not positively known to-day. They took no seconds with them. It was a simple agreement to fight out their differences, that the distance parting them should be but a few paces, and that the shooting apparently should continue until one or the other, or both, fell. The desperate nature of the duel is evidenced by the fact that Jackson was dangerously wounded in both knees and Wells was killed on the spot. When found by friends Jackson lay helpless but a few feet from the body of Wells. Surgeons sought to amputate, but Jackson refused to consider the sacrifice of a limb. Exigencies of the service forced the surgeons away and Jackson remained a cripple for months, returning to active duty as quickly as his physical condition allowed. His biographer, Charlton, searched thoroughly for an explanation of the duel but to no avail. All that rewarded him among Jackson's papers was a memorandum lamenting the necessity of the meeting which had been forced upon him by Wells' overbearing disposition. Resuming his posi-

tion with the army, Jackson took part in the retreat through
South Carolina and the other operations of the closing
months of hostilities. So high a premium was put upon his
patriotic services that to him was accorded the honor of
being the first American soldier to enter Savannah on July
12, 1782, when the British evacuated and the patriots took
possession of the city.

Next of Jackson's duels was probably that with Thomas
Gibbons, Savannah's most noted lawyer of that period. This
was a political duel. In 1789 Jackson was elected to represent in the First Congress the First Georgia District, then
commonly referred to as the Lower or Eastern District.
When he came up for re-election two years later the opposition elements induced Gen. "Mad Anthony" Wayne to op-
pose him. General Wayne had accepted from the State the
gift of a plantation near the city and made it his home.
He was Jackson's old commander and there was no personal
ill will between them. Wayne's campaign was largely managed by Gibbons, an astute politician, and Jackson's defeat
was brought about, it was charged, by corrupt practices in
Camden and Effingham counties. Gibbons had made his
home temporarily in Effingham in order to be on the ground
and personally direct the maneuvers. In that county, it was
charged, nine more votes were polled than there were names
on the registration list, while the return for Glynn was
alleged to have been suppressed and a false return made in
favor of Wayne, showing a larger vote than there were
adult male inhabitants in the county. For misconduct in
this matter the Superior Court Judge there was subsequently impeached and by unanimous vote of the legislature deprived of his office and denied the privilege of holding office
in Georgia for thirty years.

Jackson and his friends naturally resented his defeat
as a result of such illegalities and a contest was filed at
Washington. The hearing was held before the House of
Representatives at the national capital, beginning March
12, 1792, and Jackson appeared for himself. He carefully
avoided utterances that might seem to attack the honor of
Gen. Wayne or to wound him. But Gibbons was not spared.
In his early remarks he referred to Gibbons as one "whose

General "Mad Anthony" Wayne,
Hero of the Revolution and Second Representative in Congress
From the Savannah District

soul is faction, and whose life had been a scene of political corruption; who never could be easy under government." Here he was called to order. After apologizing to the House Jackson continued with the statement that the "proofs were strong against Gibbons of abominable corruption; that this corruption was in a great measure of his charges; that Gibbons had gone out of his own county, not merely to use an undue influence with the electors, but to corrupt even the magistrates themselves." Gibbons, it was claimed, induced two citizens, not magistrates, to preside at the Effingham election, that minors were permitted to vote at his behest, and that the very election return was drawn up by the Savannah attorney. Knowledge of the ignoble part Gibbons had played during the revolution did not lessen the intensity of Jackson's feelings or the severity of his strictures.

What had occurred in Effingham, Jackson declared, was minor compared to "a scene of iniquity in Camden," where names of persons unknown had been added to the poll and the judge had become "the tool of a faction."

Many years later, in a letter to the "Georgian," Charlton told of the applause Jackson's fiery oratory aroused in the gallery of the House and of the visible evidences of approbation from the members on the floor, many of whom in the former sessions had come to know and appreciate his high qualities of manhood and statesmanship.

On a motion to seat Jackson the vote stood 29 to 29. The Speaker of the House voted in the negative, and a resolution was then adopted declaring "the seat of Anthony Wayne as a member of the House" vacant. A new election was ordered. Jackson and Wayne both declined to run in this and John Milledge, Jackson's intimate friend and political lieutenant, was elected. Wayne soon after left Georgia to assume the duties of commander-in-chief of the American army, to which he was appointed by President Washington a month after losing his seat in Congress. He died three years later while forcing the Indians of the Ohio territory to submission. As Chappell said in his "Georgia Miscellanies", "There was never any imputation against Gen. Wayne in connection with the election of 1791. It was the not uncommon case of a candidate's partisans, without his participation or privity, doing wrong things and going criminal lengths for him from which he himself would have revolted."

Little is known about the subsequent duel between Jackson and Gibbons except the statement that they exchanged three shots and neither was hit. They are said to have become friends later. Gibbons is described as "a man of very strong character, great courage and ability, and much noted throughout a long and prosperous after life." His income as a lawyer is said to have been $15,000 a year, probably equivalent to $60,000 to-day, his earning power at the bar exceeding that of any other Georgia lawyer unless it be Jackson himself, who abandoned a practice equally as lucrative to serve the public. A man of Gibbons' position and temperament could hardly afford to rest tamely under Jackson's charges before the House of Representatives, and the duel, only an allusion to which has come down to us, doubtless occurred soon after the unseating of Wayne. Gibbons was mayor of Savannah (1791-92) at the time of the Jackson-Wayne campaign, retiring from that office the day the hearing began at Washington. He and Mayor Mitchell alike fought political duels shortly after their terms in the City Hall expired. Their predecessors and successors in the mayoralty were fortunate enough to avoid the necessity of resorting to the code, although some of them were equally hot-headed and courageous and went through campaigns of intense bitterness.

Gibbons served as mayor again in 1794-95 and in 1799-1801, and as an alderman in 1795-98. On the expiration of his term as the city's chief executive in 1795 his fellow citizens nominated and elected him an alderman, and then delivered an address to him urging that he occupy that position. "Sensible that the prosperity of the city depends greatly on the wisdom of its Council", said they in their memorial, "They trust, Sir, that on the present occasion they may not be deprived of your abilities, so eminent, distinguished and useful." This was signed by many citizens. Gibbons replied: "I cheerfully concur and will to the best of my abilities execute the duties", a somewhat different spirit from the reluctance and refusal of many men of affairs to-day to assume civic responsibilities.

It has been generally believed that Jackson exchanged shots with Gen. Gunn, but no authentic record of any meeting exists. No one questions that ample provocation existed on both sides to provoke hostilities. But there were other duels to Jackson's credit, in one of which he was severely wounded, and a personal encounter that almost took on the appearance of an attempt at assassination. This grew out of the repeal of the Yazoo land grant act. Jackson, it will be recalled, did the unparalleled thing of resigning from the United States Senate, at the request of the citizens of Savannah, to run for a seat in the legislature and assist in overthrowing the ring that had put through the sale of the public lands for a pittance. In a letter to Josiah Tattnall Jackson denounced this as "A confiscation of the rights of unborn generations to supply the rapacious graspings of a few sharks. Two-thirds of Georgia will be owned by residents of Philadelphia in six months." Largely through his instrumentality the transaction was wiped from the state's records. His signal success in this almost cost him his life.

Enemies galore were the result. Men who saw fortune slipping from their grasp, or political influence forever disappearing, as a result of his exertions in the General Assembly to thwart and undo their work, conceived the most intense hatred for him. One of these enemies, Robert Watkins, of Augusta, made an atrocious assault upon Jackson as he was leaving the state capitol at Louisville, to which he had gone to get some papers soon after the legislature had adjourned. This was in 1796. Jackson told the story in a letter to Milledge and once more we are furnished a vivid picture of the personal vindictiveness of the political strife of that time and of the brutality that lay thinly veneered among many public characters.

Watkins awaited Jackson outside of the capitol with "a posse of his Yazoo friends" to assist him.

As Jackson came out Watkins said to him: "General, the session is now over. I do not mean to act the assassin, but the gentleman. I consider you the leader of a damned venal set or faction who have disgraced their country".

"This was done to draw on dispute", wrote Jackson. "Flesh & blood of such texture as mine would not bear it, & the lie and stick involuntary flew on him; until my little Lucas stick broke, I finely frapped him, but the third blow it broke in my hand & till then he had not struck me; but now at his mercy I received one blow on the head which for a moment stunned me, & I Fell.

"I rose and my blood rose with me—I made at him & was told he had pistols. This made me recollect one I had carried, apprehensive of an attack from John Greene who I had been under the necessity of telling was a damned lyar a night or two before, & I immediately exclaimed, ' 'Tis well, we are on a footing. Clear the way.'

"It was proposed by Flournoy, one of his partisans, for us to fight in the morning—I replied that I never fought a base assassin but on the spot. I met him & ordered him to take his ground.

"I should have killed him, for I fired as soon as we were open to each other, but my hand was knocked up by one of the party, & as soon as I fired he ran at me with a bayonet at the end of his pistol. We closed and twice I threw him.

"I soon found that I was his Master as to strength & was beating him handsomely, when a scoundrel by the name of Wood turned Watkins on me and the Assassin strove to gouge me. Driven to necessity I was compelled to put one of his fingers in my mouth which made him relinquish his attempt after skinning my eye.

"He then sprung another bayonet, for the first one was either taken from him or returned to him, & he had a pair on purpose, & stabbed at me repeatedly. I was all the time unarmed. He stabbed me in the left breast which fortunately entered my collar bone and ran me through my shirt and grazed my ribs a second time—a half inch lower in the breast the Doctors pronounced, would have finished my business.

"The nature of this infamous attack, as I had sent Tattnal three weeks before with an assurance that any private matter could be accommodated when Mr. Watkins pleased—his eating and drinking in company—his telling our worthy friend Jones (who went to him the day before solicitous for my safety, as he had heard an attack was intended on me, but did not suspect Watkins, but Greene & who went unknown to me) with a 'Pshaw, who would attack General Jackson', and laughed at it—all these argue a blackness and depravity of mind horrid in so young a man.

"A single line would have carried me to any rendezvous he chose to appoint—but he was deceived. I could whip two of him at any time, and notwithstanding my wound I was turning on him the third time when a few of my friends collected & tore me from him. Yazoo made out a tale for him, but the mass of the people despise the attack as pitiful, dastardly and assassinating."

The allusion to Watkins striving to "gouge me" recalls that gouging out an eye with the thumb when an opponent was on the ground was one of the pleasant features of physical encounters then and until a very much later period in Georgia history among a certain type of men, but it was not to be expected that those of high standing would indulge in it, no matter how much they despised and hated one another. Even among the lowest, though, it was not ethical to gouge out an eye if the victim had already lost one.

Jackson's political foes were not willing to let matters stand with a mere thrust or two of a dagger affixed to a pistol. They sought his life. On April 11, 1796, he wrote to Milledge:

"They are anxious to get me to Duelling, & would not quit until I was put out of the way. The wife and five children—the sixth I have reason to believe will shortly be in existence—are powerful reasons to prevent engagements which may not only be fatal to myself, but those who have right to look to me for support.

"I have fear respecting Tattnal. I know that he will put up with no improper conduct of Mr. Gunn. My resolution as to this champion of the party's is taken. I will fight him if he demands it but if he takes any other measures I am resolved to take their own steps with him."

As stated, there appears to be no positive evidence that Jackson and Gunn ever fought, but it is regarded as very probable that they did exchange shots, the temper and courage and mutual attacks of the two men seeming to render a meeting inevitable. But Watkins came back and before long he and Gen. Jackson confronted one another, awaiting the signal to fire, with ten paces between them.

Watkins had been a supporter of the bill for the sale of the Western lands, although, unlike many of the others, he is said not to have been guided in his vote by the gift of a large block of stock through Senator Gunn. He and his brother had for some years been engaged in a compilation of the state's statutes, of which no digest then existed, and the need of which was apparent to all. In 1799 the legislature appropriated $1,500 to further the work. When it was completed, though, and found to contain the obnoxious Yazoo act, despite the fact that it also gave the rescinding act, Governor Jackson's wrath broke loose again. He refused to sign the warrant to cover the appropriation, fought the acceptance or recognition of the digest in an official way by the state, and revived the vindictive hatred that had merely slumbered after Watkin's murderous assault of four years before.

This time, though, the bitter animosity could not find expression in an ambuscade like that of 1796. Recourse was had to the formalities of the code and under its provisions three meetings are said to have taken place, in the last of which, on the third shot, Jackson received a severe wound in the right thigh, incapacitating him from continuing the duel. The governor was then in the full vigor of manhood, but forty-four years of age, with indomitable courage strengthened and sustained by an impetuously passionate temperament.

Under the impact of the bullet from Watkins' pistol the governor sank to the ground, but the second quickly assisted him to his feet and he announced himself ready for another exchange of shots. Only the insistence of the surgeon and the expostulation of his friends forced him to desist and permit himself to be carried from the field. The story goes that Watkins helped to bear his antagonist away, perhaps with some polite fiction of hope that the wound would not prove serious, whereupon Jackson observed:

"Damn it, Watson, I thought I would give you another shot."

A study of Jackson's character convinces one that the governor's regret that he could not have another chance to wing Watkins was keener and more sincere than any expression which may have dropped from the lips of Watkins.

Shipp says in his "Life and Times of William H. Crawford", that, in this last of the three duels fought by them, "Jackson and Watkins conversed with great elegance and entire politeness on different matters, while the seconds were arranging the terms of the combat that within the next minute was expected to put an end to at least one of them." Quite a contrast with the scene at the old capitol when Watkins assailed him as the leader of a "damned venal set" and sought to gouge out Jackson's eye when the wounded statesman had him down. The two pictures give a color of truth to the statement that the code prevented murderous brawls and, in that tumultuous period, saved instead of destroying life.

One of the duels fought by Jackson and Watkins grew out of the adoption of the State Constitution in 1798. An old pamphlet, written by Watkins, states that Gen. Jackson and Watkins were both delegates to the convention that was to prepare a constitution for Georgia. Watkins, than an officer in the militia, was not satisfied with certain features of the constitution as finally presented to the convention for adoption. "Unwilling to withhold my signature," said he, "I claimed and exercised the privilege of giving to the country the following emphatic declaration" of the features objectionable to him, "and signed the constitution accordingly." Not a great while after, Gen. Jackson having been chosen Governor, issued the following:

"Executive Mansion, Louisville, Ga., 12th July, 1798.

"It is further ordered that the conduct, &c., of Robert Watkins, Lieutenant-Colonel of the Richmond militia, with his declaration published June 30, 'that he shall never feel himself bound in any situation to support certain parts of the Constitution' be laid before the Legislature at their next session."

Map of the Yazoo Land Grants

Showing Enormous Western Territory of Georgia Granted By the Legislature in 1795 to Speculating Land Companies For $500,000—Alabama and Mississippi Have Been Carved Out of This Princely Domain

The Governor goes on to say that the Legislature is to determine whether Col. Watkins and two others who had assumed the same attitude "ought to hold commissions under the Constitution, considering the circumstances." There ensued a long correspondence, conducted with asperity on both sides, out of which grew a duel between the Governor and Watkins.

From the governor's chair Jackson returned again to the United States Senate and died in that service in 1806. His body lies in the Congressional Cemetery at Washington. Col. Thomas Benton paid a tribute to this great Savannahian, saying in part: "He was a man of marked character, high principles and strong temperament—honest, patriotic, brave, hating tyranny, oppression and meanness in every form; the bold denouncer of crime in high as well as in low places; a ready speaker, and as ready with his pistol as his tongue, and involved in many duels on account of his hot opposition to criminal measures. The defeat of the Yazoo Fraud was the most signal act of his legislative life, for which he paid the penalty of his life, dying of wounds received in the last of his many duels, which his undaunted attacks upon that measure brought upon him."

The original holders of lands under the Yazoo act were quick to "unload" large areas at enormous profits. Whereas they had secured thirty-five million acres of land at less than one and one-half cents an acre, large tracts were disposed of in the North at ten to fifteen cents an acre. The vast domain the Georgia legislators had sought to transfer to the speculating syndicate is described as extending from the Chattahoochee to the Mississippi and from the thin fringe of the Spanish territory on the Gulf to the border of Tennessee. Innocent purchasers, of whom there were many, after the succeeding legislature annulled the act, sought redress from Congress. For years the question was fought out there. In one of his noted speeches, John Randolph, referring to the right of a State to set aside a contract made by a corrupted legislature or officials, said: "When the governors of a people shall have betrayed their public trust for their own corrupt advantage, it is the inalienable right of that people to abrogate the act thus endeavoring to betray them."

The Virginian's sentiment appealed to the people, but the logic did not appeal to Chief Justice John Marshall, when the question finally came before the Supreme Court. Another Georgia case had protected a sovereign state from suit. By indirect methods a case between individuals North was finally made and brought to the highest legal tribunal. Marshall upheld the "fundamental principle of the law of public contract" and gave another great basic opinion to the country. Backed by this favorable decision, the friends in Congress of the holders of deeds to lands under the Yazoo act triumphed and in 1814 that body appropriated five million dollars to settle all claims against the lands, the vast territory having been transferred by Georgia to the United States. The Georgia legislature, though, in 1807 had placed itself unequivocally on record as opposed to this when it adopted resolutions declaring that when the cession of the territory was made it was not the intention "to evince any desire to compromise claims that originated in fraud and which were rendered invalid by the State sovereignty."

Daniel Webster, then serving his first term in the House, was one of those who assisted in putting through the measure that recompensed the holders of the Yazoo land certificates. Many New Englanders had invested in Georgia lands sold by the legislature to the speculating companies, and Webster was ardent in having their claims for millions of acres lying beyond the Chattahoochee redeemed by the national government.

"The Yazoo bill is through, passed by eight majority," wrote he. "It excited a great deal of feeling. All the Federalists supported the bill, and some of the Democrats. Georgians, and also Virginians and Carolinians, opposed it with great heat. Our feeling was to get the Democratic support of it."

Referring to this great Georgia case, Beveridge closed the incident with this statement:

"Thus John Marshall's great opinion was influential in securing from Congress the settlement of the claims of numerous innocent investors who had, in good faith, purchased from a band of legislative corruptionists. Of infinitely more importance, however, is the fact that Marshall's words asserted the power of the Supreme Court of the United States to annul State laws passed in violation of the National Constitution, and that throughout this Republic a fundamental principle of the law of public contract was established."

One is tempted sometimes to wonder whether John Marshall would loom quite so large as a Chief Justice if Georgia and Georgians had not provided the cases on which he could base his "epochal decisions."

There was one time, and perhaps only one time, when James Jackson deliberately turned down a challenge. There is an element of pathos in the story—politics severing what should have been a close relationship for life, charges of ingratitude by Jackson, offensive personalities on each side of the controversy, and the approach of the grim spectre of death closing a too prolonged correspondence.

Jacob Waldburger, of South Carolina, was placed in Jackson's office by his half-brother and guardian, David Keall, in 1783, to study law. There he remained four years, at the same time living with Jackson's family on terms of close intimacy. When he entered on the practice of his profession for himself Waldburger seems to have quickly dug a chasm between himself and Jackson by allying himself in a measure with the general's political foes. Waldburger's explanation was that he found Jackson's fighting temperament had brought him into disputes with many Georgians, that he did not think it incumbent on him to avoid these people because of this, and that he selected friends and political associates without regard to Jackson's sentiments toward them.

Doubtless through Jackson's influence Waldburger was sent to the legislature. This was when the first bill for the sale of public lands was up. He opposed it, not on account of the policy itself, but because he considered the price too low. Being absent from Savannah at the next election, on his return he found himself dropped from the legislature. Going to Augusta he became one of the purchasers of stock in the new Yazoo company, but soon sold out at a profit.

The fight Jackson made on the Yazoo act has been told. The papers held columns of vituperative anonymous attacks. Jackson was no less caustic in his replies. Letters attributed to him abounded in classical allusions. Characters from ancient history and mythology were drawn upon to depict the characters of his enemies. In one such letter, signed "Gracchus," there were allusions so pointed that the public accepted them as referring to young Waldburger. Waldburger took them to himself and believing his old law mentor was the author sent Capt. James Robertson, of the Chatham Artillery (April, 1796), with a letter asking if he were the author. General Jackson regarded this as an impertinence. He not only declined to give the information but continued in his letter to berate Waldburger, whom he connected with certain letters signed "Civic." In one of them Jackson had been assailed as an "exotic," and not a native American. Referring unmistakably to Waldburger, Jackson said: " 'Civic' may be one of those poor consumptive objects who some ten years since came into the state and in the most submissive manner begged even Gracchus's assistance for admission to the bar to gain his daily bread." Further allusions followed of the most bitter type, such as "big with ingratitude and treason," "grinding his neighbors for pelf he cannot enjoy himself," and as being "allied with traitors who, with many others, owe their return from banishment to the humanity and exertions of the man you take Gracchus to be, and who was told at the time those exertions were made he would live to regret them." At the close the General dismissed Waldburger as "meriting only the school boy lash."

The correspondence covered many columns before the affair closed. Jackson had been accused by his enemies of helping to transfer the confiscated Zuberbuhler property— which had been set aside for the Chatham Academy—to Waldburger as one of the legal heirs. So bitter did he feel toward his former law student that he intimated that Waldburger himself "might have lent a hand in the composition of these attacks." "Had you possessed the generosity your affected valour would seem to imply, you would before this day have given the lye to the assertion." Further, in his opinion, the descriptions in the letter by Gracchus were a close fit for Waldburger. "I took you, Sir, a little boy and treated you with all the affection of a parent and maintained you without reward with the best my house afforded. * * * * Did you not with tears in your eyes assure me that you esteemed me as a father? * * * * How did you return this parental conduct?" The general then declared Waldburger had "joined with a (political) party to break down my character and reputation."

"I suppose you may be so angry at this plain talk that you may think of a challenge—to cut it short and prevent your wasting paper on the occasion, be pleased to remember that if I enter the lists it cannot be with an ungrateful boy, who may wish to repair a shattered character. I shall not avoid any proper invitation. To keep my word with Capt. Robertson I have taken this notice of you—any further correspondence is inadmissible."

Waldburger was too sensitive to stand this and sent Capt. Robertson to Jackson, who declined to accept either a written or verbal challenge. Waldburger then published a card setting forth the facts from his viewpoint, declaring that the attack on him "was wanton and unprovoked," that he was absent from Savannah when "Civic's" attacks on Jackson were published, and inasmuch as Jackson had "utterly refused to receive a challenge, or give me that satisfaction due from one gentleman to another, I therefore pronounce General James Jackson an ASSASSIN of reputation AND A COWARD."

Jackson had gone to Louisville before this card appeared. On his return he published a short reply: "My letter inserted (in the Columbian Museum) by my friend Mr. J. Benj. Maxwell, will convince the world what impropriety there would have been in my noticing Mr. Waldburger as a gentleman. His publication only excites in my breast emotions of pity and contempt, instead of resentment. The story at Augusta might well be remembered—I mean the patience with which this hero bore the whip of Mr. Seagrove," an allusion to an encounter Waldburger had when in the Assembly.

This called for further angry recriminations and further explanations. Waldburger pointed out that the as-

sault on him took place in 1788, "when I was really but a
boy although a member of the legislature." He published a
letter from Seaborn Jones, stating that Jones had borne a
challenge from Waldburger to James Seagrove, who refused
to meet Waldburger. "Then Waldburger posted him (Seagrove) in the customary manner in one or two of the most
public places in Augusta. Mr. Waldburger acted with great
propriety and firmness on that occasion." Referring to the
private griefs of Jackson, in the loss of members of his
family, Waldburger caustically closed: "It would not be
amiss how soon the Great Author of nature consigned him
(Jackson) to his original condition."

Four newspaper columns were required by Waldburger
to review the whole unpleasant story. His pride was touched
by Jackson's intimation, as he thought, of his having been a
pauper student-at-law. His mother, he pointed out, was a
woman with a handsome competency, and he had property
of his own. Although in Jackson's law office, he asserted
he was really most indebted to George Walton for his legal
learning. There was an allusion to the paucity of Jackson's
law library and a covert sneer that the General had little
practice, as well as at the character of the bar in 1782-83.
General Jackson denounced this. At that time "John Houstoun, Mr. Stebbins, Mr. Howley, Mr. Stirk were among the
practitioners—men of accepted ability." "As for my practice, trifling as it may have been considered, as my books
will prove, it afforded me from 3,000 to 3,500 lbs. sterling
per annum."

The mental strain of the conflict with Jackson had re-
acted on Waldburger's physical condition, he suffering from
tuberculosis. It seems most cruel to-day, but Jackson closed
his last letter with an allusion to the fact that the doctors
had informed him that Waldburger was at the point of
death: "Let him depart in peace, and I hope he will meet
with more mercy at the tribunal he is soon to appear than
he had tenderness for my reputation." A few months later
Waldburger died in the Bahamas.

CHAPTER V.

A TRESPASS SUIT INSTEAD OF A DUEL.

HOW SAVANNAH'S FORMER MAYOR WAS MULCTED IN THE
SUM OF $5,000 BY A NEW JERSEY JURY—AN AMUSING
OUTGROWTH OF HIS FAMOUS DISAGREEMENT AND
LITIGATION WITH EX-SENATOR OGDEN—GIBBONS'
NAME PERPETUATED BY ONE OF CHIEF JUSTICE MAR-
SHALL'S GREAT NATIONALIZING OPINIONS—HIS EX-
PERIENCES WITH SOME POST-REVOLUTIONARY ENE-
MIES—GROWTH OF SAVANNAH'S COMMERCIAL IM-
PORTANCE.

ONE of the peculiar and unexplained features of Mayor
Thomas Gibbons' early life is his failure to espouse
the patriot cause, to which other members of his family
were attached. He was one of the Savannahians who took
the oath of allegiance to George III. As a result, he was
among those attainted of high treason by the legislature in
1782. Under the act those named were to be arrested and
held as prisoners until they could be transported to the
"British King's Dominions". If they persisted in returning, "death without benefit of clergy" was to be their portion.

Many of those who had not taken up arms on the British side, or otherwise rendered themselves particularly obnoxious, sought to have the penalty of banishment removed
and their citizenship restored. Among them was Gibbons.
The records of the House of Assembly show that on January 11, 1783, a petition was presented from "Thomas Gibbons, attorney-at-law, with a number of affidavits, setting
forth his humanity to the distressed inhabitants of this
state while in the power of the British, and praying to be
admitted to the liberties of a citizen of this state."

Two members of the Gibbons family were in the General Assembly and the family was one of high influence in
Georgia. On July 24, 1783, at the meeting of the House
there was considered "Petition No. 35. From Thomas Gib-

Thomas Gibbons, Once Mayor of Savannah,
A Virile Figure in the Early Life of the City, Whose Memory Is Perpetuated
By Chief Justice Marshall's Famous Opinion

bons, attorney-at-law, praying to be taken off the Act of
Confiscation." It was "Resolved: That the said Thomas
Gibbons be taken off the Act of Confiscation and put on the
Bill of Amercement." Others regarded as having been
transgressors against the patriot cause in a minor way were
similarly favored, some of whom became, like Gibbons, men
of local standing and service to the community. They were,
however, not to be permitted to vote, or to hold public office,
for fourteen years, with a special provision in the case ot
Gibbons, that he "shall not plead or practice in the courts
of law of this state," for the same period.

The efforts in behalf of Gibbons and others were bitterly resented by many of the old American soldiers. "The
Citizens Society" vehemently fought such clemency and
adopted resolutions thanking those members of the Assembly who "had strenuously opposed" the resolution. The
committee drafting the thanks included Dr. John Waudin,
Benjamin Lloyd, John Lindsay, Charles Odingsell and Joseph Woodruff. A mass meeting of citizens held in October,
attended "by a great majority of the inhabitants of the
county", protested against the return of any of the banished, and appointed a committee composed of Maj. John
Habersham, Capt. John Morel, Mr. Samuel Stirk, Mr. Houly,
Col. John Martin, Dr. John Waudin, Mr. Charles Odingsell,
to call on the State's officers to "order them to depart the
country in fifteen days". Then the "Association of the
County of Chatham", Maj. John Habersham, chairman, met
every Thursday to receive information as to such parties
and to carry the resolution into effect. Attorney-General
Samuel Stirk held that the legislature's resolution did not
suspend the operation of the Act of Confiscation and Banishment, as no Bill of Amercement was adopted after the
passage of the resolution.

The security that Thomas Gibbons felt, despite the violent protests against all who had been attainted by the legislature, is shown in the appearance in the "Georgia Gazette",
under the very notice of the "Association", of an advertisement signed by him requesting the owner of a negro taken
up on his mother's plantation to call on him. Some of Gibbons' lands were at the same time being advertised for sale

by the Commissioners of Confiscated Estates. Yet six years later Gibbons was a member of the General Assembly and elected by it as one of the State's Executive Committee. In February, 1787, he was readmitted to "all the rights and privileges of a free citizen, any law to the contrary notwithstanding", and quickly assumed a leading position in public affairs.

The favor Thomas Gibbons met in after years from his fellow citizens clearly indicates that extenuating circumstances satisfactorily explained his failure to take up arms with his kinsmen in the revolt against the British. There were a number of families in which similar cases occurred. In one or more instances, though, it has been intimated that the family division was premeditated and carefully conceived with a view to protection of property interests no matter which side won in the arbitrament of war.

Success in Savannah's political life did not lessen the animosity of some of Gibbons' old enemies. The most damaging and damnable charge adroitly circulated against him, without ostensible parentage, was that he had betrayed the confidence of Gen. Benjamin Lincoln and disclosed the location of the American forces to the British. The opportunity came in September, 1789, to forever squelch this accusation. General Lincoln came to Savannah on his way to the Creek country to negotiate a treaty with that tribe, and from his office in Market Square Gibbons wrote him as follows:

"My character has suffered exceedingly in this State by a number of men, some of them industriously circulating that I had been in your camp when you commanded the army at Purysburg, in the State of South Carolina, that I had acted as Secretary, or was otherwise employed in your service; that I had injured the cause of America by making known the situation of your army".

He then appealed to Gen. Lincoln to sustain his statement that he was never within the limits of his camp nor was it in his recollection "that he had ever seen him."

Gen. Lincoln was prompt and decisive in his reply:

"I do not recollect that I have ever had the pleasure of seeing you; certainly you were never employed by me in any capacity whatever. If these observations shall remove any false impressions I shall be happy that an opportunity has been given me of making them."

For fifteen years or more Gibbons was a prominent figure in the political affairs of Savannah and of Georgia. Then, while maintaining a home here, and keeping his Georgia property intact, he located for the greater part of his time in New Jersey, where he had a handsome country seat at Elizabethtown. There he became interested in steamboat navigation, then in its infancy, and his name as a result has become associated with the initial case in the Federal courts involving transportation rights, establishing principles in opposition to monopoly in interstate commerce, and confirming those powers of the general government over trade between the states which have gathered power and momentum from that day until this.

The theories as to the constitutional rights of Congress as set forth in the case of Ogden vs. Gibbons are said to be the base upon which all of the subsequent American decisions regulatory of public transportation have been built. And out of the causes of this suit came an effort on the part of Gibbons to force one of the most prominent figures in the public life of New Jersey into a duel—an effort that had a somewhat ludicrous denouement, viewed from the perspective of to-day, and furnished probably the first, perhaps the only, instance in American life where a would-be duellist was haled into court and mulcted in heavy damages for the offence of posting an enemy on his own premises.

Aaron Ogden was one of the big men of his state in that day. New Jersey had delighted to honor him. As a young man he had served throughout the revolution with distinction, winning the rank of major by hard and gallant service. It was he who carried to the British the suggestion of Lafayette that Benedict Arnold be exchanged for Maj. Andre, only to receive the reply from Clinton that the British did not give up deserters. At the bar he became a prominent figure, entered politics and was in the United States Senate, 1801-03. In 1812 he served his state as governor. New York state had created a monopoly in the privilege of using steamboats on its waters, a monopoly in favor of Robert Fulton and his wife's uncle, Robert Livingston. This had been a joke when its only foundation was the hope of Fulton that he could invent a steamboat of practical value, but when the "Clermont" demonstrated the final success of his dream the exclusive rights became of immense importance and similar rights were quickly created in other states, including Georgia and South Carolina, by legislative enactment, Fulton and Livingston selling their patent rights to the local monopolies thus established.

Ogden was one of those who foresaw the profits to be derived from steamboats and with Daniel Dod started a line between Elizabethtown and New York, which was speedily put out of commission by the action of the New York legislature. In retaliation Ogden had the New Jersey legislature create a similar monopoly within the waters of that state. In the end New Jersey rescinded its action and Ogden secured from the Livingston monopoly the privilege of running into New York.

"The Judicial and Civil History of New Jersey" says that Thomas Gibbons now appeared on the scene. From then the former Savannah mayor figured as a trouble maker on a large order. Gibbons, says the history referred to, "was a lawyer of consummate ability, a man of large means, of untiring energy, of iron will, and capable of employing means to attain an end which some honest men thought questionable."

Working arrangements were perfected between Ogden and Gibbons, who had been operating a boat line between New Jersey points under a Federal coastwise license. By this arrangement passengers were exchanged between their lines for the points reached by them and a joint agent maintained in New York to book traffic. Gibbons had originally denied the right of the monopoly to prevent his boats from moving in New York waters. His arrangement with Ogden speedily brought them into conflict with the Fulton-Livingston interests. Chancellor Kent enjoined Gibbons but refused to enjoin Ogden, and Ogden then broke off his connection with Gibbons. The former Savannahian, with every drop of his fighting blood aroused, immediately established his own line as a direct communication between Elizabethtown and New York City, with the future "Commodore" Cornelius Vanderbilt as one of his steamboat employes, and soon gave to Ogden a taste of genuine competition. Ogden sought to restrain him through the courts. Gibbons had lost none of his ability as a lawyer, or of his aggressiveness, by his removal from Savannah to the North. His characteristics had not altered between 1791 and 1818. The New York courts sustained Ogden and the Fulton-Livingston monopoly rights. Gibbons promptly appealed to the Federal courts and in this way, through the former mayor of Savannah, as Beveridge puts it, "Was John Marshall given the opportunity to deliver the last but one of his greatest nation-making opinions."

The eyes of the country were centered on the case. Already the public, and especially the expanding trading interests of the land, realized that the steamboat was to be the great factor in the transportation of passengers and freights, and that if held within the vise of a monopoly the development of the country would thereby be seriously hampered and checked. Especially was this true of the newer sections where good roads and canals did not exist and the rivers formed the only highways for the easy movement of merchandise. Gibbons, a rich man and endowed by nature with the fighting attributes, secured the services of two of the greatest lawyers of the day, Daniel Webster, of Massachusetts, and William Wirt, of Virginia, attorney general of the United States. The monopoly employed the great Pinckney, of South Carolina, but ill health prevented him from serving. Its attorneys before the court were Thomas J. Oakley, attorney-general of New York, and Thomas Addis Emmet, the Irish patriot, who had risen to a high place at the metropolitan bar.

"Of all Webster's arguments," says Beveridge, "that in the steamboat case is incontestably supreme." "Oakley, Emmet and Wirt exhausted the learning then extant on every point involved in the controversy." To quote again from the admirable "Life of John Marshall", by the former Indiana senator, "On March 2, 1824, Marshall delivered that opinion which has done more to knit the American people into a nation than any other one force in our history except-

ing only war. * * * * In Gibbons vs. Ogden he welded that
people into a unit by the force of their mutual interests. * * *
The specific question to be decided was whether the New
York steamboat monopoly violated that provision of the
national constitution which bestowed on Congress the power
to regulate commerce among the several states. The earliest
exposition of the commerce clause of the constitution by
any eminent national authority, therefore, came from
John Marshall. In his opinion in Gibbons vs. Ogden he
spoke the first and last authoritative word on that crucial
subject. * * * * After almost a century Marshall's nation-
alist theory of commerce is more potent than ever; and
nothing human is more certain than that it will gather new
strength as far into the future as forecast can puncture."

This final verdict in the Supreme Court in favor of
Gibbons dealt a death blow to the steamboat monopoly, not
only in New York but in Georgia and other states. The
former Savannahian had won not only a personal triumph
over his recent associate in the transportation business but
had brought about a declaration of the right of Congress
to regulate commerce between the states that has been the
bed rock on which judicial decisions and congressional
actions along that line have ever since rested.

Gibbons fully appreciated the vital importance of the
case. Referring to it in one of the footnotes to his "Miscellanies of Georgia," Chappell a half century ago wrote:

"The case throughout its long pendency was regarded
as one of immense public, political and commercial importance, and excited, consequently, a strong and unusual interest, and Mr. Gibbons himself came to be everywhere viewed
as the champion of free trade between the States, and indeed
somewhat in the light of a great public benefactor by having
taken upon himself the burden of the magnificent, costly
and finally victorious litigation.

"In 1824, not long after Mr. Gibbons' triumph in the
Supreme Court, I heard Judge Berrien say in conversing
with some gentlemen about it, that Mr. Gibbons, whilst the
case was yet pending, made his will and appropriated $40,000
to carry on the suit in case it should not be ended before
his death. Upon some one present expressing surprise,

Judge Berrien remarked that Mr. Gibbons was a very able lawyer and felt great pride in having his opinion on the constitutional question sustained."

Chief Justice Marshall prepared and delivered an opinion in this noted case and the name of the former Savannah mayor, politician and duellist may be said to have become almost immortalized thereby. Day after day had been given up by the court to the learned arguments of the attorneys in the case on the mooted question of the scope of the power of Congress to regulate commerce. The Chief Justice held that "This power, like all other powers vested in Congress, is complete in itself, may be exercised to the fullest extent, and acknowledges no limitations other than are prescribed by the constitution." The Court held that "steamboats could no more be restrained from navigating waters and entering ports which are free to vessels using sails than if they were wafted on their voyage by the wind instead of being propelled by the agency of fire." And in his memorable conclusion Marshall paid his respects to the attorneys who had sought to deny or restrict the rights of the general government in the interest of the authority of the states:

"Powerful and ingenious minds, taking as postulates that the powers expressly granted to the government of the Union are to be contracted by construction into the narrowest possible compass, and that the original powers of the state are retained, if any possible construction will retain them, may, by a course of well digested, but refined and metaphysical reasoning, founded on these premises, explain away the constitution of our country and leave it, a magnificent structure, indeed, to look at, but totally unfit for use. They may so entangle and perplex the understanding as to obscure principles which were before thought quite plain, and induce doubts where, if the mind were to pursue its own course, none would be perceived. In such a case it is peculiarly necessary to recur to safe and fundamental principles, to sustain those principles, and when sustained to make them the test of the arguments to be examined." And judging from the fact that Marshall's opinion has pre-

vailed for a century it is evident that he "recurred to safe
and fundamental principles" in the preparation thereof.

The greater part of the space of the Savannah "Georgian" for two days was given up to the publication of Marshall's opinion. Interest in this city in the case was two-
fold. There was the natural personal sympathy his fellow
townsmen felt for Gibbons in the long fight he had been
making in the courts. Then there was the even greater
interest arising from the fact that Savannah's business was
being slowly throttled by just such a monopoly as Gibbons
was contesting through the courts. The legislature of Georgia in 1814 had created a similar monopoly in the use of
steamboats on the Savannah river, in the incorporation of
The Georgia Steamboat Company, $800,000 capital, in 1,600
shares of $500 each, with Samuel Howard of Savannah as
a chief incorporator, giving to it the exclusive right for
twenty years to transport merchandise upon Georgia waters
on all vessels or rafts towed by steam craft. The penalty
for infringing on this right was a fine of $500 for each of-
fense and the forfeiture of the boat and its machinery.
South Carolina likewise imitated New York in conferring
similar exclusive rights to the company so far as the Savannah river was concerned. Savannah's general commercial interests were adversely affected and there was intense
opposition to the existing conditions among those not directly affiliated with the monopoly. Gibbons' fight against
the New York monopoly was recognized as a gallant fight to
break the shackles elsewhere, and Savannah quickly bene-
fited by the decision of the Supreme Court. Steamboat
navigation of all waters was thrown open to healthful
competition and the effect was soon apparent.

Diversion of freights to Charleston, business men of
which city had quietly secured a controlling interest in the
Georgia Steamboat Company, had been brought about by
discriminating lower freight rates from Augusta and other
points to that city than to Savannah, the much nearer port.
This discrimination now ceased and the natural trade of
Savannah came to Savannah once more. A writer in the
"Augusta Courier" in 1827 stated that a dozen steamboats
then "paddled between the cities of Savannah and Augusta,

a new one is building in Augusta, and in New York an elegant one is in prospect to ply by the side of the George Washington and the Carolina so as to give us a steamboat passing up and down the river every other day. The Washington goes down and comes up frequently within the week, having gone down in twenty-four hours, its actual running time a little over seventeen hours."

Frequently a steamboat towed down five or six barges loaded with the commodities of the upper part of the state and the importance of Savannah as a port was not to be gauged by its small population. A few months later, in December, a correspondent at Charleston wrote that he "perceived a great change in the tone of the public in that city when speaking of Savannah from that noticed last year. They are now convinced, by a somewhat dear bought experience, that nature has been too bountiful to Savannah for it to fear Charleston or any other city wresting from it a trade so long enjoyed." And in April, 1828, as new and unmistakable evidence of the spirit of Savannah, the "Georgian" told of the building at the upper yard, of the Georgia Steamboat Company, by John Cant, of a steam packet to run between Savannah and Augusta, "the boat to be of two hundred tons burthen and one hundred and twenty feet long." This was the first steamboat built at Savannah, was completed in forty-five days, and the "Georgian" expressed the feelings of all when it said: "We are proud to find that this first exercise of the art in Savannah has been productive of so fine, complete and beautiful a craft." It is also interesting to note that at that time the charge for bringing a bale of cotton from Augusta to Savannah by boat was 35 cents, with delivery in less than three days.

Still further proof of the progressiveness of the Savannah of that period, once the grip of the monopoly was torn away, is found in the fact that there was built in the North the same year, for a local company, the steamboat John David Mongin, named after the largest stockholder. This was designed especially for the Savannah-Charleston route and to carry many passengers and considerable freight. It was equipped with every comfort and luxury of the day, and is described as "the most commodious and elegant boat yet seen in the South." Its running time from its wharf here to its wharf at Charleston was fourteen and a half hours, including an hour's stop at Beaufort, and on the outside run it made eighteen miles an hour. Other steamboats were built at Savannah from year to year and until the Civil War its shipyards had an enviable record for well constructed craft of moderate size, steam and sail.

The victory of Gibbons had not been effected, though, without the creation of intense personal feeling between him and Ogden. From the very inception of the trouble there was bitterness between them. This antagonism would have early culminated in a duel if Gibbons could have brought it about. He tried no devious ways to affront his enemy but resorted to the most direct method of letting him and the public know his sentiments as regards Ogden. Invading the grounds of Ogden's home at Elizabethtown, Gibbons deliberately posted him in language that ordinarily would have meant a duel within as short a time as customary preliminaries permitted.

Instead of the usual challenge, though, Ogden countered with a suit for trespass. It is needless to go through its course or furnish details. Suffice it to say that "the long depending cause," as it was described, came on for its final hearing before the Chief Justice of New Jersey in September, 1818. The plaintiff had the most distinguished counsel of the state in his service, J. C. Hornblower, T. Frelinghuysen, and Richard Stockton. The attorney for Gibbons was William Halsey, with Gibbons, of course, largely assisting. A verdict of $5,000 was returned against Gibbons and sustained.

Commenting on the case the Newark, N. J., Centinel said:

"One word more. The jurors of Essex spoke a caution to duellists in accents as loud as thunder. Invitations to the bloody field shall not escape with impunity—nor shall the crime of duelling, so offensive to God and odious to man, go unpunished. High minded and honorable gentlemen may here learn to resist the bloody combat, how to sustain a character worth a thousand honors of murdering a fellow man. Instead of appealing to the sword, appeal to the laws of the land. We have enlightened courts—we have independent jurors—and they will award impartial justice to the oppressor and the oppressed."

Col. Ogden, his New Jersey biographer says, "was dogged and persevering in his attempts to secure his rights. No aspersion could be justly made against his character; that remained untarnished; but in the end he was defeated after a most harassing conflict. He lost his fortune, his wife died, and he never recovered the position he formerly held." In 1829 he was thrown into jail in New York for debt, and his case is said to have been largely responsible for legislation prohibiting imprisonment for debt of an officer or soldier of the Revolution. It is remarkable that in our own country, nearly a hundred years after Oglethorpe founded Georgia as a refuge for unfortunates imprisoned for debt, veterans of the war that freed the colonies and constituted them into a republic were cast into prison and held there indefinitely because of financial embarrassment.

Col. Ogden was one of the founders of the Society of the Cincinnati and at his death in 1839 was the president of the General Society. In the last years of his life he held the office of Collector of the Port of Jersey City, created for him through the sympathy of Congress.

Daniel Dod was interested with Ogden in his steamboat line. This Dod was the noted engineer of his day, who built the engines for the famous steamship Savannah, which sailed from this port for Liverpool in 1819. It was doubtless through Gibbons that the designing and building of the engines for the steamship was placed in Dod's hands. The Savannah's machinery was constructed and installed at Elizabethtown, where Dod had built the engines for Gibbons' boats.

Gibbons, whose plantation near Savannah, Whitehall, is still in the hands of his descendants, never resumed his place in the life of this city, although he held large property interests here and always manifested a keen interest in its affairs. It was doubtless through him that Dr. Henry Kollock, described as "profoundly distinguished for his remarkable eloquence, which was unsurpassed in his day in the American pulpit," came to the Independent Presbyterian

Church. Kollock was ordained at Elizabethtown and served in the pastorate there. Another man who uniquely connects with the story of Ogden and Gibbons is Eli Whitney, who was a cousin of Ogden. It is clearly within the range of probabilities that his removal to Savannah may have partly come about through knowledge of this section that came to him through Gibbons' relationship with Ogden.

Savannah's former mayor became so fat and unwieldy in his old age that it was with difficulty he could stand for any length of time and in court he was granted the privilege of being seated. This was so on one notable occasion in the Supreme Court of New Jersey. Speaking of it, the author of the "Judicial History" of that State says that Gibbons was remarkable for wit and sarcasm, in the use of which, in cases where he appeared as counsel, he excelled the most of men. "At the time of one of the many controversies between him and Gov. Ogden his own son-in-law, John M. Trumbull, had been subpoenaed as a witness, but had failed to appear. Gibbons, who had quarreled with Mr. Trumbull, as in fact, with almost all the members of his family, seized the opportunity to wreak his vengeance and applied to the Supreme Court for an attachment for contempt. He appeared before that tribunal in support of the motion. Richard Stockton representing Mr. Trumbull, injudiciously reflected upon the character and motives of Gibbons. This opened the door for a witty and sarcastic reply. Gibbons requested permission from the Court to remain seated, and poured out volumes of invective which even the dignified Chief Justice Kirkpatrick and his associates were unable to withstand. The court, the counsel and the spectators indulged in roars of laughter until the court room resounded with the peals. Joseph Warren Scott, then in the prime of his life, and a distinguished counsellor, left his seat and ran to a place where he was concealed from the view of the judges, danced up and down, and clapping his hands shook with uncontrollable mirth. It was some time before the dignity of the court could be restored."

From this one might infer that the other New Jersey lawyers wished to verbally castigate the great Stockton but that it took the Georgian to "trim him" to their hearts' content.

Gibbons died North in 1826. His estate is said to have been of the value of over a million dollars, an enormous amount for that day. Indeed, he is reputed to have been the wealthiest man in the South. He carried his pugnacious spirit into his will, on file at the Chatham county court house, in his efforts to keep certain parties from sharing in the estate.

They were bitter haters, those Savannahians of a century ago, and no one better illustrates this temperament than Gibbons. Every page of his will bristles with intense hostility to Trumbull, who had married his daughter Ann. Time after time he repeats that none of his valuable holdings in Georgia, South Carolina, New Jersey and New York, shall ever become the property, by gift or inheritance, of Trumbull, his children, or their descendants. And at the close, to make assurance doubly sure, he compresses his wishes into a few almost venomous lines:

"And I do pray to God, before whom I am shortly to appear, that I have been enabled to so devise and bequeath my whole estate, real and personal, that no event may or possibly can arise in all the changes of this changing world, that will enable John M. Trumbull, or any one of his children, or any person descended from them, to be benefitted one cent, or the value thereof, from my estate, meaning and intending that they shall be forever excluded to the end of time."

Gibbons furnishes a most interesting picture in the gallery of early Savannah portraits of men of forceful action.

General Nathaniel Greene,
Chief Lieutenant of Washington, Who Sustained His Refusal
to Accept a Challenge From Captain Gunn

CHAPTER VI.

WHEN GUNN SOUGHT GEN. GREENE'S LIFE.

REVOLUTIONARY TROUBLE LEFT A BITTERNESS THAT SOUGHT SATISFACTION THROUGH THE CODE—WASHINGTON'S PART IN THE AFFAIR—A SAVANNAHIAN THE FIRST APPOINTEE TO PUBLIC OFFICE TO BE REJECTED BY THE UNITED STATES SENATE—HOW GEORGE M. TROUP CAME TO ASSAIL THE EDITOR OF THE "MUSEUM"—GEORGIA URGES A RECALL AMENDMENT—OBNOXIOUS FEDERALIST EDITOR MOBBED BY REPUBLICANS AND MAYOR ISSUES A PROCLAMATION.

MANY personal antagonisms which developed during the struggle for independence cropped out in later years. One of the most notable of these locally was the difficulty between Capt. James Gunn and Gen. Nathaniel Greene.

Gunn was a man of obscure origin, born in Virginia in 1739. He became a lawyer there, joined the patriot cause, served as captain of dragoons under General Wayne, engaged in the movement for the relief of Savannah, and after the war made this city his home and took up the practice of his profession.

He was one of the original members of the Georgia Society of the Cincinnati.

Gunn had become incensed against Greene as a result of the course pursued by the general, as his commanding officer, in 1782.

Gunn had sold a horse belonging to the army, without orders. When the matter was brought to Gen. Greene's attention he directed a Court of Inquiry. This court exonerated Gunn. Gen. Greene refused to approve of its action. Gunn looked on this as evidence of personal hostility. The correspondence was sent to Congress, which approved of Greene's conduct and condemned that of Gunn, who ever after cherished a bitter grudge against the general.

On the termination of hostilities, when Gen. Greene came to reside on the plantation, "Mulberry Grove", presented to him by the State of Georgia, Gunn's animosity found speedy expression in a cartel through Col. James Jackson, who soon withdrew from the affair on ascertaining the merits of the case.

Judge Johnson, one of the early biographers of Greene, held that Jackson's consenting to carry the challenge for Gunn arose "from the highly chivalrous state of feeling which existed among American military men at the close of the revolutionary war, and in no part of the United States was this feeling in such excess and so frequently developed as in Savannah".

Gen. Greene wrote to Col. Jackson detailing the facts in the case and explaining why he would not receive a challenge from Gunn:

"If an officer had the right to sell public property without authority, so had a private soldier. Capt. Gunn demanded a confirmation of the proceedings of the Board in justification of his conduct. At first I could scarcely suppose him serious, but finding him persistent in the thing, I was obliged to give him my sentiments on the subject, however unpleasant to his feelings or opposite to his wishes. But no man ever heard me use language that would disgrace a gentleman. My sense of his proceeding was that it was criminal and altogether unwarrantable." Greene pointed out that he could have brought Gunn before a court-martial and forced the loss of his commission but had no desire to so degrade and punish him.

Gen. Greene having ignored this challenge, Major Benjamin Fishbourne, another revolutionary soldier, became the friend for Gunn in a second challenge.

Jackson was colonel at the time of the First Regiment of Chatham County Militia, Gunn was lieutenant-colonel, and Fishbourne was major.

Again Greene refused to consider the challenge, taking the broad ground that a superior officer could not be held accountable in such a way for acts involving discipline of subordinate officers. The general recognized that such a precedent would be subversive of all discipline and tend to a constant embroilment of commanders with subordinates.

It was a day when few men had the moral courage to decline a challenge from one considered a gentleman.

To refuse satisfaction rendered one subject to the charge of cowardice—the unforgivable sin—and to the probable loss of public esteem.

Gen. Greene appreciated this keenly, and, fearful that his brother officers might misinterpret his conduct, laid the history of the affair before Gen. Washington, and asked for his opinion.

"If," said he, "I thought my honor and my reputation would suffer in the opinion of the world, and more especially with the military gentlemen, I value life too little to hesitate a moment to accept the challenge."

It seems incredible that Greene could have believed, after the years of service he had given his country on the battle field, that any one associated with him could have considered the taint of cowardice applying to their old comrade.

The pressure of public opinion, as regards the right to demand personal satisfaction if one felt injured by another, was so strong that the Quaker, who had forsaken the teachings of his faith at the militant call of patriotic duty, wavered in his convictions.

But George Washington, with his clear insight and ability to pierce to the heart of a question and lay bare its essential points, was prompt and decisive in his judgment.

His answer left no ground on which any possible enemies of Greene could stand for an attack upon his action.

"I give it as my decided opinion," wrote Washington from the privacy of Mount Vernon, "that your honor and reputation will stand, not only perfectly acquitted for the non-acceptance of his challenge, but that your prudence and judgment would have been condemned by accepting it; because, if a commanding officer is amenable to private calls for the discharge of his public duty, he has always a dagger at his heart, and can turn neither to the right nor the left, without meeting its point. In a word, he is no longer a free

agent in office, as there are few military decisions which
are not offensive to one party or the other."

Backed by the overpowering influence of Gen. Washington on the public mind, it was needless for Gen. Greene
to go further.

Gunn knew this as well as Greene. But Gunn was a
man described as "violent, aggressive, overbearing." To
Greene went the threat that his enemy would satisfy his
aggrieved "honor" by a personal assault.

Greene's answer was cool and to the point:

"I always wear pistols and will defend myself."

When he rode into Savannah from his plantation the
General wore his pistols ready for immediate use.

This was in 1785. A year later Greene died. It is interesting to note that one old writer, explaining why the
General rode through the intense heat of the mid-day sun,
intimates that he feared assassination after dusk, from
some old Tory or other enemy. But Gunn never attempted
his threatened personal assault.

This Gunn-Greene "near duel" is referred to by old
writers on the code as one of the striking evidences of the
force of popular sentiment.

Sabine says that while Greene's courage had never
been doubted, "he dared not act definitely and finally without the assurance of the most illustrious man in history
that his 'honor' and his 'reputation' would not suffer by dis-
regarding the call.

"No wonder that persons in the common walks of life
yielded against their convictions, in cases of aggravated injury, when a gentleman of Greene's lofty character and
standing in every sense, hesitated whether to meet an inferior officer under the circumstances related."

These old duels bring one into contact with strong
men whose memories have unfortunately vanished. They
also allure one to stray into other by-paths of history. It
is so in this instance. Who recalls Major Benjamin Fishbourne to-day? He had served bravely through the war
and in 1783 married Nancy Wereat, daughter of John
Wereat, one of Georgia's illustrious patriots and "recognized

as one of the most useful men of his generation." Yet Fishbourne was the first and only man nominated to office by President Washington who was rejected by the United States Senate, bringing to that body a letter from Washington in endorsement of this Savannahian such as probably no other president ever wrote in favor of any other rejected candidate.

The Senate had assigned no cause for its refusal to approve Fishbourne, who had been nominated as the first collector of the port of Savannah under the new Federal government. Washington acquiesced, but took occasion to inform the Senators as to the type of man Fishbourne was.

The Savannahian, the President stated, had served under his own eyes "with reputation as an officer and a gentleman." At the storming of Stony Point he had distinguished himself. General Wayne sent him as messenger to Washington with the news of the mutiny of the Pennsylvania troops in 1781. Chatham county had shown its confidence in him by electing him repeatedly to the Georgia Assembly. The militia had selected him as their lieutenant-colonel. He had been a member and president of the Executive Council of the State, and under its appointment had served in practically the same position as collector of the port.

"It appeared therefore to me," continued Washington, "that Mr. Fishbourne must have enjoyed the confidence of the militia officers in order to have been elected to a military rank—the confidence of the freemen to have been selected for the Council, and the confidence of the Council to have been appointed collector of the port of Savannah." Major John Habersham's name was then sent to the Senate, the appointment confirmed, and he served as collector of the port until his death, ten years later.

Gunn lived for sixteen years after his vain efforts to force Gen. Greene into a duel. That incident gives an insight into the vindictiveness of his nature and his uncompromising disposition, and would also indicate that he was not over-scrupulous in his methods.

He was undoubtedly a man of unusual strength of character and genuine ability, as otherwise he would not have

been a state leader in the days of strenuous political conflict that began with the inauguration of Washington and
ran on for several decades in Georgia without regard to tne
"era of good feeling" under Monroe. He became Brigadier-
General of the State's forces and served twelve years in the
United States Senate, 1789-1801, associated there with General James Jackson, who had carried his first challenge to
Gen. Greene. If he had been less the man of unyielding determination and domineering power he would not have left
the national capital and coming to Augusta used every influence at his command, legitimate and otherwise, to assist
those who were forcing through the "iniquitous" Yazoo act,
albeit it is now a revised version that Jackson and his allies,
by their hue and cry, somewhat exaggerated the "iniquity"
thereof for their own political ends, which seems not at
all surprising to those who know the devious ways of politicians and statesmen even until this day.

Gunn is described as a sort of field marshal for the
campaign to seduce the Georgia legislators, and is pictured
as striding about the streets of Augusta "arrayed in broad
cloth, tan boots and a beaver hat, commending those who
favored the bill and abusing those who opposed it. In his
hand he carried a loaded whip, and with this the burly
United States Senator actually menaced those members
who objected to the scheme." But it does seem just a bit
strange in turning over the musty pages of the past to sud-
denly realize how, even in death, this same picturesque, even
if ruffianly, Gunn came near to forcing other Savannahians
to the duelling field, and how harsh reflections upon his
character, as he lay hardly cold beneath the sod in middle
Georgia, involved a future governor and senator in an assault with a loaded whip upon a Savannah editor, with a
soon-to-be judge of Chatham as aid and abettor—if the
editor told the truth—the editor posing as the defender of
the liberty of the press to publish anonymous personalities
and yet refuse to divulge the identity of the writer.

It all came about in this way. Gunn died at Louisville
on July 30, 1801, his term as Senator having expired on
March 3. Old English customs still lingered in Georgia and
we find designated as the official "mourners" at his funeral

Capt. Merriwether, Capt. Shellman, and Maj. John Berrien, the latter the State Treasurer and father of John McPherson Berrien, who became the most prominent Savannahian of his day, United States Senator, Attorney-General of the United States, and otherwise a commanding figure in national affairs. The "Columbian Museum", Savannah organ of the antagonists of the Jeffersonian party, sadly commented:

"Gen. Gunn is now beyond the reach of friendship or of hatred, nor can his ashes be affected by censure or by praise. May be rest in peace, 'And if charity and good nature open not the benevolent lips let the finger of silence rest on the tongue of malevolence and detraction'. "

Gunn had been the target of ceaseless attacks from Jackson and other Republican leaders and their assaults and the repeal of the Yazoo act were credited with hastening his sudden death. But the "Museum's" appeal for the "finger of silence" was of no avail. Attacks on the deeds and misdeeds of Gunn continued, and his friends came to the rescue of his memory. They were embittered by their political defeats and not inclined to spare the lash any more than were their enemies. An anonymous contributor, signing his letter with a Q, said:

"That he (Gunn) had his faults his warmest friends will not deny. He, however, served his country faithfully and bravely in our Revolutionary war, and shall we allow any of these mushroom officers, these gewgaws, to insult his memory? To the shame of one of the gentlemen be it told, that he wrote to Gen. Gunn requesting the appointment of aide-de-camp." The writer intimated that another of Gunn's revilers wanted to be Judge. "If it is their object to get in the Legislature, for God's sake send them", he concluded.

There was no question as to the parties referred to. David B. Mitchell was major of the First Battalion of the Chatham Regiment and candidate for State Senator; George M. Troup was an aspirant for the House; Thomas U. P. Charlton was captain of a militia company and, youthful though he was, suspected of having judicial aspirations. They were all active leaders of the Jeffersonian Republi-

Governor George M. Troup
As a Young Man He Assaulted the Editor of the "Columbian Museum"
of Savannah

cans, selected and groomed by Jackson himself. Troup and Charlton had been anonymous contributors to the Savannah papers on political subjects.

Charlton and Troup replied to Q in the "Museum." Their letters are interesting disclosures of their style of attack and of the personal virulence that marked the politics of that day.

"Mark how a plain, unvarnished tale will set this libellous scoundrel down and throw the lie into his teeth," said Charlton, and then he pointed out that while friends had sent a request to Gen. Gunn to make him an aide, and he had been told that Gunn on his return to Georgia would appoint him, he "felt that even an abstract relation with Gen. Gunn, even the military connection of aide, might be construed by the people into a partial dereliction of principles, which, with my honor, I hold dearer than life, and to preserve which I have sacrificed interest and everything that savors of selfish calculation."

Troup was not less severe in his answer:

"Whether I am a mushroom or a gewgaw, I will hunt the coward from his obscurity and expose him to the public infamy.

"I am not the persecutor of the dead. My malignity reaches not the peaceful silence of the tomb. My resentment is against the living enemies of my country."

Referring to the Federalists, Troup said: "I have always delighted in the exposure of their crimes, and when their sins had brought upon them the vengeance of their injured fellow citizens, when they had fallen never to rise again, it was my triumph to insult them with their vices and to humble them in repentance."

"We told them of a leader, the very Hercules of his faction, concentrating in himself the strength, the virtues and the confidence of his party, stealing from the closet of secrecy the conspiracies of his friends and betraying them to the world."

This was a reference to a charge that Senator Gunn had divulged caucus secrets to Duane, the notorious vituperative editor of the "Aurora," of Philadelphia, chief of Republican organs.

"Such a party was worthy of such a leader," concluded Troup. "Oppression, insult and injury had followed in their footsteps, and the last scene of their political life closed with the treachery of faithless friendship."

Peremptory demands went from Charlton and Troup to Seymour and Woolhopter, editors of the "Museum", for the name of the writer of the article signed Q.

The request was denied. The editors held that "where injunctions had been laid upon them to keep the real names of correspondents out of sight" "we have been faithful to the trust," and that Troup and Charlton themselves had published articles in the "Museum" without exposure of their identity.

"But we have not expected (them) to resort to assassination in these enlightened days of special liberty and equal rights to compel us to violate our engagements and to a surrender of the privileges time immemorially assigned to and enjoyed by editors."

The publication in the "Museum" which "arraigned the illiberal and unjustifiable conduct of the two young men who had aspersed the character of the late Gen. Gunn," the editors said, brought a demand for its author, which, "with perfect integrity and propriety we refused." "The paper was open to them for vindication. They came forward with replies, with their names annexed. Not satisfied with this they insisted with violent threats upon the disclosure of the author of Q, and were still denied.

"One of them, George M. Troup, assailed the unarmed editor with a loaded whip, was disarmed and failed in the rencounter, and would have met with his deserts had not interference been made.

"Though we shall never become the aggressor in any assault, we shall be prepared to repel it at the hazard of our lives, and have no apprehension from individual attack.

"But we are told that these high mettled young men (Troup was then but 21 and Charlton 22) are stirring up the multitude, to do us evil and destroy us; and that they are

determined to make bloody war upon us, till they compel us
to a forfeiture of our integrity, honor and independence as
men, or procure our deaths.

"We do not profess ourselves Samsons, to encounter
armies, and we confidently hope that the good sense and
strength of this community will not be idle spectators of
our demolition, for preserving to ourselves the character of
men and of Americans."

The appeal seems to have had its effect. Either the
influential Federalists rallied to the support of the editors
or the Republican chieftains held in check the too zealous
game cocks of their party. But the incident pictures most
graphically the political conditions under which the nineteenth century opened in the little city of Savannah, with
its 2,800 white folks and 2,500 negroes. There was no room
here for the Laodicean. All men blew hot, and without
mental reservations.

So it was throughout this section. Politics ruled and
disturbed every community. Writing from the country, a
correspondent of the "Columbian Museum" in 1798 gave
this graphic description of what one had to contend with
from the political ardor of his neighbors:

"In this little community there are no less than six
classes of politicians. We have the Republicans, Aristocrats, Aristocratic-Republicans, Republican-Aristocrats,
Democrats, and a few called Hell-Fire Republicans, and
when three or four of the different classes meet, by chance,
at a poor man's house, like mine, they never leave off dis-
putation as long as there is a drop in the bottle; and the
longer they dispute the hotter it grows, till sometimes my
wife and myself are obliged to go out of the cabin to avoid
having the drums of our ears broken."

A few days after the trouble with the editors of the
"Museum" the election came and the Republicans swept
the county, sending Mitchell to the Senate and Edward Harden, Joseph Bryan and Troup to the House. The following
year Charlton went to the House and Bryan to Congress.

It may not be amiss to recall that Senator Gunn's participation in the "barefaced corruption" of members of the
legislature, as it was described by his enemies at the time,

led to Georgia becoming the first state in the Union to suggest a recall amendment to the Federal constitution, antedating William Jennings Bryan and others in their support of such a measure by more than a century. The General Assembly of 1796 was thoroughly in control of the enemies of Gunn and of the Yazoo grants, and resolutions were adopted urging an amendment to the constitution "authorizing the legislature of any State to recall a senator in Congress therefrom whenever the same may be deemed necessary". It needs no very vivid imagination to recall quite recent times when Georgia might have been tempted to avail itself of the recall if it had been grafted on the constitution as the State urged in its indignant impotence to rid itself of Gunn.

Charlton was Solicitor-General 1804-09 and Judge of the Eastern Circuit 1821-22. Troup went to Congress in 1807 and served four terms in the House, until 1815, when he was elected United States Senator, serving 1816-18 and again in 1831-33. He also served as governor in 1823-27. When Senator James Jackson picked Charlton and Troup, before they were of age, as of the calibre from which big men are made, he showed the unerring sagacity that marked all of his political judgments.

The bitter antagonism between the Republicans or Democrats and the Federalists of Savannah continued for many years, in fact until the final disappearance of the fragments of the latter party in the new and greater Whig organization.

Seymour and Woolhopter were not the only Federalist editors who were threatened with, or suffered from, mob violence. Federalism became more than ever obnoxious when the country was involved in the difficulties which led to the second war with Great Britain. Savannah stood foursquare to the winds in its support of the national government. Common prudence should have dictated to the Federal handful of the city that they refrain from antagonizing this overwhelming sentiment of the community.

Partisanship overcame their discretion, though, and a newspaper began a brief and stormy life as the organ of opposition to the administration at Washington. It was

dubbed "The American Patriot", and its course was limited
to sixteen numbers, two a week for eight weeks, from
April 14, 1812, to June 5, 1812.   John S. Mitchell and Charles
M. Pratt were the publishers and editors.   They stood, they
declared, for the principles of Washington and Hamilton,
and their restoration in the conduct of the government.
They "would endeavor", they stated, "to place in a clear
point of view the misconduct of the present public servants
in attempting to cajole, deceive and mislead the people,
thereby to maintain the high posts of honor, which their
measures prove them incapacitated to fill."

The "Patriot" and its editors were the centres of a
growing storm of hatred from the first issue.   They were
pro-British and anti-French.   Jefferson was lampooned as
"Terrapin Tom", Madison, then president, was held up as a
poor, abject, servile tool.   The administration was "characterized by hypocrisy and deception, imbecility and folly."
The embargo and non-intercourse policies were ridiculed, re-
cruiting for the approaching war was opposed, the Republican leaders were scorned as men of "dark and ignorant
minds, instigated by debased passions", and their utterances
as "waves of Democratic slander and scurrility", while Congress was "but little better than a factious club of dema-
gogues".

The nullification-secession tendencies of certain Federal
leaders of New England were endorsed.   "All New England
arises in the majesty of her strength and says she will no
longer be imposed upon."

The anger of the Savannah Republicans grew hotter
and hotter as each issue of "The Patriot" poured its broadsides into their beliefs and their admired leaders.   Finally
came the explosion.

A mass meeting was called to consider the questions of
the day and to express Savannah's attitude as regards them.
From the City Hall it adjourned to the old Independent Pres-
byterian Church.   Mayor William B. Bulloch presided.   The
feeling was intense.   Savannah was represented among the
"Patriots" who had seized East Florida from the Spanish.
Resolutions were presented endorsing their actions.   The
Republicans triumphed in their passage, despite the opposi-

A Proclamation.

CITY OF SAVANNAH.

Whereas, it is represented to me, that JOHN S. MITCHELL, late editor of "The *American Patriot*," has surrendered himself into the hands of the Sheriff of Chatham County, and sought the protection of the laws—

I do hereby call upon the Citizens, generally, to abstain from violence, of every description; and they are hereby most earnestly enjoined to do so; and respect the laws of our Country. The Officers of the Police are required to be vigilant in preserving the peace of the City.

In witness whereof, I have hereunto set my hand, this 8th day of June, 1812.

W. B. Bulloch,

Mayor.

Mayor Bulloch's Proclamation
To Quell Republican Violence to a Savannah Federalist Editor

tion of Judge Berrien and John Y. Noel. Resolutions were introduced endorsing the acts of the government at Washington. Col. Habersham, a veteran of the revolution, introduced a substitute urging the administration to pause "until they had ensured to themselves the means of rendering the conflict with Great Britain honorable and decisive to this country".

Alderman T. U. P. Charlton, ardent Republican, urged that the division be on party principles, and the Republicans defeated the substitute and passed their own endorsement of Madison and his policies.

"The American Patriot" erupted one time more in its brief history, the day after the meeting. According to it the Federalists at the mass meeting were persons "of eminent standing in society, and warmly interested in the country, from both property and family." While there were "some very honorable and respectable characters" on the Republican or Democratic side, there "was a considerable number of foreigners, entirely uninterested in our welfare, either from family, or property", "If character were considered the principles of Washington" would have triumphed.

This was the last issue of "The American Patriot." The "Republican" denounced it as a "traitorous print." "The common herd" and "the foreign rabble", as its editors considered the majority of the Jeffersonians, arose in their wrath before the hour came for it to go to press again. That very night a mob gathered. The city administration was Republican and the guardians of the peace seem to have had pressing business elsewhere for the time being. The house where Mitchell and Pratt lived was invaded. Leaders of the assailants, according to Mitchell, were "Burke, an Irishman", Pitcher, Ash, Greer and John Bulloch, nephew of the Mayor." Mitchell's pistol failed to discharge; Pratt fired a shot and ran for assistance. Mitchell was clubbed and then, to quote his language:

"These degenerate cowards, were not content with bruising, but must drag me out of my own dwelling, into the street, where I was surrounded by a large mob, the very filthy dregs of corrupt Democracy, who hurried me along with abuse and blows to an adjoining pump, where they gratified their hellish malice."

This was set forth in a broadside which Mitchell printed and scattered over the city the next day. The editor had his nerve unshaken to that extent. He threw fresh fuel on the flames and the mob spirit flamed up in a more dangerous mood. His life and perhaps other lives were imperilled thereby. Urged by friends and supporting Federalists, Editor Mitchell placed himself in the hands of the Sheriff for protection, and probably for the first and only time in the history of Savannah its mayor had printed and distributed throughout the city a handbill reciting this fact and urging the citizens to abstain from violence, and calling on the officers of justice to be vigilant in preserving the peace of the city. Accompanying this proclamation was another handbill, the obituary of "The American Patriot":

TO THE PUBLIC.

The paper lately published in this place under the title of The American Patriot is discontinued from this moment and the firm of Mitchell and Pratt under which it was edited hereby dissolved, John S. Mitchell ceasing henceforth to have any interest in it.

J. S. MITCHELL,
CHS. M. PRATT.

Savannah, June 8, 1812.

Ten days later Congress declared war against England —the war that Woodrow Wilson has pronounced "a war of arms brought about by a programme of peace"—and Savannahians, sinking their factional differences, ceased to be Federalists or Republicans and became simply Americans.

It must not be thought that Savannah was alone in this brutal outbreak of political passion, or that it was the only city wherein a mob vented its hatred of the Federalists in violent attacks upon an editor. Sitting in the Council Chamber of the Savannah City Hall one day, Miss Mary Custis Lee, daughter of Gen. Robert E. Lee, looking at the magnificent painting of that illustrious chieftain, spoke of his father, Gen. "Light Horse" Harry Lee, and of the movement then under way to remove his body from Cumberland Island to the soil of his native Virginia. Incidentally she told of stirring incidents in his life and among them of the injuries he suffered at the hands of a Republican mob in Baltimore, injuries that crippled the Revolutionary hero for the remainder of his life and were a contributory cause of his death six years after.

In Baltimore, as in Savannah, many of the leading men of affairs were opposed to the war with Great Britain and supported a newspaper, "The Federal Republican," set up in opposition to the administration and edited by one Hanson. "Lewd fellows of the baser sort," as they were described by the Federalists, destroyed the newspaper plant and put a temporary stop to its publication. This outrage brought to Hanson's open support men of distinction and the paper resumed under the protection of prominent Federalists, including Generals Lingan and Lee. A mob again attacked the office and the two old soldiers with a party of friends sought to protect it. They did not hesitate to fire upon the assailants and some were killed. Under the assurance of protection given by the Mayor the defenders surrendered and were placed in prison. On the following night the mob again assembled, broke open the jail, with little resistance on the part of the authorities, beat General Lingan to death, left General Lee senseless and grievously injured, and clubbed and mutilated others, leaving nine of them on the prison steps supposedly dead.

Savannah at least did better than Baltimore in the way it suppressed "right of free speech" run to dangerous license at a time when the country was facing a powerful foe and needed union among its people, regardless as to what their original views had been as to the policies that lead to the hostilities. Can any one believe that in 1917 Savannah would have been more tolerant of a newspaper started here for the express purpose of antagonizing the government and of neutralizing its efforts to prosecute the war with Germany?

CHAPTER VII.

DID THEY FIGHT, OR DID THEY NOT FIGHT?

PECULIAR INSTANCES OF PROMINENT MEN LIBELING
EACH OTHER IN PUBLIC PLACES WITH OPPROBRIOUS
EPITHETS, BUT WITH NO EVIDENCE OF THEIR SUBSE-
QUENTLY MEETING ON THE FIELD OF HONOR—GUNN
vs. WELSCHER, SHICK vs. SARZEDAS, McINTOSH vs.
CUTHBERT, PUTNAM vs. WOOD, LEAKE vs. MILLER,
—HOW JOHN HOUSTON McINTOSH HANDLED A SPAN-
IARD—NO MAN IMMUNE FROM THE TONGUES OF
SLANDER.

DID they fight, or did they not fight?
This is the question that often puzzles one in study-
ing the published correspondence in the early newspapers,
in which two Savannahians denounce each other, apply the
epithets "coward", "liar", "scoundrel", "rascal", or something else equally as unpleasant to face in cold print and
realize that everyone in the community is discussing it.

There are the letters setting forth the trouble, each
one's version of it, and there are the vituperative remarks
by the contending men—and then there is an utter absence
of any further information.

It was not a time when men tamely submitted to private reflections upon their manhood, let alone to wholesale
advertising of such charges. Generally the parties to the
disputes which are spread before the readers of the "Gazette", or later newspapers, are recognized as men of bravery. In the years immediately following the revolution
they are found to be those who had served their country
courageously in that struggle.

Reading the notes that passed between them and the
final statements to the public, generally closing with the
posting of one or the other, or both, in the most opprobrious
manner, one is constrained to believe that they must finally
have resorted to the code and for the satisfaction of their

"honor" taken a shot or two at one another. Neither being seriously wounded or killed, the newspapers simply refrained from mentioning the meeting; after a few days further discussion the minds of men and women turned to other subjects, and with the passing of that generation all remembrance of the affair faded away.

Take the trouble between James Gunn, then Colonel of the Chatham County Regiment, and Joseph Welscher, Captain of the West Company of that regiment. Welscher was not popular with his men and there was talk of their appealing to the line officers for his removal. He was unquestionably unpopular with Col. Gunn.

At the Fourth of July celebration in 1787, after the regimental parade and review, there was the customary dinner. All were more or less mellowed by the popular liquors of the day when Welscher arose to sing a song. He rendered one written before the War for Independence. In the song were allusions that were offensive to Gunn and other officers. It was evidently an unwise selection. Some officers hissed and Gunn peremptorily ordered Welscher to sit down. There were all the elements for an affair of honor.

Capt. Welscher later said:

"The company prest me to sing it—that it would give no offense—wherefore I began:

" 'It was in the gates of Calais, Hogarth tells' "

Col. Gunn and others loudly groaned.

Welscher stopped and explained that he had apologized for the song before he began it. He had been called on to sing and it was the only song he knew, so he continued "The Roast Beef of Old England", as it was called, a popular song of the years before the country had tried the issue of freedom with the mother land.

Sentiment with regard to the song had changed. At one time its "hits" at the French and the Irish had brought forth uproarious applause. But the French had become allies instead of enemies and the cause of Ireland was now looked upon with a favorable eye. But Welscher made the room ring with offensive lines:

"Then Britons be valiant, the Moral is clear;
The Ox is Old England, the Frog is Monsieur,
Whose Puffs and Bravadoes we need never fear.

    *   *   *   *

His Fellow-Guard, of right Hibernian Clay,
Whose brazen Front his Country did betray,
From Tyburn's fatal Tree had hither fled,
By honest means to gain his daily bread."

Col. Gunn's wrath was up. "Damn your song and you, too," said he.

Then Welscher's feelings were aroused. "Col. Gunn, that is language which I am not used to, nor ever receive."

Col. Gunn abandoned his position as presiding officer and rushed at Welscher. Other officers interfered, and when the colonel ordered the captain to leave the room Mr. William Stephens interposed and told Welscher he should not go.

Whereupon Gunn told Stephens that he was now "the ostensible person and he should call upon him."

"Whenever you please, Sir," replied Stephens.

Here was the opening for a second duel.

After this Gunn, by entreaties and arguments, was persuaded to resume the chair until the party broke up about midnight.

The more serious trouble came later. On his way home Capt. Welscher passed Col. Gunn's house. As Welscher told the story, Gunn called from his piazza: "Mr. Welscher I want to speak with you."

Welscher waited and his colonel came out.

"I have been waiting for you the whole night, Sir," said he. Snatching Welscher's sword, which the captain was carrying under his arm, the colonel threw it in his house, called for a whip, and fell upon the captain. After beating him Gunn called for the swords and ordered the captain to take one and defend himself.

Mrs. Gunn sent a servant posthaste for Maj. Berrien, living close by.

When the major arrived he found the two swords sticking in the ground and Gunn commanding Welscher to take his choice of them. Major Berrien wrested the sword from Welscher's hand, without trouble, and after a struggle got the one from Gunn.

Col. Gunn put Capt. Welscher under military arrest, made two formal charges against him of conduct unbecoming an officer or a gentleman, and a court-martial convened with Maj. Frederick Shick as president, the other members being Capt. Josiah Tattnall, Capt. James Bulloch, Capt. Thomas Elfe, First Lieut. William Lewden, Second Lieut. Wm. H. Spencer, John Eppinger, and Justice Justus H. Scheuber. Added to the charge of failing to act as an officer and gentleman should have done in the affray with Col. Gunn, there was the additional accusation that he had permitted James Simpson to disarm and assault him without properly resenting it—again an instance of too much liquor at military events in the old days. The court exonerated him of the charge in his trouble with Col. Gunn, doubtless on the score that at the time he was in no condition to defend himself, but held that his conduct as regards the affair with Simpson was highly censurable and recommended that he should be severely reprimanded.

We shall meet with both Gunn and Welscher in later affairs of honor. The incident related did not injure Welscher with the public, it seems, as he became very popular and prominent in local politics and at the bar. Some years later, with George M. Troup as his second, he calmly faced a political foe and almost fatally wounded him. There is no evidence, though, that after the court-martial brought on by Gunn he further resented what his commanding officer had done.

A few weeks later one finds Maj. Frederick Shick, presiding officer at the Welscher court-martial, being advertised by Dr. David Sarzedas, whom Shick had refused to honor by accepting an invitation to adjust their personal troubles with duelling pistols. Strange to say, the same Capt. Edward Cowan who figured as second for Welscher in an attempt to bring Gunn to accept a challenge from Welscher the day after their midnight affray, is found representing Dr. Sarzedas, who charged Shick with "unbecoming conduct to him in the street".

Sarzedas, it appears, hired a slave from Maj. Shick's parents for domestic service, and, as Shick charged, had failed to pay for the services except with physical abuse of the negro. He had also failed to pay a note on which Shick was endorser. In an encounter in the street the major whipped the doctor for this combination of offences, and when challenged replied:

"When you pay the note you gave William Welscher, and the debt you owe my father, I shall talk to you of satisfaction."

Sarzedas published the letters that passed between them and as a final shot informed the public that "The character of Maj. Shick I hold in abhorrence; his conduct on the present occasion shall be the criterion whether he merits the appellation of the soldier, gentleman, or coward, which I shall leave men of honour to determine."

Maj. Shick threatened to chastise Dr. Sarzedas again and the physician left for Charleston. On his return he stated that if Shick was satisfied he was, but that if assaulted he would be found prepared. Shick closed the affair with a letter to the editor of the "Gazette", which is useful as showing the position sometimes assumed in these personal affairs:

"When a man conducts himself beneath the character of a gentleman or a man of honour, I do not hold myself bound by any custom to risk my salvation with him, but, on the contrary, the man whom I esteem in a different point of view, I shall ever conceive myself highly honored by attending his invitation. I am equally as bound to pay every respect to the gentleman as I am to chastise the rascal whose conduct merits abuse."

If the major and the doctor met to satisfy honor with bullets or sword pricks it does not appear. Major Shick had an excellent revolutionary record and no one questioned his bravery. Sarzedas was an officer in the Light Dragoons of the First Regiment of Chatham County Militia. The correspondence serves to show that men could say very harsh things at times, have street encounters, and still apparently fail to actually meet on the duelling ground, challenge or no challenge.

Nine months later, in June, 1788, came the falling out between Maj. William McIntosh, Jr., and Col. Seth John Cuthbert, both men of local prominence, and both with war records that proved they were men of personal bravery. This affair grew out of a court trial in which McIntosh's father, General McIntosh, was making a defence in an action brought against him by John Cuthbert, Sr. Maj. McIntosh claimed that Col. Cuthbert "acted in a most unjustifiable manner, interrupting the general at a very inappropriate time, and declaring the general's assertions to be 'infamous falsehoods.'" The general, he pointed out, was referring to things that had occurred before Seth John Cuthbert was born, and of the truth of which he could not know. Gen. McIntosh had referred to the senior Cuthbert's "attempt to learn the cooper's trade, without possessing either industry, frugality or temper." Either the allusion to his father having been a cooper, or the accompanying remarks in derogation of his efforts to learn that trade, grievously wounded the younger Cuthbert.

When called on, Cuthbert promptly admitted what he had said in the court room. "The words were forced from him," he said, "by the most illiberal and personal reflections on myself and my nearest connections that I have ever experienced."

The offending words having been admitted, and no apology forthcoming, McIntosh sent a challenge at once:

"I demand satisfaction at 11 o'clock tomorrow morning at the Fort, where I shall attend with a gentleman."

The "Fort" was old Fort Wayne, at the foot of the Bay, where the gas works now stand. It was a favorite resort for the duellists of that day.

The challenge was not accepted. Seth John Cuthbert felt himself bound "in reason and honor to answer no person but your father in any personal dispute between him and myself." He declined the challenge but stood ready to accept one from Gen. McIntosh. "There is a much greater similarity in his situation in life and my own, than there is betwixt yours and mine," said he to Maj. McIntosh, "and it is unreasonable to accept your challenge because, on the same principle that you demand satisfaction, it might be demanded by every member of your family in succession."

McIntosh repeated the challenge. The next morning Mr. Clay, Jr., acting as the friend of Cuthbert, waited on Mr. Gibbons and informed him that Col. Cuthbert wished to refer the question of acceptance of Maj. McIntosh's challenge to two persons, and mentioned Mr. Gibbons and Dr. MacLeod as proper persons. Maj. McIntosh finally agreed and accepted Mr. MacQueen to represent him. MacQueen unexpectedly left the city and the board gave no decision. Then McIntosh published the correspondence and added that he had posted Col. Cuthbert, under the vendue house on Sunday afternoon, in the following words:

"I do declare Seth John Cuthbert to be a coward. My reasons shall be made known in the publick Gazette.

"WM. McINTOSH, Jun."

Was there a hostile meeting between the two? It would seem almost inevitable that the former patriot officers should have met at ten paces at Fort Wayne after this public posting. Seth John Cuthbert died a few months later, in November, the "Gazette" states, "after a tedious and painful illness", which leads one to infer he may have been an ill man at the time of the trouble with Maj. McIntosh. The "Gazette" said he "was among the first who stood in the cause of their country. In 1776 he was appointed major of the Second Continental Battalion." He also represented Chatham in the legislature and served acceptably as State Treasurer in 1784. The "Gazette" speaks of his "amiable qualities and brilliant abilities."

It was an age when self-restraint appears woefully lacking. Next appear Henry Putnam and Lieut. John Wood. Putnam sent a note to Wood, through Dr. Geoghegan, accusing him of slandering him. Wood verbally denied this to the doctor and sought his friend, George Throop. Throop called on Dr. Geoghegan and asked him what should be done in the matter:

"Your man must make an apology or else take a crack in the field," was the reply.

'He is determined not to apologize and our pistols are ready," was Throop's message.

Wood anticipated what Putnam would probably do and the vendue house speedily bore this placard:

"Having received a note from Mr. Henry Putnam by his friend, and having sent an answer thereto by my friend, I do declare said Putnam a coward and not worthy the notice of any gentleman.   "JOHN WOOD."

Putnam was in bed ill and Maj. McIntosh called and informed him of the posting. Putnam then called in Maj. Hopkins and this is the card he bore to Wood:

"My friend, Major Hopkins, will point out the ground, time and mode of settling the business. Although you have been so expeditious as to publish to the world my deficiency, let the test prove the fact."

Lieut. Wood stuck the note in his pocket when Maj. Hopkins handed it to him. "I have posted my answer already at the vendue house," said he. He then expressed a willingness to meet Maj. Hopkins at Fort Wayne and give that gentleman satisfaction, but Hopkins declined to assume his principal's quarrel.

Another note at the vendue house gave the public something to talk over. It read:

"Mr. J. Wood having published me yesterday as a coward &C. the public will please to suspend their opinions till Thursday next when by a state of facts they will find him a liar, coward and no gentleman.

"HENRY PUTNAM."

Savannah, 11 June, 1791.

Wood then advertised Putnam and concluded:

"I drop him into that contemptible state from which he endeavored to emerge by a seeming display of courage, though unfortunately it forsook him when called to exercise it."

Did they fight? It was only five minutes walk to the vicinity of Fort Wayne where more than one duel had been fought under less provocation. If they fought, neither was killed.

By This Wall of Old Fort Wayne,
Now the Savannah Gas Works, a Hundred Years Ago Savannahians Met
in the Early Morning to Adjust Their Difficulties With Pistols
Or Rifles Under the Code

Duelling had become a fad, or perhaps a passion might more suitably express it. Even the free negroes became infected with the spirit. One of the most amusing items in the "Gazette" about this time is the account of two well known Savannah negroes who put on "white men's airs":

"So prevalent has the practice of Duelling become lately, that Major Small and Capt. Qua, two men of color, some few days past agreed to meet at a time and place appointed, each attended by a friend with a pair of pistols, to decide a dispute which happened betwixt them.

"Copy of the challenge: Capt. Qua tink himself injure by Major Small, esq. and require satisfaction for insult. Major Small must eider beg pardon, or fight to-morrow on pistols. My fellow servant Dick fix a place, and will let me know where. You must eider do one oder of the two tings, Mind, me say so. Afternoon near dark."

"To Major Small, Esq., Gentlemen's Barber, Savannah."

"The Answer: Major Small informs Capt. Qua that he has received his challenge and will accordingly meet him agreeable to appointment, in order to put out of the world a rascal and a thief that does not deserve to live in it. By gar. 9th June, 1790. To Capt. Qua."

The major, though, failed to appear and the angered Capt. Qua, imitating white men, armed himself with a whip to flog the major. Then the law intervened.

"O wad some Pow'r the giftie gie us,

To see oursels as ithers see us!"

The "Gazette" facetiously observed: "Both of the gentlemen got their titles from the British during the late war."

Most bitter of all the cards published in the one hundred and fifty years, 1732-1882, were those in 1798 between Richard Henry Leake and John Miller. Leake was an attorney of prominence, Miller apparently a business man of standing. There was no preliminary peppering with small arms in their dispute. They spent no time in voluminous correspondence and the publication thereof in the local papers. Two cards only appeared, but they left nothing to be said. Each knew what he had in mind and each said it in unmistakable English. As the most virulent specimens of this class of public denunciations they are given:

"For the assertion of repeated falsehoods, and the highest provocations, I thought proper to send a message to John Miller, formerly of Belmont, by my friend Capt. John Lyons, requesting him to meet me, and give me that satisfaction I was entitled to demand. I therefore proclaim to the world, that the same John Miller, refusing to accept my said message, has evinced himself a lyar, a scoundrel, and a cowardly assassin.

6th June, 1798.   RICHARD HENRY LEAKE."

"ATTENTION

"I DO proclaim RICHARD HENRY LEAKE, Attorney-at-Law, to be an infamous LIAR AND VILE DEFAMER. Fathers of families, if you value the reputation of your daughters, suffer him not to enter your doors.

"JOHN MILLER."

Not a line as to where and when they fought, nor what with, nor the result of the meeting. It was practically impossible for two men to live in Savannah after such cards as these and fail to wipe out the stigma through the code unless they resorted to a "recontre" on the public streets.

Nowadays no newspaper would permit the publication of such cards. It is safe to say money could not buy the space. Even the Savannah journalists of that time felt a bit squeamish about it. Seymour & Woolhopter, publishers of the "Columbian Museum", thought it advisable to protect themselves and stated in their journal: "We do not attempt to regulate or criticise the language of our advertising customers. We should hope, therefore in future, to be spared the trouble of being considered in any respect as parties between persons who may chuse to apply to each other (through the medium of our paper) the most scurrilous or indecent epithets."

Some years after this (1807) Leake disappeared. What became of him was never known. He may have been murdered. For some times he was advertised for broadly. Then his property went through the usual disposition. Nearly a century later it was found necessary again to re-establish, in some Northern court, that he had been diligently sought and no trace found, and Mr. William Harden furnished the proof and affidavit as to the ancient legal notices.

The McIntoshes have already figured in three duelling stories, but two more remain to be told—perhaps more, if the records of all duels and challenges were available.

John Houston McIntosh, grandson of John Mohr McIntosh, had all of the antipathy of his race to the Spaniards. His clan had suffered severely in the earliest days of Georgia in the border struggles with the Spanish. Old John Mohr McIntosh, who had led them after Culloden out of the mountains of Scotland to the far-away wilderness of the Altamaha, and Col. John McIntosh, grandson of the Highland chieftain, had lain in the darkness of Spanish dungeons for months. No McIntosh could forget that. There was no love, either, on the part of any of the frontiersmen of Georgia for the rulers of Florida. When the war came with the British in 1812 there was a well-defined fear that the Spaniards would turn Florida over to them and that it would become a source of great danger to the southern coast and country.

Relying on assurances from Washington, a little army of Georgians and Floridians, "with all the woodchoppers and boatmen in the neighborhood of St. Mary's," formed a provisional government and chose the Georgian, John Houston McIntosh, as Director of East Florida. They organized as patriots seeking to establish republican institutions. United States gunboats came to their aid and Fernandina and Amelia Island were surrendered to them. Congress was disinclined to support the venture, the president finally disclaimed the acts of his agents, and the seized territory was returned to the Spaniards.

The Spanish leaders were intensely indignant over the invasion of their territory, and especially of the action of the "Patriots" in setting up an opposition government. One Don Manuel Solana sent a challenge to Director McIntosh "to fight him by day or night, on foot or on horseback, with

any weapon." McIntosh despised and disdained the Spaniards. His reply was cutting in the extreme:

"Was he a private man and Don Manuel Solana (whom
he did not even know) a decent character, he would meet him
by day, with any weapon but a knife or stilletto, but as Mr.
McIntosh had lived among the Spaniards long enough to
know that those among them who have any honor left are
great sticklers for etiquette, and as he is the Director of East
Florida and is extremely solicitous to retain the love of his
dear and honorable friends in St. Augustine, he could not
condescend to accept a challenge from any individual in that
place but Colonel Kinderland (Kintelan), Governor of all the
town and castle of St. Augustine."

No challenge appears to have been forthcoming from
the Spanish governor of St. Augustine and Don Manuel Solana, not being acceptable as a substitute, was left to fume
and fret over the sneering tone of the communication that
had come in response to his challenge. In Savannah and in
all the country to the St. Mary's there were doubtless many
hearty laughs over the manner in which McIntosh had
handled the presumptuous and bombastic Don.

This quintette of difficulties between leading white men
of the community amply illustrate the spirit of the closing
years of the 18th and the opening years of the 19th century
in Savannah and nearby country, the methods pursued, and
also explain the somewhat frequent essays in the "Gazette"
and "Museum" condemning duelling and deprecating the
readiness shown to resort to it in this city and vicinity.

There was a reason for this readiness to appeal to the
code. All too often slander went broadcast through the
community. A man's social or business standing, or even
the magnificent patriotism he had shown, was no protection
from the defiling tongues. No less a man than Col. James
Jackson, to whom the Georgia legislature two years before
in appreciation had presented the Tattnall home, was accused of accepting bribes while in the legislature in the interest of Tories, eager to escape from the dreariness of exile
and seeking to be restored to citizenship and their properties.

He scorned the libels, but in the end found that public
repudiation of the tales was necessary. There was no one

of position on whom he could pin direct responsibility and publicly brand as a "liar." In the "Gazette" he denounced the "infamous reports" being circulated that "he had been bribed by Dr. MacLeod", and a second report that he "had received sixty guineas from Mr. Thomas Young to serve his purpose". Mr. Young, of Liberty county, had presented to the Assembly a petition "signed by many staunch Whigs" for his reinstatement in American citizenship. This slander, Jackson found, had made an impression on his friends in the country, going the rounds as it had done without specific denial from him.

A young man for whom Jackson had done much, and whom he did not dignify by naming, had industriously circulated the report and declared Jackson "a secondary planet in Mr. Young's business", an intimation that he had played second fiddle to some corrupt and more influential member of the Assembly. This seemed to sting worse than the general charge of corruption. "Did he know me," cried Jackson, "he would be convinced that my pride, however deficient I may be, will never permit me to rate myself second to any at the Georgia Bar, and therefore, was I to be bribed, it would take as large a purse to buy me as any of the profession." He then published an affidavit, drawn in the strongest possible terms, vigorously denouncing the charges, and concluding, "He had many and repeated tempting offers, which he had rejected as frequently."

Two young men, afterwards well known, James Benjamin Maxwell and Jacob Henry Waldburge(r), clerks in Jackson's office, who had "access to all his papers and were privy to most of his transactions", told that they knew of applications to him to "speak to points in the legislature, which he always refused, declaring it repugnant to the duty he owed his country." They remembered especially one letter from a rich Tory, offering him one plantation out of two, or both, if he would use his endeavors to re-establish him and "get him off the Bill of Banishment and Confiscation"— a revelation of the means resorted to by the more obnoxious Tories to recover their lost positions in the country they had failed to defend. This especial proposition came from

Philip Dell, large owner of lands on the Savannah river, then a refugee with the British in Florida.

If a gallant and popular officer like Col. Jackson could not escape the calumniator, what could a former pro-British surgeon like Dr. MacLeod expect? That able surgeon, progenitor of a number of well known Savannahians of to-day, had already been through the agonies of a campaign of slander and once more was forced to undergo the fiery ordeal before his enemies allowed him peace of mind. No less atrocious charge was made against him than that of putting powdered glass in drugs prepared by him for the Americans wounded in the attack on Savannah in 1779. The accusation had been investigated before the Assembly and proved false, but that did not prevent its being revamped more maliciously in 1784 by a Dr. Rehm and others. MacLeod proved by affidavits from former officers and privates that he had never compounded drugs for the Americans, that in his capacity as surgeon for the British he had secured improved conditions for the American sick and wounded, that he had been recognized among them for his humanity and kindness. For a while, at least, he silenced the serpents' tongues, and the next year he was restored to citizenship. One wonders if the scurrilous reports of all sorts were originated by old and bitter Tories, not all of whom had left the community. Perhaps the Grand Juries of this and other counties thought so when they recommended that those who had been antagonistic to their country, and who would probably be a disturbing element in the great work of reconstruction ahead, should be sent to other realms, and returned special presentments against those "who harboured persons banished from Georgia or any other State."

Savannah, like other places, in the period of evolution that followed revolution, was far from being a paradise of fraternal affection. Malice and envy and hatred and slander and selfish ambition were strong forces at work, and the lifting of the lid at times tells of the seething passions and harsh bitternesses that were the inevitable aftermath of a war that wrought so complete a political change and left for several years chaotic conditions.

CHAPTER VIII.

WHEN JEFFERSON USED THE GUILLOTINE.

VINDICTIVE BITTERNESS OF THE OUSTED FEDERALISTS OF
   SAVANNAH—HOW AN AFFAIR BETWEEN THE NEW
   COLLECTOR OF THE PORT AND AN ENEMY WAS AD-
   JUSTED ON THE FIELD OF HONOR—A FUTURE GOV-
   ERNOR KILLS A POLITICAL FOE—CITY COUNCIL POLI-
   TICIANS SQUABBLE, BRINGING AN ALMOST FATAL
   MEETING.

ANDREW JACKSON is generally credited with introducing the spoils system, but Thomas Jefferson anticipated both Jackson and William Jennings Bryan in appreciation of the virtues of "deserving Democrats." Federal head after Federal head fell into the basket, giving
more force than ever to the Federalist cry of "Jacobins"
against their enemies.

Senator James Jackson expressed the Jeffersonian
party idea as to the proper use of the party guillotine when
he wrote to John Milledge in September, 1801: "It will not
do to be squeamish. Those fellows would have cut your
throat and mine six months ago."

The houses of Savannah Republicans had been brightly
illuminated to express their great joy over the election of
Jefferson and a subscription festival held under the auspices
of Mitchell, Troup and Charlton. The faithful clamored for
the loaves and fishes.

Savannah proved no exception to the rule of displace-
ment. It was then the maelstrom of Georgia politics. Capt.
Ambrose Gordon, United States Marshal for the District of
Georgia, was removed without ceremony, and Benjamin
Wall appointed. Henry Pitman became commander of the
revenue cutter here in place of John Howell. A new navy
agent held that lucrative post. But more grievous than all
others was the dismissal of James Powell, collector of the
port, to give room to Major Thomas DeMaltos Johnson. All
government positions were soon Jeffersonianized. Jubila-

tion reigned among the Republicans and the disconsolate
Federalists deplored the ruin being brought upon the country.

The big business men of the city were largely Federalists. They united in a published appreciation of the services of Collector Powell, and objected to his enforced resignation. Forty-six leading men of affairs comforted him
with the thought that "You have the consolation of quit-
ting public life accompanied by some of the best patriots of
our common country." One paper, signed by many, attacked Jefferson personally. Truly, it may be said, the
Federalist cup of bitterness overflowed. But Jefferson was
establishing a party and its principles and routing the enemy from the vantage ground they held as office holders.
Even the sustained accusation that he had thrown on the
charity of the world many old revolutionary soldiers and
officers was void of effect.

A few weeks after assuming office Major Johnson, Collector of the Port, pistol in hand, stood facing a defamer
in South Carolina, one of the earliest parties to cross the
river, there being no law then against duelling in Georgia.

Among the disgruntled Federalists was Captain
Gresham, of Greene county, evidently a man of position.
One day while in Savannah a discussion came up in the
store of George Ponsonby about the bogus bank bills then
in circulation and the men held in jail charged with their
printing and issuing.

As Ponsonby told the story, Gresham observed that
"these men were not at the bottom of it, and that if the
business were properly investigated it would be found that
a man lately put in office in Savannah would also be impli-
cated."

On asking him if he alluded to Major Johnson, recently
made Collector, Capt. Gresham replied "Yes."

Doubtless Gresham gave his views unsolicited to others.
News of his remarks came quickly to Johnson's ears, a challenge was prepared and delivered by T. U. P. Charlton, now
become a major, and accepted by Gresham, with Robert
Fisher as the latter's second.

Dr. James Ewen, only recently arrived from Virginia, accompanied them as surgeon. In view of the seriousness of the remarks made by Gresham there was every reason to expect the surgeon's services to be required before the affair was over.

It was on November 25, 1801, at an early hour, that the parties met at the appointed spot.

"Every arrangement being adjusted, usual in an affair of honor, it was the expectation that an exchange of shots was inevitable," wrote the seconds later, "but at this crisis the surgeon, Dr. Ewen, requested permission to interfere and speak to Captain Gresham."

Major Charlton informed the doctor that such permission could only be given by Mr. Fisher. Gresham's second having consented, the surgeon held an interview with Captain Gresham, the upshot of which was that the captain "was disposed to make any concessions not incompatible with his honor."

The day preceding Major Charlton had prescribed the terms of an apology to his principal, and would consider no adjustment save a denial from Capt. Gresham that he had made the assertions reflecting on the honor and integrity of Johnson, and "if he had made the assertions that they were unfounded, false and malicious."

To this Capt. Gresham assented, and moreover added "that he might have expressed himself improperly in an inadvertent hour, and that he would call on Mr. Ponsonby, whom he understood to be the original author of the defamatory report, and tell him what he had propagated he had very much misrepresented."

The seconds signed a statement that "no man placed in a similar situation could have conducted himself with greater coolness and determination than Major Johnson, or have acted with more candor than Capt. Gresham."

This left George Ponsonby, Federalist, in an awkward position, and he added a little fuel to the rancorous hatreds engendered by politics in Savannah by stating that Capt. Gresham had informed him that "Mr. Johnson was a damned rascal", and "that he would furnish papers that would astonish me." "Gresham's apology has been couched in language intended to injure my character, but it cannot suffer by the shafts of such malicious insinuations, which are themselves groundless and contradictory."

And as a further illustration of the lack of brotherly love in Savannah in those days, let me quote this one more expression from Ponsonby:

"Mr. Johnson in his letter to Capt. Gresham calls me a British Tory merchant. I have always before supposed myself to be an American; to be a merchant is no disgrace, and that I am a Federalist and despise Jacobinism I will never deny."

The feeling that is expressed in these lines continued between the two contending political parties for several years. The Federalists were "Tories", the Republicans were "Jacobins"; the Federalists were "royalists" or "imperialists", the Republicans were the red-capped guillotinists of property rights and intelligence and integrity.

The country fairly reeked with political prejudice and passion. In that fierce clash of contending ambitions and principles one could hardly retain a passive neutrality. Conditions political were still mirrored in the picture George Walton drew in 1779 when he wrote: "The demon Discord yet presides in this country, and God only knows when his reign will be at an end."

When on May 1, 1802, St. Tammany's Day, dedicated to the patron Indian saint of America, the military had their annual celebration and closed the observance with dinners, the Chatham Troop of Light Horse gathered around the banquet board at Gunn's tavern on the Bay in honor of their own anniversary, with Capt. Ambrose Gordon at the head of the table. They closed their formal toasts with one purely political and Federalist in character:

"To Timothy Pickering: The upright man amidst a host of enemies."

Pickering had been dismissed from the Secretaryship of State by President Adams, largely because of his efforts to promote the presidential aspirations of Alexander Hamilton. That the Chatham Troopers, smarting under the President's dismissal of their captain from the marshalship of Georgia, should show their displeasure by a toast to a New Englander of the rankest Federalist type, and whose views were extremely obnoxious to the Republicans, shows how political factionalism invaded every phase of life in the Savannah of that period.

Out of such unrestrained villification and personal antagonism came many duels in Georgia and throughout the country in the next decade or two. At Savannah there were several bloodless affairs. In one, though, a prominent citizen and politician was slain, and in a succeeding meeting another man of local note was severely wounded.

Nowhere in the opening years of the nineteenth century was there more of this political hatred than here. In the Federalist ranks were the greater number of the leading business men of the city, those of large commercial and property interests. The Federalists were making a losing fight, here as elsewhere, and this did not decrease the acrimonious sentiments they entertained for the opposition leaders who were overthrowing their conceptions of strong, centralized government and superior class control. The bitterness of the party antagonisms ran into every phase of politics, and it was deemed just as necessary to have Federalist or Republican mayor and aldermen as to have one's party dominating at Washington. Out of these conditions grew two of the most dramatic duels in the history of the city.

Prominent among the political figures of the town when the century opened were David Bradie Mitchell and William Hunter. Mitchell was a Scotchman, born in 1766, who had come to Savannah in 1783 to look after property that had been left him by his uncle, Dr. David Bradie, an old resident of Georgia and one of the patriots outlawed by Gov. Wright and his Tory legislature. The freedom and opportunities of the new world appealed to him and he remained, to become one of the most distinguished of Georgians.

He studied law under Hon. William Stephens, became a member of the legislature, voted against the Yazoo act in 1795, was active in the agitation for its repeal in 1796, was elected solicitor-general by his fellow legislators (1796-98),

Governor David B. Mitchell
Who Soon After Leaving the Mayor's Chair Shot a Political Antagonist
Through the Heart in a Duel

and then judge of the Eastern circuit (1798-1804). In 1801 he was elected mayor of Savannah for the year ending July 12, 1802. In military life he also forged rapidly to the front, and passing through the various ranks by 1802 had become colonel of the First Chatham regiment, succeeding Josiah Tattnall when the latter became governor. Although the revolutionary war was over before he came to Savannah, Mitchell was intense in his feelings and expressions against Americans who had failed to align themselves with the patriots, and in his early years in the legislature in a noted speech declared: "If I ever find it in my heart to forgive an old Tory his sins, I trust my God will never forgive mine." A feeling almost as bitter he displayed toward the Federalists.

Hunter was a man of business affairs, largely interested in shipping and in imports and exports. In 1802 he took James Hunter in partnership with him and the firm was one of the leading factors in the thriving, progressive life of the little city. He served on the directorate of the Bank of Discount and Deposit, composed of the leaders of the Savannah business world. He was one of the commissioners of pilotage and in 1802 with Robert Bolton represented those Savannahians who had spoliation claims against the French government. He was also active in local politics and in 1798-99 served as an alderman. In May, 1801, he was appointed Navy Agent for Georgia, succeeding Ebenezer Jackson, whose resignation was forced. As Jefferson had assumed office sixty days before this the natural conclusion would be that Hunter had supported his candidacy. He held the office but a year, though, as one of the little news items of the "Columbian Museum," June 22, 1802, was: "We are informed William Hunter, Esq., has resigned his appointment as navy agent for this port."

What brought about the meeting between Mitchell and Hunter is not now known. One might infer from the resignation of Hunter that he had differed with the Jeffersonian administration, perhaps returned fervently to Federalism as a first love. Not a clew is obtainable in the local newspapers of the day, which discreetly refrained from referring to the affair. Be the causes what they may, two months after Hunter's resignation as Navy Agent, and but a few weeks after Mitchell retired from the mayor's chair, they faced each other, on August 23, 1802, duelling pistols in hand, at the Jewish cemetery, then in the open country beyond the city limits, now at Stewart and Guerard streets. In the New York Daily Advertiser of September 6, I found a brief story of the duel.

The depth of the antagonism between the two men may be measured by the conditions under which they fought. Starting at ten paces, or thirty feet, they were to advance two paces after each shot. At the first fire the ball from Hunter's pistol struck Mitchell's side, evidently but a glancing shot, and was stopped by a fold in his shirt. Mitchell's shot entirely missed. Moving forward two paces each, bringing them twelve feet closer, the second shots were exchanged with the duellists but eighteen feet apart. The bullet from Hunter's pistol struck Mitchell in the hip, but again passed through his clothing without injury to him. Col. Mitchell's aim had been more accurate and more deadly. Hunter fell to the ground a corpse. The bullet had gone through his heart. "Mr. Hunter's funeral was attended by the most respectable citizens of Savannah, by whom he was highly esteemed and respected."

On the next Fourth of July, 1803, when the military celebrated the natal day of the republic, with parade and review, and then gathered for their dinners, in separate commands, the Troop of Light Horse once more had a significant toast, this time to one of its officers who had more than surrendered a public position at the behest of partisan politics, a toast to one who had forfeited his life to political convictions.

In fancy one can see Capt. Gordon and his company standing at attention in the dining room of the old tavern, and drinking in sorrowful silence:

"To the memory of our invaluable citizen and brother soldier, Lieut. William Hunter—his virtues were rare, may his example be ever present and influencive with us."

Hunter had been the first lieutenant of the Troop from 1781 until his death.

At another tavern not far removed, where the glasses clinked and good cheer reigned, where toast succeeded toast until one wonders how men could withstand the liquid strain, Col. David B. Mitchell, surrounded by applauding admirers, drank, among many and other toasts, to "Thomas Jefferson. May that virtuous Republican statesman continue to deserve the title of the 'Man of the People' ".

But the comrades of the dead Lieut. Hunter drank no toast to the then President of the United States.

Mitchell went on to higher and higher honors. Two years after he had slain Hunter he became United States District Attorney, a position he resigned after a few months service. The preceding year (1803) he succeeded Tattnall as Brigadier-General of the Georgia Militia. In civil life he was active in all that pertained to the welfare of the city. In 1806-07 he was president of the Union Society. In 1809 he was elected governor of Georgia, filling that office in 1809-12 and again in 1815-17, resigning to accept the appointment by President Monroe as agent to the Creek nation. He died at Milledgeville in 1837.

Whether Mitchell ever felt compunctions over the killing of Hunter no one can tell. That he did not approve of duelling may be construed from his action as Governor when, on December 12, 1809, he signed the Georgia law against duelling. This act made it unlawful to extend or accept a challenge or be concerned therein as principal or second. On conviction the parties were excluded from the right to hold any office of trust, honor or emolument in the State.

What a strange sequel, the scene in the Governor's office at Milledgeville on that winter day when Mitchell appended his name to this act, to the picture presented that mid-summer day seven years before, when, with the smoke oozing from the barrel of his pistol, he looked down upon his political foe, lying prostrate in death in the old Jewish cemetery at Savannah.

In December, 1804, Mitchell was one of the five arbitrators who adjusted the difficulty between Gen. John Clark and William H. Crawford, between whom a challenge had passed and been accepted.

The killing of Hunter by Mitchell may not have been the first baptism with blood of the Jewish burying ground. It was not the last. Situated convenient of access, enclosed by a recently constructed heavy brick wall, and with few graves, it seems to have been selected as a suitable spot for the settlement of political and other disputes. There was no public sentiment against duelling in Georgia then, and no necessity to leave the state to avoid indictment. Five minutes from home, a walk of a half mile brought the duellists to the selected spot, as free from intrusion in the early morning as though they had gone miles away. Another warm summer morning, a year later to the very day, on August 23, 1803, two other prominent figures in Savannah politics faced each other at the same place, each ready to take the other's life.

Again the newspapers fail to give an inkling as to the cause of the meeting. Everybody knew it, why print it? That was the local newspaper attitude of the day. But fortunately the old City Council proceedings are still in existence and in their brown and musty pages the story can be traced. It is the old tale of political maneuvers to secure a party advantage, with consequent bitterness rapidly developing a position that forced the chief figures to the duelling ground.

Perhaps it may be well to formally introduce the principals to the Savannah public of to-day.

Joseph Welscher was an active Republican. In 1802-03-04 he represented Washington ward in the City Council. In those days each of the aldermen represented one or more especial wards. In 1803 he was elected to the legislature along with George M. Troup and Thomas U. P. Charlton, Edward Harden going to the Senate, a quartette of staunch Republicans, or Democrats as we would call them to-day. Welscher was also active in professional and business circles.

Samuel Howard was a Federalist, a man of greater commercial prominence than Welscher. A number of vessels came consigned to him, and he was largely interested in the import and export trade. In 1803 he was elected as alderman from Warren ward.

Out of this municipal election of 1803 grew the duel of that August. When the box at the polling place in the new market house was opened, Thomas U. P. Charlton and Samuel Howard had an even number of votes. A new election was ordered and Howard was elected. The minutes of Council say: "July 25, 1803, Samuel Howard, Esq., attended and produced the return of his election as an alderman to represent Warren ward and was thereupon qualified and took his seat in Council."

The Republicans were still in the majority in the aldermanic board. Howard took a step calculated to upset this predominance and give the Federalists control. At the very next meeting after his installation he introduced a resolution: "Whereas, the law of the State expressly enacts that no person holding an appointment under this State or the United States (except Justices of the Peace and officers of the militia) shall be eligible to the appointment of aldermen, and whereas, it appears to Council that Joseph Welscher and Edward Stebbins, Esquires, hold the office of Commissioners of Bankruptcy, an appointment under the United States, Resolved, that Joseph Welscher and Edward Stebbins, Esquires, are by law disqualified from acting as aldermen of the city of Savannah."

An amendment to defer action resulted in a tie vote, and Mayor Charles Harris, whom Charlton a few years later described as "distinguished by devotion to Republican principles", voted in its favor. Nothing further was heard of the Howard resolution. Two weeks later its author lay at the point of death with a bullet wound through his intestines. Welscher had challenged him and the challenge had been accepted.

Welscher's second was George M. Troup, member of the legislature, afterwards representative in Congress, United States Senator and Governor. George D. Sweet, alderman from Reynolds ward, acted as Howard's second.

Could it have been more than a coincidence that this second duel between representatives of the bitterly contending factions was set for the same day of the year and at the same place as the previous one, and that in both instances there was an apparent determination to shoot to

Old Jewish Burial Ground
Where Several Noted Savannah Duels Were Fought Early in the Nineteenth Century

kill? Those were not mollycoddle days in Savannah politics and men staked their lives on their opinions and their words.

Again the local papers disappoint the searcher after facts. Nothing is told of the duel at the time. But by one of those strange peculiarities of the journalism of that day a flood of light is thrown on this and the Mitchell-Hunter duel, and on the feeling of the political parties toward each other, two months later in the republication in the "Columbian Museum" of a letter from a Savannahian to "The Hornet", of Frederickton, Md., a letter reproduced without a word of comment. The letter was dated Savannah, August 23, 1803:

"This day, at 12 o'clock, a duel was fought by Capt. Joseph Welscher, barrister-at-law, and Mr. Samuel Howard. The subject of dispute arose in the City Council, of which they are both members. Mr. Howard was dangerously wounded, by being shot in the belly. He has since been brought to town, his wound examined, and it is expected he will recover. Col. George M. Troup was Welscher's second, and Mr. George D. Sweet was Howard's. The place of action was at the Jews' burial ground (or as the Republicans call it 'The Jews' Holy Ground' for certain reasons). What is very remarkable, the very day of the month the year before, a duel was fought between Col. David B. Mitchell and Mr. Hunter, at the same place, when the latter was killed on the spot. Politics was the cause of both of these duels—the Republicans are not to be trifled with in this part of the world.

"In giving you a short history of this unhappy circumstance it may not be improper to mention that however desirous the Republicans in this quarter may be to live upon terms of friendship with those who differ from them in opinion, yet they are determined never to court it by tame submission to the haughty, insolent and overbearing conduct of the despicable few whose views, had they but the power of putting them into operation, would lead us to misery, desolation and death. We have gotten them in the background—far away—and there we shall keep them.

"Capt. Welscher is a man of amiable manners, a truly honorable character, highly beloved by a number of respectable friends and acquaintances—hated by none but Tories—the worst of Tories—the enemies of Washington and Jefferson—the enemies of sound order, peace, liberty and happiness. But, as I have mentioned just now, we have got them in the background, far away, and there we shall keep them."

If this had been originally published in a Savannah paper and the author had been made known another duel would have been the inevitable result. The reference to "Tories" recalls that at this time the Savannah "Republican" having made a threat to publish "a list of old Tories", and having failed to do so, the editor of the "Columbian Museum" stated that the "Republican" editor had probably received "a cautionary hint for its suppression". If he had no such list, though, "and wanted one, the Museum would furnish it if he would really publish it". The list was never made public. In a day when a duelling pistol was considered an essential part of a gentleman's equipment "discretion was the better part of valor."

The partisan politics behind both duels is clearly shown in the remarks of the Federalist "Daily Advertiser", of New York: "The place of action was the Jews' burying ground, where our friend Hunter gloriously but unfortunately fell".

Howard recovered from his wound and lived for years, a prominent member of the business world. He served again in Council in 1805-06. He was elected one of the directors of the Office of Discount and Deposit of the Bank of the United States, perhaps filling the vacancy caused by the killing of Hunter, and served for several years. Welscher was in Council until 1806, and during the same years continued to represent Chatham in the State legislature. He died during the session of the Assembly at Milledgeville on November 30, 1806, aged 45 years. His popularity is shown in the fact that in the 1806 election he led the Republican ticket. His strength with the Republicans was doubtless increased by his meeting with Howard. Shortly before he died he had the law regulating the election of aldermen and city officers changed, doing away with the property qualification. "This places a poor man on an equal footing with the rich. The Republican electors will therefore now have full opportunity of selecting men whose principles are congenial with their own and in whom they can place implicit reliance." So commented the editor of the "Republican". But already, in 1804, the editor of the "Republican" had relished the sweet joy of announcing that "The Aldermanic Board now stands eight to four in favor of the Republicans".

If any one questions the acerbity of Savannah politics in those days or the fact that their forebears here took their politics very much to heart, let them read and ponder these two extracts from the "Republican" in 1806, when Welscher and Morel and Harden triumphed over John M. Berrien, and Chatham retained its prestige as a Republican stronghold by sending another solid delegation of that faith to the legislature:

"On election day, Republicans, it will become you to de clare to the world your strength. On that day be at the polls, exercising the inestimable rights of freemen, on that day convince your opponents that you are jealous in a good cause, that you are mighty in strength, that you are a free and independent people."

And the morning after the election: "The Federalists have been unusually active. They have left no means untried. They have traduced the characters of the Republican candidates, they have endeavored to incense the good people of the city against men whose reputations defy the most poisonous arrows. Notwithstanding all their cunningly devised artifices, the Sons of Freedom have baffled their attempts."

The only wonder is that there were not more duels.

Twenty years later a writer in the "Georgian" proudly declared that "The representatives of Chatham in the legislators have been Democrats since 1775, with one exception only."

CHAPTER IX.

AN ERA OF NUMEROUS HOSTILE MEETINGS.

SAVANNAH'S ATTITUDE TOWARD THE BURR-HAMILTON DUEL AND ITS RESULT—FORMER SAVANNAHIAN, ONCE CONSIDERED FOR SECRETARY OF STATE, SECOND TO ALEXANDER HAMILTON—SENTER SLAIN BY JOHN RUTLEDGE—TWO YOUNG MEN MEET DEATH AT ONE ANOTHER'S HANDS—POSTING ENEMIES AT THE VENDUE HOUSE OR IN THE NEWSPAPERS—GRAND JURY PRESENTMENTS WITHOUT EFFECT—SOUTHERN STATES MOVE TO CHECK DUELLING.

L IVING in the atmosphere they did, Savannahians naturally showed a tolerant and indulgent spirit toward duellists elsewhere. This was illustrated in the Burr-Hamilton duel.

Burr had visited Savannah, had kinspeople and many political acquaintances here. When he became Vice-president with Jefferson as President, instead of Jefferson as Vice-president with Burr as his chief, by the intervention of divine providence working through the instrumentality of Alexander Hamilton, as good Democratic Republicans later came to believe, Burr was popular with his party in Savannah.

When he came here in 1802 Burr was the honored guest of the municipality. Private lodgings were provided for him and his suite, but the Vice-president preferred to be the guest of his niece, Mrs. Montmollin, at her home, still standing on West Oglethorpe avenue.

The Republicans were in control of the city administration. They had elected Mitchell as Mayor, in July, 1801, and were in the first flush of their municipal, state and national victories. An address was prepared in which the City Council set forth that of Burr's "Republican virtues" it had "long entertained the most exalted opinion." "In common with the friends of liberty this corporation rejoiced on the ever memorable fourth of March, 1801, which gave

Vice-President Aaron Burr
From Painting By John Vanderlyn, Owned By the New York Historical Society

to America Jefferson as president and yourself as vice-president—auspicious day for the freedom of this now happy land. They most sincerely wish, sir, that the virtuous principles of the present administration may be perpetuated to succeeding generations."

As Burr declined to make a written reply to this address it was withdrawn and Council called on him in a body and presented its verbal congratulations. Describing the "festival" given in his honor by the Savannah citizens, the "Columbian Museum" said: "The brilliancy of the entertainment, the number and respectability of the company, and the harmony which universally prevailed, have never been exceeded, perhaps never equalled here on any former occasion." Yet this was months after the charge had been made that Burr had conspired with the Federalists to defeat Jefferson and secure the presidency for himself, and that political office and political support had been freely promised to that end.

When Burr killed Hamilton two years later, in the duel of July 1, 1804, it would be more than erroneous to say the prevailing sentiment in Savannah was that of shocked horror. True, the fragments of the old Federalist party expressed indignation, but the mass of the people were no doubt indifferent, if not callous. They had seen their own local Republican leaders calling out the Federalists. The duel had been conducted in accordance with the regulations. Hamilton had an equal chance with Burr. Hamilton was the victim. That was Hamilton's misfortune. Hamilton had figured as a second in the duel between John Laurens and Gen. Charles Lee, had challenged Commodore Nichols, had almost forced a duel on James Monroe which Burr, as Monroe's friend, had amicably adjusted. And his death had removed the ablest man in the Federalist party, the one man who might have held the rank and file together and welded them into a powerful political force once more. Jeffersonian Republicans in Savannah, as elsewhere, may be considered as breathing easier when Hamilton fell on the heights of Weehawken.

Bitter though the political tone of Savannah was, not a public man here ever assailed the memory of the slain statesman with the venomous virulence of the old Federalist leader and recent president of the United States, John Adams, a vitriolic hater if there ever was one, who referred to Hamilton as "A caitiff come to a bad end", and held that "Fifteen years of continued slander against Burr provoked a call to the Field of Honor, as they call it, and sent him, pardoned I hope in his last moments, to his long home by a Pistol Bullet through his spine." When one recalls that only two years before this Hamilton's son had likewise been slain in a duel, the two tragedies that sorrowed the one home bring into clearer light the Adams' lack of the "milk of human kindness".

The tendency to-day, though, is to do more equal justice to both men, to regard Burr as something else than an arch-devil and Hamilton as not entirely akin to an archangel. Beveridge sums up perhaps as well as any one the opinion of many, "That Hamilton's pursuit of Burr was lifelong and increasingly venomous. It seems incredible that a man so transcendently great as Hamilton—easily the foremost creative mind in American statesmanship—should have succumbed to personal animosities such as he displayed toward John Adams and toward Aaron Burr."

Burr came south soon after the duel. In the Savannah papers one gets a glimpse of him now and then:

"The Vice-president, Col. Burr, is now within this state, at the plantation of Major Pierce Butler, on the island of St. Simon's about sixty miles to the southward. He came there by a small schooner from Philadelphia."

"The Vice-president has been residing on St. Simon's for some time, owing to a badness of weather which forbids his traveling. Before coming to Savannah however, he had visited our southern counties for the first time in his life, and proceeded as far as the St. Mary's river. He was received at St. Mary's with a Republican salute of seventeen guns, and generally in his travels received every attention from Republicans it was in their power to pay."

In the early days of October he reached Savannah. In an editorial announcement on October 5 the "Republican" said:

"The Vice-president has received the most respectful attention from the Republicans of this city and has been waited on by all our public characters."

This was three months after the duel with Hamilton, about which full details were published at the time in the Savannah papers.

Finally, in the "Republican" of October 9, 1804, is this item:

"Col. Burr set out from the city on his way to the seat of government on Friday last. We understand his early departure was owing to a desire of taking his seat in the senate at the opening of the session."

The Burr-Hamilton duel is the one American duel that all know about. One looks in vain in the Savannah papers for adverse editorial comment. The fact that he slew Hamilton one may well conceive was a relatively small factor in Burr's downfall. The seed for his political ruin had been laid in the unprincipled ambition that led to the maneuvers to overturn Jefferson, the leader ever toasted by the Savannah Republicans as "The Man of the People". The local organ of the party in after years stressed the charge that four members of Congress "had been offered any gratification they might wish for themselves or their friends if they would vote for Mr. Burr for president in preference to Mr. Jefferson."

And Jefferson did not forgive or forget.

There is one feature of the Hamilton-Burr duel, though, that few are aware of.

Hamilton's second was a former Georgian, a Savannahian to whom almost came the honor of filling the office of Secretary of State in President George Washington's cabinet.

There are dramatic pages in the life of Nathaniel Pendleton, as in the lives of many notable early Savannahians, that are well worth recalling.

Born in Virginia in 1756, he became an ardent patriot, espoused the American cause in its inception, fought bravely in its armies, served for a time on Gen. Greene's staff, and for gallant conduct at Eutaw Springs received the thanks of Congress.

With Greene and Wayne and others who had served in Georgia and appreciated the opportunities here offered, Pendleton located at Savannah when the British evacuated in 1782, and soon began the practice of the law. Such a leading position had he assumed at the bar, as a citizen and in the General Assembly, that in 1787 the Assembly elected him Chief Justice. He declined to act and Henry Osborne was elected. Pendleton was elected as Osborne's successor in January, 1789, and was the last man to hold the office of Chief Justice of Georgia under the Constitution of 1777.

Pendleton was a man of considerable persuasive power as an orator. One incident of the forceful use of this talent is told by Governor Gilmer.

It appears that a few years after the Revolution a horse was stolen from Gen. Elijah Clark. Horse stealing at that time was a whit worse than murder. Clark had a trifling fellow in the neighborhood arrested and had him charged with the offense before the grand jury at the next Superior Court.

"The testimony was insufficient for finding a true bill and the prisoner was discharged. Gen. Clark, not doubting his guilt, took the discharged man into his own custody, marched him to a convenient place, followed by the posse comitatus, judge and jury, and was about hanging him to some limb when Judge Pendleton made so eloquent an address in favor of law and order that he succeeded in doing by words what he could not through the officers of the Court."

It was from Pendleton's residence on the Bay, between Whitaker and Barnard, that the funeral of Gen. Greene took place.

When the convention met at Philadelphia in 1787 to draft the Federal Constitution Pendleton was one of Georgia's six representatives. For months, it will be recalled, Washington presided over the deliberations, in which Alexander Hamilton took a prominent part. More or less intimate acquaintanceships sprang up between the members. If Pendleton attended the sessions his personality and ability were such as to attract favorable attention. There is no doubt that as a former Virginian and brave soldier Washington knew of and respected him.*

When the Federal judiciary was established Washington appointed Pendleton as the first United States Judge for the District of Georgia. Four years later Thomas Jefferson resigned the office of Secretary of State and was succeeded by Edmund Randolph, another Virginian, who retired in a storm cloud in August, 1795, leaving a nest of thorns for his successor. The country was torn with dissensions, divided into almost warring factions as to its attitude toward the French Republic. Patrick Henry, of Virginia, Thomas Johnson, of Maryland, Governor Pinckney, of South Carolina, when approached declined the honor of filling the vacant secretaryship. Sorely perplexed Washington turned to his chief adviser, Alexander Hamilton:

"What am I to do for a Secretary of State," wrote he, "private and confidential": "I ask frankly and with solicitude, and shall receive kindly any sentiments you may express on this occasion."

Seven days later, on November 5, Hamilton wrote the President: "The following characters, in the narrowness of the probable circle, as to willingness, have occurred to me: Judge Pendleton, of Georgia * * * * Judge Pendleton writes well; is of respectable abilities, and a gentlemanlike smooth man. If I were sure of his political views, I should be much disposed to advise his appointment under the circumstances, but I fear he has been somewhat tainted with the prejudices of Mr. Jefferson and Mr. Madison, and I have afflicting suspicions concerning these men."

The world knows there was no political love lost between Hamilton and Jefferson. It does not recall as vividly that there was but a minimum of it between Washington and Jefferson.

Several Georgia encyclopedias, even Appleton's Encyclopedia of American Biography, state that Washington suggested the name of Pendleton. There is nothing in Washington's published letters to indicate this. The thought of Pendleton seems to have originated with Hamilton and but for the suspicion that the Savannahian was tainted with

---

* See foot note end of chapter.

Republicanism Hamilton would have succeeded in installing him as the successor of Jefferson and Randolph, in making him the third Virginian by birth to fill the office.

Whether Pendleton knew at the time that he was under consideration for the chief of cabinet positions does not appear. A year later, on August 31, 1796, he resigned his judgeship and removed to New York. His departure from Savannah may have been the result of his connection with the Yazoo land grants. Despite his position as Federal judge, Pendleton is said to have been active in urging on the legislators the passage of the act, and signed and issued certificates for the shares that, it was charged, were given to the members of the legislature of 1794-95 for their votes. He indignantly denied any wrong doing in his acts but one can readily perceive the uncomfortable position he occupied in Savannah when Jackson opened the batteries of his fiery wrath on all connected with the Yazoo affair.

In New York the acquaintanceship between Pendleton and Hamilton was renewed and ripened into a more intimate friendship. It was probably through him that Hamilton became a legal adviser for those fighting before Congress to sustain their claims to Georgia lands under the Yazoo grants. Hamilton's esteem for him had become so pronounced that when Vice-President Burr's challenge came to him he turned at once to Pendleton as his friend and second, and at the duelling ground on Weehawken Heights it was the former Savannahian, guide and adviser through all the unfortunate affair, who stood by his side and helped to bear the dying man away to his home when felled by Burr's bullet. And when Hamilton's will was read it was found that Pendleton was named as his executor.

Truly, in many ways, Savannah connects with some of the most dramatic incidents in the history of our country. The stories of its sons are illuminated with thrilling incidents. Its streets and public places are vibrant with historic life. It is hardly second to any other American city, younger though it is than some, in those colorful, picturesque events that give history its great charm. But the poet and the painter and the novelist have been absent. The full story has never been told as it should be, to grip

The Burr-Hamilton Duel
From Painting By F. Luis Mora; Reproduced From Woodrow Wilson's
"History of the American People," By Permission of
Harper & Brothers

the imaginations and leave indelible pictures on the minds of all readers.

Pendleton never came back to Savannah. His son, Nathaniel Greene Pendleton, born in Savannah, became a congressman from Ohio, and his son, George H. Pendleton, was one of the great leaders of the Democratic party, and among those considered for its presidential nomination. He was candidate for vice-president when Gen. George B. McClellan ran for president against Lincoln in 1864. He was in the United States House of Representatives in 1857-65, Senator from Ohio in 1879-85, and minister to Germany under Cleveland in 1885-89.

Other duels came in due course between Savannahians, of which no records exist, mainly political in origin. South Carolinians, too, had a habit of settling their disputes on Georgia soil and an occasional death attested the sureness with which they shot. Of one such duel the only existing data, apparently, is in the municipality's records of burials:

'F. Strace Senter, 25 years of age, physician, native of Rhode Island, January 19, 1804. Lockjaw occasioned by wound. Buried January 20. Left two brothers in England and two sisters in Rhode Island, also some property in Rhode Island. Wounded in duel with Honble. John Rutledge, Esq."

Senter's dust has long mingled with the sand of Colonial park. Strange to say, highly prominent as Rutledge was, not a bit of information can be had as to the duel and its cause. Those most conversant with South Carolina history when appealed to admitted that they had never heard of this affair. All there is with reference to it, outside of the municipal death records, is an allusion to Rutledge's having killed a man in a duel. As Mr. A. S. Sally, Jr., secretary of the South Carolina Historical Commission, wrote me: "The newspapers of the early days did not care to pry too much into a strictly private affair."

Sometimes from the neighboring world with which Savannah was closely associated by the ties of blood and of business came the news of a tragedy so poignant in its resulting sorrows that all attention was centered on it and the community as a whole felt a thrill of horror and a sense of deepest sympathy such as only come when men and women are shaken from their apathy by an incident far beyond the ordinary. Such an occasion was that of 1807, when two young men of Beaufort, well known here, met death at one another's hands. Frequent duels of a more commonplace character had hardened the public conscience, but the pathos of this affair stirred anew the fountains of remonstrance, and the newspapers found courage and room for an account of the meeting in which the writer gave full vent to the protests against the taking of life in such a way. From the "Republican" this account is taken:

"Departed this life on Monday afternoon, Mr. Arthur Smith, and on Tuesday morning, Mr. Thomas Hutson, and yesterday the remains of these young gentlemen were deposited in the tomb. On Monday morning they arose in all the vigour of youth and health; in a few hours both were bleeding on the field of honor. A challenge had been given and accepted—a duel was fought—and both were mortally wounded. Such, honor, are thy triumphs! Come hither, duellist, and regale thy senses! See two young men, the joy of their parents, levelling the deadly tubes at each other— they fire—they fall. See them groaning on a death bed; and now they breathe their last. Hear the distracted outcries of a fond and doating parent—the heart-piercing lamentations of affectionate sisters and the more silent though equally deep grief of loving brothers—are these pleasing to thine eyes, or music to thine ears? Yet, these, duellist, are the fruits of honor, so called.

"Oh, thou idol who delightest in human sacrifice; who snuffest up blood as sweet smelling incense; when will thy reign cease. Oh, ye votaries of the Moloch, ye abettors of murder and bloodshed, remember that that day will assuredly come when you will know whether you are to frame your actions by the laws of honor or the laws of God."

On the following Sunday a union service was held at the Episcopal church in Beaufort. The rector took as his text: "Let not the sun go down upon thy wrath; neither give place to the Devil." The graves of the two young victims of the code duello were in view of the worshippers as they heard the appeal from the pulpit for the suppression of duelling by the force of Christian opinion. But the impression proved only too fleeting. The hold the custom had upon the public was too strong to be broken. For seven decades to come other young and older men met as these two youths had done, some to fall never to rise again.

The Hutson family name is occasionally met in the Savannah papers of the early part of the century as resident here.

Fencing masters located in Savannah in the early years of the century and the young bloods became their apt pupils. "The polite art of fencing," as they termed it in their advertisements, became quite popular. But the sword could never usurp the place the pistol and the rifle had long held in the public esteem. Occasional ebullitions of feeling against duelling are noticed with resulting legislation aimed at the custom, but it was all to no purpose. Perhaps earliest among the southern states to seek to check the spreading practice of recourse to the code was Tennessee. Its legislature in 1802 passed a law under which he who killed another in a duel was held a murderer and "to suffer death without benefit of clergy", with a fine of $50, imprisonment for sixty days, and forfeiture of rights of citizenship for one year, for sending, carrying or receiving a challenge. North Carolina the next year followed suit, but the "aiders and abettors" of a duel resulting fatally were likewise to suffer the death penalty, while a fine of £100 attached to sending or carrying a challenge. It is interesting to recall in this connection that the man who was most instrumental in putting through this law was Frederick Nash, grandfather of Edmund S. Nash, of New York, once resident here, and the great-grandfather of J. C. Nash, of Savannah. So effective and beautifully expressed was his speech in the House of Commons, although he was then but 22 years of age, that it was incorporated in one of the early reports of the State. He was the son of Abner Nash, second governor of North Carolina, and afterwards became a Superior Court judge and Chief Justice of his state.

Encouragement to this opposition sentiment was furnished the Savannah public by occasional publications of protests from other sections, and in one of the "Columbian

Museums" of 1803 is found a three column letter from an English bishop vigorously condemning duelling.

It was not until 1809, though, that Governor Mitchell affixed his signature to a rather weak Georgia act. But neither before that nor after was there a predominant sentiment here to sustain prosecutions. When William Ploudon awoke one morning and found staring in his face, in the columns of the "Columbian Museum", this announcement:

"I pronounce WILLIAM PLOUDEN a COWARD and a LIAR.
June 15, 1802.   GASTON BACKLER."

what was there for William Plouden to do, if he wished to remain in Savannah and not have the finger of scorn pointed at him as he walked along its streets, but to immediately dispatch a friend with a challenge to Backler? Nor was there any expedient other than the duel whereby Francis Welman could save his sense of personal honor and satisfactorily refute the charges, when the Savannah "Republican" of June 21, 1809, held this card:

"I hold Francis H. Welman a Liar, Coward and Poltroon.   John Moorhead."

While there is no record that Plouden and Backler and Welman and Moorhead settled their difficulties with bullets, it is reasonable, in view of the spirit of the day, to believe they at least fired one shot at each other. The burial records tell of no resulting deaths.

Readers of the old "Gazette" also found this graphic portraiture of one of their fellow-citizens confronting them on its news page one morning:

"To deal in calumny accords with the lineaments of this gentleman's contracted phiz and phlegmatic constitution; the features of his countenance appear clouded with malignant passion; his soul is prone to false invective; and though the insidious smile should now and then relax the furrows in his brow it bears no claim to benevolence,"

A shot or two under the circumstances must have greatly relieved the strain and imparted a new and different smile to the "contracted phiz"—provided it was not put beyond the pale of smiles forever by a well-located bullet.

Even to-day such an unvarnished picture of a well-known Savannahian, wart and all, would be calculated to provoke a street brawl, if nothing worse. In those days the pen portrait painter invited an invitation to the nearest duelling ground.

At times a man was posted at the vendue house, which stood on the Bay near where the City Hall now is. There the public sales of the city were advertised. Amid the miscellaneous offers of negro slaves and plantation lands, of stocks of merchandise and of schooners and other vessels, of rewards for runaway apprentices and slaves, the angered Savannahian boldly and openly nailed the paper on which he gave to the world his final verdict as to the character of his erstwhile friend. His sketch was in a few simple words and no one who could read could misunderstand them.

In the very heart of the city's business district, surrounded by the offices and warehouses of its merchants, he pilloried the man who had refused to accept his challenge, or whom he desired to provoke to hostilities.

Quickly the news spread within the small limits of the town and before nightfall in every Savannah home there was a discussion of the merits of this latest antagonism of two leading citizens and its probable final outcome. When the victim of the posting came forth on the morrow he saw in every face the language of his foe and realized that, for the time being at least, he was the subject of general inquiry and comment, and that all awaited his action.

Posting at the vendue house was equally as effective as posting in the newspaper. It was as though the town crier, drum beating and a pack of barefooted children at his heels, had gone up and down the sandy streets loudly proclaiming the insults that were heaped upon the white placard that stared at every passer-by on the Bay. It was the acme of humiliation and of affront, firing the blood to the fighting temperature.

Sometimes the man posting another stood by the placard, pistol in pocket, ready to draw and shoot if any one essayed to remove the obnoxious paper. It was unsafe to interfere in such an affair, except through the regular channels prescribed by custom.

The Grand Jury presentments of 1808 throw a flood
of light on the local situation as to duelling, leave no doubt
that hostile meetings and rumors of meetings kept the
community alive with gossip, and prove conclusively that
the then existing laws did not check the habit, unsupported
as the statutes seem to have been by any strong favorable
public sentiment. Said that august body to Judge Walker:

"We present the too frequent and irreligious custom
of duelling. As we view it with horror, we recommend some
penalty that may effectually restrain it.

"We regret that persons in the commission of the peace
have not been prevented thereby from carrying challenges,
which is directly in violation of the laws they are bound
to support."

From this one might infer that the officers of the law
were more interested in arranging for meetings under the
code than in suppressing them—a conclusion that is justified by other official pronouncements. Wounding a man's
honor by seducing his wife, or slandering his integrity, or
sneering at his courage, was not an offense to be disposed
of in the Superior Court with a damage verdict for so many
dollars and cents. There were some things that could not
be translated into terms of money and public opinion proved
paramount to legislative enactment. Grand juries did not
indict for violations, and if they had done so petit jurors
would hardly have convicted. As for the judges on the
bench, well, is it improbable that they would in the main
have echoed the viewpoint of Judge Fletcher, in England,
who, in charging a jury in a duelling murder case, said:

"Gentlemen, it is my business to lay down the law to
you, and I shall do so. Where two persons go out to fight a
duel, and one of them falls, the law says it is murder, and I
tell you by the law it is murder, but at the same time a
fairer duel I never heard of in the whole course of my life."

The Society of the Cincinnati, of which Alexander Hamilton was President General at the time of his death, embrac-
ing as it did many of the most prominent men of Savannah
and other communities, the remaining officers of the revolutionary struggle, admitted that although under the common
law homicide in a duel was murder, the law was a dead let-

ter and obsolete, and that "All the decisions in the courts of justice turned wholly on the fairness with which the duel was conducted." In the North, where duelling is popularly supposed to have been under the ban much earlier than in the South, one finds the Legislature of New York in 1819 refusing to pass a bill making it a crime.

Regarding duels, even when death resulted, as "purely private affairs", the Savannah newspapers refrained from noting them. But the frequency of their occurrence is once more made apparent by the action of the Grand Jury in January, 1819, of which Steele White was foreman. In its presentments it unveiled the situation locally:

"The frequent violations of the law to prevent duelling have made the practice fashionable and almost meritorious among its chivalrous advocates. We will express it as our opinion that the law has been violated in repeated instances with impunity, when a knowledge of the cases were, or have been, known to its constituted guardians, and in the next instance the character of our city was wantonly disregarded, the laws of social order and of the state unblushingly set at defiance. Viewing the subject, as we do, of such magnitude, we deem it our duty to present the negligence and indifference of the officers whose duty it is to take cognizance of such matters as proper subjects of which to make examples."

[Referring to the Pendleton family, on page 129, Hon. George H. Pendleton visited Savannah in January, 1876. The "Morning News" said of him: "His name in this section is familiar as a household word, and is connected with recollections of many defences of the South." A public ovation was extended the visitor in front of the Pulaski House. Introducing Mr. Pendleton, Gen. Henry R. Jackson said: "His voice has ever been raised in defence of constitutional liberty, and his best endeavors have been devoted to the furtherance of the interests of the South." Addressing the thousands of citizens who crowded the street and square in front of the hotel, Mr. Pendleton referred to Savannah as a city "which for many years he had ardently desired to visit. In his early boyhood, he might say in his early infancy, his father had called him to his side and pointing on the map to the city of Savannah, told him that there he had been born and his father had lived before him." Referring to George H. Pendleton, Alexander H. Stephens said: "He is one of the brightest and brainiest men on this continent."]

* From Pendleton's letter to President Washington, soliciting appointment as Federal Judge for Georgia, published in the Georgia Historical Quarterly, September, 1923, it is evident that he had never come into personal contact with Washington, sustaining the opinion that Pendleton did not attend the Constitutional Convention. His uncle, the noted Virginian, Edmund Pendleton, who presided over the Virginia convention and was potent in having it ratify the Constitution, and who was afterwards Chancellor of Virginia, used his influence in behalf of his nephew for the District Judgeship and afterwards in an unsuccessful effort to secure his appointment on the bench of the United States Supreme Court.

CHAPTER X.

POLITICAL FEUDS AND RESULTING DUELS.

A STRIKING ILLUSTRATION FURNISHED IN THE TROUBLES
  BETWEEN THE McINTOSHES AND HOPKINSES, LEAD-
  ING FINALLY TO A SHOOTING AFFRAY, WITH ONE
  KILLED AND ONE WOUNDED, A TRIAL FOR MURDER,
  A CONVICTION FOR MANSLAUGHTER, AND ESCAPE TO
  EUROPE—A PICTURE OF LIFE IN THE BORDERLAND
  OF SOUTHEAST GEORGIA WHEN NEARLY EVERY MAN
  CARRIED A PISTOL OR BOWIE KNIFE, OR BOTH—DUELS
  BETWEEN HOPKINS AND KEITH, AND HOPKINS AND
  FLOYD.

FEUDS that soon embraced all the members of a family
frequently led to challenges and duels, or sometimes to
encounters in which code formalities were dispensed with
and pistols and knives were quickly brought into deadly
play.

In the first three decades of the last century it is said
that only two men in McIntosh and Camden counties—and
doubtless other counties, as well—appeared in public at any
time unarmed. To church or to social functions, to market
or to political gatherings, pistols and bowie knives went as
their inseparable companions. Two pistols were frequently
carried in the inside coat pockets and by a quick double
movement both could be brought into the open and to bear
upon an adversary. The bowie knife was the weapon for a
close encounter. If the two shots that the single barrel
pistols supplied were ineffective the pistols were sometimes
thrown at the enemy's head and the knife drawn for further hostilities.

No more striking illustration could be had of the bitterness that sometimes sprang up between those once enjoying
the most cordial relations, and the aftermath of violence,
than is afforded by the Hopkins and McIntosh families.

Both were of prominence in eastern Georgia, with their
roots firmly planted in the soil of McIntosh county and
branches cropping out in Chatham and other counties.

To tell in full detail the origin and incidents of the troubles between members of the families would require a book by itself. Mainly political in origin, their animosities increased in bitterness quickly, and what had been a state of friendly intercourse became one of envenomed antipathy that led to challenges and finally to a street brawl, with a McIntosh left dead upon the ground and a Hopkins wounded and prisoner. Members of the family and others in Savannah were involved in a way, and the succession of dramatic incidents stirred the city as it had seldom been disturbed by such occurrences beyond the confines of Chatham.

It was in 1817-19. The dramatis personae included several figures of note in their section of the state. They were: Gen. Francis Hopkins, a prominent planter, and his son, Col. John L. Hopkins, at one time an officer in the navy, and at the time of the difficulties with the McIntoshes a planter on Sapelo Island; Gen. Lachlan H. McIntosh, Capt. William R. McIntosh, who had also served in the navy; his brother, Dr. John McIntosh, and their cousins, William Augustus McIntosh and McQueen McIntosh.

It is not necessary to sketch the pedigree of the McIntosh clan. The Hopkinses were an early family, whose descendants to-day occupy positions of prominence in Georgia and other states. The first of the family in America was Francis Hopkins, an officer in the British navy, who married Mary Martinangelo, daughter of Filippo Martinangelo, one of the first settlers of Daufuskie Island, better known as Capt. Philip Martinangelo, of the Loyal Militia of South Carolina during the Revolution. Their only son, Francis Hopkins, was born near Bluffton, in 1772. Before the revolutionary storm broke Francis Hopkins, wife and child, removed to the West Indies, where he died in 1780. The mother and son returned to Daufuskie Island and in the first census of the United States, that of 1790, Francis Hopkins, aged eighteen, appears as the head of the family of two, his widowed mother and himself, in the Beaufort district. In April, 1794, he married Rebecca Sayre, daughter of Benjamin Sayre, formerly of Elizabeth, N. J., and Elizabeth Fripp, of Hilton Head, S. C. They lived with his mother on a large plantation on May river until the terrible storm

of 1804, which wrought great destruction to property along
the coast. Soon after this, his friend, Thomas Spalding, of
McIntosh county, persuaded him to move with his family
to that section of Georgia. Among the children he brought
with him was the oldest, John Livingston Hopkins, born
near Bluffton in 1795.

Francis Hopkins served in the Georgia legislature,
1808-13, when he resigned to enter the military service of
the State for the war then in progress with Great Britain.
He was given the title of Major. After the war he is frequently referred to as General Hopkins, but the exact origin
of the higher title does not appear. Six of his sons served
in the legislatures of Georgia or Florida.

John Livingston Hopkins when a youth enlisted in the
United States navy as midshipman and saw service on the
frigate Constitution, on the African coast, in the war with
the Barbary States. On the return of his ship to home
waters it was stationed at Hoboken. There, a correspondent
tells me, he became involved in a difficulty with a lieutenant,
named Keith. It seems that an amusing caricature of this
brother officer was circulated, much to the annoyance of
Keith. He became obsessed with the idea that Hopkins,
who was clever with his pencil, was the artist, and called
him to account in an insulting way. Hopkins was innocent
of the charge, but feeling outraged by the grossness of the
lieutenant's attitude resigned his commission and sent him
a challenge, which was accepted. In the duel Hopkins slew
Keith. Strange to say, several years later, in McIntosh
county, another caricature drawn by Hopkins came very
near involving him in a duel with a prominent citizen there,
and only prompt and proper explanations avoided such a
meeting. It was a day when men were sensitive, and pictures or comments which put them in a ridiculous or ludicrous attitude before their friends and neighbors were a sufficient cause for a cartel.

After the duel with Keith young Hopkins returned
home, studied law, and was admitted to the bar. In 1817
he was elected as one of the representatives from McIntosh
county in the Georgia legislature. From his service therein
came many months of personal and political discord. His

aggressive attitude at the capital and at home antagonized many of the older, conservative citizens, including his father's friend, Spalding.

At this session of the legislature Capt. McIntosh also represented McIntosh. The establishment of free schools in that county came up for consideration. Hopkins spoke in favor of the bill if sufficient funds could be provided under the plan proposed. When the next election came the charge was made that he had opposed the measure. This became a hot issue of the campaign. Major Hopkins, or General, as he was called, had previously been active in establishing the McIntosh Academy, and this doubtless had its bearing on the acute situation which developed.

Prior to this, ugly feeling between members of the McIntosh clan had shown its head. At a militia rally the cousins, Capt. William R. and William A. McIntosh, had a difficulty, weapons were drawn, and the latter requested Col. Hopkins to carry a challenge to Capt. McIntosh. When Hopkins called on Capt. McIntosh he met with a rebuff:

"Sir," said the captain to the colonel, "Your friend is not upon a footing with me; I shall treat him with contempt, as I have ever intended to do."

Accepting this as a personal reflection and insult to himself—as it was under the code—Col. Hopkins drafted a note demanding an honorable apology from Capt. McIntosh. This was done at the Darien postoffice. Coming out of that building, the captain and his brother, the doctor, were met. Hopkins, as he told the story, presented his pistols to the captain and asked him to take his choice, intending to settle the trouble then and there. The McIntoshes, he stated, refused to accept the tendered weapon.

"I shall post you on the highway and in the town of Darien," said Hopkins.

"Do it at your peril," was the reply from Dr. McIntosh.

That evening Col. Hopkins carried out his threat and posted McIntosh.

General McIntosh sought to reconcile the matter at a dinner at his home. Capt. McIntosh declined to meet Col.

Hopkins there. Eventually this particular trouble was seemingly settled at a conference at the court house

McQueen McIntosh had not been on good terms with the other members of his clan. His associations with Col. Hopkins had been pleasant and after the peaceable adjustment of this difficulty he spent the summer at the colonel's home.

"We were generally alone, but always surrounded by a good collection of books," writes Col. Hopkins. "At length the spoiler came and peace and happiness eloped." One day McQueen McIntosh visited Capt. McIntosh. There, while under the influence of liquor, he indulged, as the report came to Hopkins, in "virulent abuse of the Hopkinses, father and son," although he returned to the Hopkins house that night.

Col. Hopkins overlooked the incident so far as McQueen went, but felt that it showed the continued enmity of Capt. W. R. McIntosh.

Soon after this politics awakened in McIntosh. Legislators were again to be chosen. The McIntoshes began a quiet campaign for the election of Mr. Dunwody over Col. Hopkins. McQueen McIntosh warned Hopkins of this, and that Senator Allen B. Powell had been told by Capt. McIntosh of what was going on and "had smiled thereat." Finding all three men together, Powell was called to account by Col. Hopkins, and denied the story. McQueen McIntosh adhered to his statement.

Col. Hopkins afterwards said that until then he had implicit faith in McQueen McIntosh. "A few months previous to this unpleasant interview I had borne the brunt of a fight for him in which I had received three dangerous stabs, two in the head and one in the breast, from which I was confined to bed for seventy days."

Enraged at his cousin for betraying political plans, Capt. McIntosh attempted to strike McQueen with a club. Col. Hopkins and his father protected him. Dr. John McIntosh then threatened the life of McQueen, and it was understood those two cousins were to meet in the vicinity of Darien and fight a duel the next morning. Hopkins declined to act as McQueen's second. He recalled an expression of General Hopkins, that "The McIntosh quarrels are frequent and soon made up." As expected, when the McIntoshes met, instead of shedding each other's blood, "Their animosity was wiped away with the Tuscan sponge," as Hopkins expressed it.

Political slander now became rampant, it seems. The fight became a more open one. Stories came to Col. Hopkins that Major McIntosh had declared him a drunkard, that Capt. McIntosh had called him a fool and a coward, and that some young ladies influenced by them had called him a "cyclop," because he had lost his left eye.

The free school issue came to the front. Senator Powell charged Col. Hopkins with having opposed it. Hopkins held his reputation had been unjustly assailed, and "addressed a note to the Senator, not a challenge express, but an epistle of the same purport," "to which the Senator very properly replied, verbally, that he had a wife and children and was consequently not in that situation from which he would be censured for refusing to fight." This was carried to General Hopkins by some one, with "delectable additions," evidently meaning reflections on the Hopkins family.

Of course a challenge went then from Gen. Hopkins. Seconds were appointed and the day selected. Capt. Mc·tosh "Ground his cane sword" to a sharper point, "loaded his pistols, and hurried to Darien" to participate in an affair with which "he had no earthly concern"; and with the avowed purpose of settling his accounts with Col. Hopkins. Col. Hopkins and his father met all the parties interested at the Exchange in Darien. A verbal quarrel began between the older Hopkins and the Senator, then a physical altercation, and Capt. McIntosh drawing his sword rushed on the General. Col. Hopkins seized the sword. From that time there could be nothing but enmity.

The difficulty between Gen. Hopkins and Senator Powell was amicably adjusted, and with friends the Hopkinses turned in to dine at the Darien hotel. Capt. McIntosh came in, and took a seat. A quarrel ensued. Col. Hopkins threw a glass of wine in his face and McIntosh threw a bottle of wine at Hopkins' head—a waste of good wine on both sides.

Hopkins was induced to enter another room. McIntosh and his father sought to enter and Hopkins drew a pistol. "Lachlan H. McIntosh, of Savannah, requested that he give up his pistol and sword cane," pledging that there would be no further attempt at violence. This he did, but later when the McIntoshes endeavored to force themselves into the room the weapons were returned to him.

McIntosh posted Hopkins at Darien as a coward.

Hopkins posted McIntosh at that place, claiming that McIntosh was derelict in leading his forces to the Wayne county border where there had been trouble with the Indians.

Hopkins became exceedingly bitter in his comments:

"You posted me at Darien, hero, while I was at home fifteen or sixteen miles off, the day after I left Darien, though I had remained there two days for you.

"I will never tremble at the frowns of such a contemptible enemy as you are.

"I have never refused to meet my equal in the field.

"Did you go to St. Mary's on your return from Milledgeville, and challenge or horsewhip the commander of the U. S. Brig Saranac for writing to the Secretary of the Navy to request your dismissal from the navy as a barbarian, devoid of human sympathy or feeling?

"Did you retort upon those who had posted your want of courage? Did you not tremble at the very smile of your enemy? How often did you reject the hazard of the field of equal combat for the most trivial causes? Did you ever resent an insult?"

Capt. McIntosh professed to regard Col. Hopkins as beneath the notice of a McIntosh.

"To the charge of cowardice, I have to reply to Col. John L. Hopkins that I never expect to establish a fair reputation by duelling with men who are unworthy the notice of gentlemen. I am always prepared to repel the assaults of an assassin. You have threatened violence to my person. At your peril make your vaunting true.

"WM. R. McINTOSH."

Hopkins closed his side of this part of the controversy with a fine specimen of the epistolary art of that day as developed by such hostile conditions. It beautifully illustrates the early Georgia method of impaling an enemy on what has been termed "a vitriolic pen."

"Go on, infatuated man," said Hopkins to his enemy. "Pursue the same contemptible round of folly, falsehood and idle boasting. Leprous with crimes, bloated with vanity, inflated with anger, and shrouded with timidity, you shall corrode and waste your substance on the wind of error."

Col. Hopkins was defeated in the election that came on soon after. He sneeringly expressed the belief that Capt. McIntosh was entirely incapable of writing the correspondence coming from him and attributed its authorship to Mc-Queen McIntosh. Capt. McIntosh's letters were referred to as "A scurrilous and voluminous compilation of the most profound fatuity."

Some days later, while at court at Jefferson, Hopkins received a challenge from his old friend and companion, McQueen McIntosh, which was accepted. The articles of arrangement are of interest, having some features not usual in Georgia duels:

Article 1st: Lieutenant of Marines Charles C. Floyd, and Doctor John McIntosh shall second challengee and challenger.

Article 2d: The parties shall meet at 10:00 o'clock a. m., on Amelia Island, each armed with a brace of pistols and sword, each pistol to be loaded with powder and ball.

Article 3d: They shall take post at 20 steps apart, holding in their right and left hands loaded pistols.

Article 4th. Their swords shall be posted within their reach and immediately in their rear, and shall be used at their option after the exclamation of the acting second, 'Gentlemen, you are ready!'

Article 5th: The combatants will fire as they please, and not be restricted from reserving their fire and advancing as near as they desire to each other, and, after the exclamation named in article the fourth, they shall receive no orders from their seconds, but fight as they please within the distance stated in article the third.

A real duel seemed to be in prospect. Accompanied by their seconds, Lieut. Floyd for Hopkins, Dr. McMcIntosh for McIntosh, the principals met at the appointed place. McIntosh objected to the swords being used in additior to the pistols. "He did not like hackling". Lieut. Floyd, for Hopkins, yielded this point.

"The fatal moment had arrived," wrote Hopkins, "which was to send one or both, for neither of us were bad shots, unannointed and unannealed into the presence of an avenging God."

Then came more objections. The pistols to be used by Hopkins had barrels two inches longer than those McIntosh had brought. An hour was given the latter to get other pistols. When they came "McIntosh snapped one, and swore he preferred to use the ones he had brought."

About this time a party of gentlemen arrived with a desire to prevent bloodshed, if possible. Among them were three Savannahians, Judge John MacPherson Berrien, Solicitor-General William Law, and Attorney George Ker. With them came Mayor Archibald Clarke, of St. Mary's.

McIntosh resumed his position, holding his first brace of pistols in his hands. Hopkins was in position, awaiting the signal to fire. Dr. McIntosh, to whom had fallen the duty of giving the word, stood ready. Then Judge Berrien and the other gentlemen urged delay and reconsideration. As a result the following papers were prepared and signed:

"I withdraw my challenge to Colonel Hopkins, together with any and every expression which I may have used calculated to injure the feelings either of Mr. Hopkins or General Hopkins, and without hostility I do implicitly believe them to be gentlemen, soldiers and men of honor.

"McQUEEN McINTOSH."

"In consequence of the above signed McQueen McIntosh, I declare that my attack upon him was predicated upon a supposed insult at that time, viz. in Darien on the 31st August.

"JOHN LIVINGSTON HOPKINS."

Unfortunately, Hopkins gave copies of these cards to a friend. Some time after, while visiting Savannah, McQueen McIntosh had an interview with this party, was chagrined to find how others looked at the card he had signed, and returning to McIntosh county the ill-feeling between the parties reasserted itself. McIntosh claimed he had been betrayed by Hopkins violating a mutual promise that only one copy of the agreement should be preserved, in General Floyd's hands, all others being destroyed.

The McIntosh clan in Georgia, like their progenitors in the Highlands of Caledonia and in early colonial days, were probably all high-strung, easily irritated, quick to take offence, and not overly courteous in language while under the stress of passion. They were courageous, as Georgia's history of a century and a half has shown, and bloodshed again seemed inevitable. But it came not through the medium of the established code.

After several incidents which intensified the bitterness, McQueen McIntosh published some correspondence offensive to Hopkins. The Hopkinses and McQueen and Dr. John McIntosh met in Darien. Col. Hopkins, according to his statement, hearing that the McIntoshes threatened his life, borrowed a pair of pistols and a sword cane. Conflicting stories are told of the meeting on the highway of the little town between the four men. Hopkins' statement said that the fight was in the open:

"Dr. McIntosh was advancing to fire upon me. No alternative was left to me but to shoot the one and throw the empty pistol at the other, or to sustain the fire of both and die."

"McQueen McIntosh and myself raised our pistols and fired together—I fired first and hit him—I threw the empty pistol at the doctor, who fired. I put my left hand to my breast, and at that moment I felt a wound in my right arm, and walked away to the hotel."

On the other hand, the McIntoshes claimed that Hopkins had concealed his body behind a corner of the building, and after McIntosh "fired without effect, Hopkins, availing himself of this concealment, took deliberate aim and shot his heroic antagonist through the body", and that McIntosh, while falling, "presented his second pistol and with well-directed ball shattered the fugitive's arm, though twelve yards distant."

McQueen McIntosh lay dead on the ground and Hopkins' arm was shattered. He was arrested and confined in jail with his father, a military guard being put over the jail to guard the prisoners from attack and prevent their rescue.

Politics were exceedingly bitter. The Hopkinses and the McIntoshes stood for contending factions. The friends of the McIntosh family are alleged to have controlled the grand jury. General Hopkins and his son were indicted for murder. They were brought to Savannah soon after and remained in jail here until October, 1819, when they were tried before Judge Berrien, at Eulonia Court House, McIntosh county. The father was acquitted but the son was convicted of manslaughter and sentenced to a term of years in the penitentiary. Judge Berrien's charge in this noted case is said to have been a masterpiece of judicial eloquence and was long referred to as evidence of the high forensic ability of the Georgia bench.

During the trial Col. Hopkins' wife died, with her twin babies, at their birth, at the old home in Beaufort. In view of these circumstances Judge Berrien permitted Col. Hopkins to visit his home at "High Point'," Sapelo Island, before beginning to serve his sentence. All of the records of McIntosh county were destroyed by fire in 1873 and the only sources of information to-day are family records, tradition, and scanty allusions in the newspapers of that time. As the accounts come down to us, Col. Hopkins' friends felt outraged by his conviction for a crime as a result of what they deemed purely an "Affair of Honor," and steps were taken to enable him to escape from the country. Judge Berrien's own son-in-law, Mr. Burroughs, father of the late William B. Burroughs, of Brunswick, who was a warm friend of the Hopkins family, without the knowledge of the Judge, is said to have been a party to the plan whereby Col. Hopkins was rowed out of Sapelo sound to the ocean, where a sailing vessel received him, and under a payment of $5,000 the captain carried him to safety in England.

Col. Hopkins, it is stated, spent three years in Europe, part of the time with a cousin on the River Thames, but for months wandering over the continent in the guise of a physician. His father died in 1821, broken in body and in spirit. A year later Col. Hopkins returned to America and Gov. John Clark issued a pardon to him. Locating soon after in Tennessee he resumed the practice of law. He became Judge of the Superior Court in Monroe county. In October, 1828, while on the way home from court he was assassinated by three men whom he had threatened to prosecute for violations of the law. In the short life of thirty-three years he had crowded dramatic experiences that fall to the lot of very few men. He had married a second time, Miss Anne Stephens, daughter of Maj. Henry Stephens, of Monroe county, Tenn. His son, John Livingston Hopkins, was born on October 5, three days before the judge was slain. He became one of Georgia's noted lawyers and jurists, dying at Atlanta in 1912.

While in jail awaiting trial for the killing of McIntosh, Col. Hopkins wrote a little pamphlet reviewing the whole circumstances from his standpoint, only one complete copy of which is known to be in existence now. Much of the bitter correspondence between them was printed in the Savannah and Darien papers at the time.

Out of the affray grew uncalled-for charges against Judge Berrien and perhaps the duel elsewhere referred to between Edward F. Tattnall, representative from Chatham, and another legislator, whose name is not obtainable, in which Tattnall was wounded.

"John Abercromby was one of the leading men of the session of the legislature of 1819," wrote Governor Gilmer. "He was a large, fat, pot-bellied man, with his head stuck upon his shoulders without neck. His mind was uncultivated by books, but quick and intelligent. His passions and prejudices were strong and indulged in freely.

"Abercromby, whose opinion of Judge Berrien was not very favorable, was excited by the report of the Judge's conduct to introduce into the House of Representatives a strongly condemnatory resolution, without any evidence but a short street conversation.

"A very angry debate took place. Col. Tattnall, who was one of the Representatives and a neighbor of Judge Berrien, was very indignant. He and Abercromby were soon in a fighting mood. Abercromby reflected upon the lawyers for the support they gave their 'Brother Chip', as he called Judge Berrien.

"He and I occupied seats and were upon very friendly terms. I succeeded in (what I am not very successful at) exciting the laugh of the House at Abercromby, and putting everybody into good humor. Col. Tattnall offered a resolution of inquiry into Judge Berrien's conduct, which was referred to a large committee. Judge Berrien was immediately notified of the proceedings of the House and came to Milledgeville, attended by several friends of the bar.

"The committee held its meetings in the Senate Chamber, after the adjournment for the day of the two Houses. A great crowd assembled below and in the gallery. Col. Tattnall, the mover of the resolution of inquiry, was chairman of the committee. Before he took his seat in the president's chair, he told me that Abercromby's violent conduct had so excited him that he believed he would find it impossible to restrain his temper if it was repeated, and requested me to move, as soon as the committee was ready to act, that he should be excused from presiding over it, and another chairman appointed.

"I did so, and nominated Col. Murray. The investigation was made upon the evidence given by Judge Berrien's friends and resulted in his entire acquittal by the committee. Abercromby was alone in his attack, and without any offensive materials to carry it on. He had to submit, but he did so with bad temper."

Such was one phase of life in Georgia a century ago.

Col. John L. Hopkins did not monopolize the duelling honors of his family. A younger brother, Edward Stevens Hopkins, fought a more famous duel, his antagonist being the redoubtable Gen. John Floyd, descendants of whom are to be found to-day in Savannah and elsewhere in Georgia. Edward Stevens Hopkins was born in 1809 and lived to a ripe old age, passing away in 1887. His affair with Gen. Floyd is generally referred to as "The Three Weapon Duel". The stories of this meeting are very conflicting—each family has its own traditions, irreconcilable in their versions as to what occurred, reflecting to this day family prejudice and family pride. Shotguns, pistols and bowie knives were the weapons. This duel has merely an incidental Savannah interest and belongs more to a volume dealing with Georgia "Affairs of Honor" in general.

Grave of James Wilde
Who Was Shot Through the Heart By a Brother Officer

CHAPTER XI.

THE SLAYING OF A POET'S BROTHER.

DEATH OF PAYMASTER WILDE, SHOT THROUGH THE HEART BY CAPT. JOHNSON—ENSIGN BRYAN SLAIN BY LIEUT. BRIDGES—THE KILLING OF AARON MENDES —HOW TEFFT THRASHED AN ASSAILANT AND REFUSED HIS CHALLENGE—TWO SAVANNAH CONNOISSEURS OF ANTE-BELLUM TIMES—ORIGIN OF THE GEORGIA HISTORICAL SOCIETY.

WHILE many duels were fought in the decade from 1810 to 1820, of only a few does the most diligent research reward one with more than meagre information. Most tragical of them all seems that meeting in which the much loved brother of Richard Henry Wilde, scholar, statesman and poet, met death at the hands of one who had been his comrade and friend. Even to-day, more than a century later, one is saddened by the story of the useless sacrifice of a noble young life.

In the old Colonial cemetery, not far from the walk which connects the two ends of Lincoln street, and directly west of the vault of the Johnston family, is the well preserved stone above the brave boy's grave. It is scanned now and then by the curious, wondering as to the tragedy of which the graven lines give but a hint. It is a strange epitaph, both a eulogy and an indictment:

This humble stone
records the filial piety
fraternal affection and manly virtues
of
JAMES WILDE, Esquire,
late District Paymaster in the army of the U. S.
He fell in a Duel
on the 16th of January, 1815,
by the hand of a man
who, a short time ago, would have been
friendless but for him;
and expired instantly in his 22d year:
dying, as he had lived:
with unshaken courage & unblemished reputation.
By his untimely death the prop of a Mother's
age is broken:
The hope and consolation of Sisters is destroyed,
the pride of Brothers humbled in the dust
and a whole Family, happy until then,
overwhelmed with affliction.

It was this stone which attracted the attention of William Dean Howells on one of his visits to Savannah and lead him to direct especial attention to it in his delightful "Savannah Twice Visited," in Harper's Magazine of February, 1919: "The duel is now apparently quite extinct. There is a record of it incomparably touching in an epitaph of that beautiful old cemetery which the city keeps for a playground of the neighboring school children, and the resort of the sympathetic frequenters. In rural grave yards everywhere the grief of the survivor is apt to express itself with unsparing passion, but here, beyond elsewhere, it imparted the pang of indignant anguish. 'He fell,' this epitaph said, 'by the hand of a man who a short time before would have been friendless but for him.' The words must have been primarily meant for the eye of the homicide, but they wrung my heart with abhorrence for the custom which wronged him and his victim alike, and made me feel its atrocity and stupidity as never before."

Only one other record than the tombstone exists in Savannah, as far as known, of this duel. Once more the old burial book at the City Hall yields from its pages, crispened by the passage of over a century, some details that but for it would not be obtainable. The official who kept that book little knew that only through its medium would some day information be had concerning not only this but many other deaths of interest to Savannahians. Here is what he wrote:

"James Wilde, aged 23, native of Baltimore, died January 16, 1815, paymaster 8th Regt. U. S. Infantry; duel; buried 17th. He was shot through the heart at the fourth discharge by his antagonist, Capt. R. P. Johnson, of the 8th Regt. U. S. Infantry. His corpse was conveyed from the fatal spot, on the north side of the Savannah river in South Carolina, to Mrs. Wilson's Boarding House, facing the Baptist Church, and thence buried with military honors."

James Wilde was the beloved brother of the poet. The incident of the duel is inseparably interwoven with the writing of Wilde's beautiful poem, "My life is like a summer rose," a poem which, as Anthony Barclay so well said, by "The pathetic and tender feelings which it conveys, the exquisite truth of its images, and the melody of its verse, con-

spired to confer upon its author a fame which nothing so
brief had previously ever secured even to the masters
of the lyre."

Barclay, a classical scholar and lover of literature, for
years the British consul in Savannah, in his little work on
"Richard Henry Wilde's Summer Rose, or the Lament of
the Captive", quotes from a letter from the poet to an
intimate friend in this city:

"The lines were originally intended as part of a longer
poem. My brother, the late James Wilde, was an officer of
the United States army, and held a subaltern rank in the
expedition of Colonel John Williams against the Seminole
Indians in Florida, which first broke up their towns and
stopped their atrocities. When James returned, he amused
my mother, my sisters and myself, with descriptions of the
orange groves and transparent lakes, the beauty of the St.
John's river and of the woods and swamps of Florida—a
kind of fairy land—interspersed with anecdotes of his campaign and companions. As he had some taste himself, I
used to laugh and tell him I'd immortalize his exploits in an
epic. Some stanzas were accordingly written for the amusement of the family at our meetings. That, alas, was destined never to take place. He was killed in a duel. His
violent and melancholy death put an end to my poem; the
third stanza of the first fragment, which alludes to his fate,
being all that was written afterward."

The third stanza to which Wilde referred read as follows:

"I, too, had once a brother; he was there
Among the foremost, bravest of the brave;
To him this lay was framed with fruitless care;
Sisters for him sigh in the secret grave;
For him a mother poured the fervent prayer.
But sigh or prayer availeth not to save
A generous victim in a villain's snare:
He found a bloody but inglorious grave,
And never nobler heart was racked by baser glaive."

The only portion of the poem that has lived, is, of course,
the "Lament of the Captive," lines which promise to endure
as long as there are lovers of the beautiful in literature.
Known to many, there may be others to whom they are
new, and so their republication be justified. Prominent

though Richard Henry Wilde was in Congress as one of
Georgia's representatives, world-wide though his recognition
was as a great Dante-Tasso scholar, his fame rests not upon
his speeches at Washington, nor his scholarly work in Italy,
but solely upon these three verses the world will not willing-
ly let die:

> My life is like the summer rose,
>   That opens to the morning sky;
> And ere the shades of evening close,
>   Is scattered on the ground—to die;
> Yet, on that rose's humble bed
>   The softest dews of night are shed;
> As if she wept such waste to see:
>   But none shall drop a tear for me.
>
> My life is like the autumn leaf,
>   That trembles in the moon's pale ray;
> Its hold is frail, its date is brief—
>   Restless, and soon to pass away;
> Yet, when that leaf shall fall and fade,
>   The parent tree will mourn its shade;
> The wind bewail the leafless tree:
>   But none shall breathe a sigh for me.
>
> My life is like the print, which feet
>   Have left on Tampa's desert strand;
> Soon as the rising tide shall beat,
>   Their track will vanish from the sand:
> Yet, as if grieving to efface
>   All vestige of the human race,
> On that lone shore loud moans the sea:
>   But none shall thus lament for me.

Lord Byron is said to have expressed the opinion that
"No finer American poem has met my eye than Wilde's
'Summer Rose'."

No local newspapers of the period of 1813-16 are to be
found in Savannah. In the Congressional Library at Washington are the files of the Savannah "Republican" of those
years, and to them I turned with the hope of bringing to
light more details as to the duel and its causes. The papers
carried a formal funeral invitation, and that alone. They
told nothing beyond the facts already in hand. Nor did in-
vestigations North in other newspapers of 1815 bring to
light the origin of the trouble between Wilde and Johnson.
Apparently it must forever remain a mystery unless some

family papers reveal it. The bitterness of the Wilde family against Capt. Johnson is apparent from the allusion in the stanza quoted from the unfinished poem, and is more clearly displayed in the inscription on the tombstone. There is no reason to believe, though, that this feeling was shared by the people of Savannah, or that they did not regard the circumstances surrounding the meeting with a less severe eye than the kinsfolk of the unfortunate young soldier.

Eight months before this the American forces stationed for the defence of Savannah had lost another young officer through the code. Again one is thwarted in the effort to discover the cause of the meeting, except that it was of small moment. "The Republican," of May 10, 1814, carried this brief account:

"DUEL—A duel was fought yesterday morning at daybreak near this place between Ensign Samuel H. Bryan and Lieut. George R. Bridges, both of the 10th regiment, with pistols, at a distance of twelve paces. The former was killed at the second fire without having fired at all, his pistol having missed fire twice. They fell out, it is said, about a trifling affair."

Two years after the Wilde-Johnson duel came another, likewise fatal, of which the only record is the notice in the burial book:

"Dennis O'Driscoll, 22 years, native of South Carolina, lawyer, August 17, 1817. Fell in a duel by John Edwards, of South Carolina. Died at and was buried from Col. Shellman's."

These parties were doubtless South Carolinians who came to Savannah to settle their dispute.

How many other duels, fatal and otherwise, were fought during this period no one know. Those in which no one was injured, or in which the wounds were not mortal, were ignored, as were doubtless others in which the results were fatal if the interested parties were influential and exerted themselves to suppress the particulars. Particularly, it is said, was this the case when a woman was involved.

On April 2, 1818, another Savannah victim was added to the list. Here again the cause and the weapons used were not divulged in the public prints. The "Columbian Museum" gave the following account, furnished by a friend of the deceased, whose signature of H was appended to his contribution:

"DIED. In this city on Monday evening, in consequence of a wound in the stomach received in a duel, Mr. Aaron Mendes, a native of Charleston. The character of this gentleman among his friends and acquaintances bore that dignity and fame which had long noted him as the polar star of virtue, honesty and sobriety. His quiet disposition was of that nature which gained him the esteem and affection of all who knew him, although the magnanimity of his courage could not brook injustice. Had the unfortunate circumstance of his untimely demise been timely circulated, friends who in the last moments of his life (left him not to die bereft) would have taken such measures as to have prohibited this unfortunate occurrence. But the deed, alas! was too precipitately concluded—yet this remains to be said: He died with that resolution which would have distinguished even the greatest hero."

The city's burial book simply records of Mendes (or Mendez): "April 2. Native of Jamaica. Died 3d inst. Fell in a duel; died at the corner of Barnard street and Bay lane."

Not far from the Cottineau graves in the old cemetery, lying flat upon the earth, on a line with the north side of Hull street, is a heavy granite slab with an inscription which frequently attracts attention. Tradition, which is so often merely the mother of "historical" lies, tells us that he who lies beneath fell in a duel. In a way this is a companion to the Wilde stone, with the difference that the latter did not give the name of the man who slew the poet's brother, while on this memorial tablet the slayer's name was deeply graven, only to be removed by some one connected with him, who properly resented the perpetuation of his memory as a homicide. The chipping of the name until it became undecipherable has done more to centre attention on the inscription and awaken comment and conjecture than if it still told the passer-by who it was that slew Odrey Miller.

Ordinarily the defacement of a grave stone would not prevent the interested from ascertaining who it was that sent the fatal bullet into the brain of Miller. Nowadays reference to the newspaper files would bring to light the full story. But ninety years ago the local newspapers kindly refrained from any allusion to the affair, not even a death notice and funeral invitation appearing. This was not uncommon, as in several instances where Savannahians were killed in affairs of honor not a line is to be found in print. "The Georgian's" columns threw no light on the slaying of Miller, and a search through the pages of "The Republican" files at Washington was equally fruitless. The burial book at the City Hall supplied the only information beyond that of the stone itself. There one learns that Odrey Miller was 33 years of age, that he was a Kentuckian by birth, a horse trader by occupation, that he was wounded in the head on July 13, 1831, and that Doctors Daniell, Arnold and Richardson gave their surgical services in vain. He was buried the next day.

Miller's profession naturally suggests a quarrel over a horse. Savannah had its jockey club in those days, its young men owned fine stock and were keen judges of the merits of horse flesh. Racing was the sport of the day and more than one quarrel finally arbitrated with duelling pistols originated at the track. Did Miller take advantage of a patron in a horse deal? Did the trouble originate in charges of misdoing at a race? Either explanation is probable. From the race track to the duelling ground, from the duelling ground to the hospital, from the hospital to the old cemetery—all in a few hours—completed the life story of the Kentuckian who had come to Savannah and lived on State street. If it had been a murder, or ordinary manslaughter, the daily papers would doubtless have alluded to it. Being a duel it came within the scope of private affairs about which good taste and ordinary prudence dictated silence. The very absence of newspaper comment sustains the tradition of a duel.

Who Slew Odrey Miller?
A Mystery of Savannah's Old Cemetery

The inscription on the tombstone, with the obliterated name of the slayer, follows:

To the Memory of
ODREY MILLER
a native of
Scott County, Kentucky
who died from a wound
inflicted by ....
on the 13th July, 1831
aged 33 years & 3 months.

A just, honest and benevolent man, is the report which his deportment among strangers has earned for him; he possessed a generous and noble spirit which could readily forgive & as readily ask forgiveness but which was ever indignant at cruelty, oppression and wholly irreconcilable to an ignoble submission. Though this stone is designed to mark the spot where they have laid him, his name and his virtues will be perpetuated in the affections and friendship of many who mourn his untimely fate.

Challenges were not always accepted, nor posting regarded as rendering a duel necessary, nor did the refusal always carry with it an implication of cowardice or injure the future position in the community of the man who declined a meeting. This was signally shown in the case of Israel K. Tefft.

In Tefft's early manhood he was a member of the Chatham Artillery, and in 1824 aspired to an election as sergeant in that company. When the election was held he was defeated through what he regarded as underhand methods by William Turner. Tefft, who resigned from the company, held that the result of the election "was not the voice of the corps," but that "new members were influenced by the intrigues of Turner."

"Had I been unsuccessful by the employment of fair means I would not have uttered a word," said he, "but who is safe against plots and combinations?"

Tefft sent a communication to the Chathams, which was read at the parade of the company on Washington's birthday. Soon after this Turner attacked him on the street, but Tefft got the better of his assailant and inflicted more punishment than he received.

Turner then challenged him, demanding "a prompt and ample apology," or "direct your friend to act in conjunction with mine."

When Tefft refused to consider the cartel Turner proceeded to post him.

Tefft held that by the code he was under no obligation to meet Turner.

"He has chosen his mode and felt the consequences," said he.

"The challenge," Tefft maintained, "was merely an effort by Turner to recover lost ground in public esteem." "I declined the glorious pomp and circumstance of a duel, but assured him that if he attacked I would defend my person and reputation."

Turner printed a card signed by fifteen of the new members of the Chathams, certifying that he had not influenced their votes. Further, he insisted that Tefft while a corporal was "a burlesque as a non-commissioned officer." and that if it had not been for outside interference he would have worsted him in the street encounter.

To remove Tefft's contention as to the street attack having put Turner outside the pale of the code, Turner apologized in the public prints for the assault and renewed the invitation to settle the affair with pistols.

Turner's posting accomplished nothing. "Mr. Turner," said Tefft, "is perfectly welcome to any advantage he may flatter himself he has derived from his posting system. The public need not be told that its importance must depend upon the truth or falsity of the assertions the paper contains." "You assailed me in the street and received at my hands the chastisement you merited," said he, in closing.

A meeting of the Chathams held that it was a personal matter between the two men and refused to have the com-

pany drawn into it further.   Evidently other friends intervened, as there is no record of any meeting.

Mr. Tefft became a very prominent citizen of Savannah.
He had been joint proprietor of the "Georgian" with the
actor Harry James Fenn in 1821-22.   In 1822 he entered
the service of the Bank of the State of Georgia as a clerk,
was for twenty years teller, and then in 1848 became
cashier.   It was he who suggested the Georgia Historical
Society and became one of its founders and its secretary
from its organization in 1839 until his death in 1862.   The
story goes that Tefft mentioned the idea to Dr. William
Bacon Stevens, afterwards Bishop Stevens, and the two
discussed such an organization with Dr. Richard D. Arnold.
Out of their conferences grew the Georgia Historical
Society.

"Dr. Arnold was the only disinterested party," said a
Savannahian of that day.

Mr. Tefft's hobby was autographs, and he keenly appreciated the value of a historical society in bringing him
into touch with men of prominence in literature, art and
politics the world over, and the opportunities it might afford
of securing rare American and foreign letters and engravings through other collectors.   Dr. Stevens, who was then
practicing medicine, was intent on writing a history of
Georgia, the need of which was appreciated by all educated
Georgians of that day.   It was the hope of his life to be in
a position where he could gratify this laudable ambition.
The backing of a society dedicated to the acquisition of historical materials concerning colonial and revolutionary days
would be of inestimable value to him.

Dr. Arnold had no axe to grind, no private motive, no
matter how commendable, to influence him.   He was, as
tradition says, the sole disinterested organizer of the movement.

Mr. Tefft's desires were gratified.   His memory still
lives as one of the leading early American collectors of autographs—probably the most widely-known of his day—and
his collection at his death had no equal in this country.   The
story is frequently told of the visit to him of Frederika

Israel K. Tefft
Founder of the Georgia Historical Society and America's Greatest Autograph
Collector; When a Young Man He Declined a Challenge
(From a painting owned by Georgia Historical Society)

Bremer, the Swedish novelist, and her delight in examining the wonderful aggregation of historical documents, signatures and portraits.

Miss Bremer styled him "The greatest autograph collector in the world." "His collection of autographs," wrote she, "is the first which I have ever been able to examine with interest and respect, not because it occupied many folios and could not be fully examined in less than six months, but because a portrait is appended to the handwriting of each distinguished person, usually an excellent copper plate engraving, together with some letter or interesting document."

Some years after Mr. Tefft's death his unrivaled collection was sold at auction in New York. Collecting had not then attained the wide vogue it now has, but the richness and variety of the Savannah collection awakened a degree of attention hitherto unknown in the metropolis. It and the famous library of A. A. Smets represented the life interests of those two scholarly companions, whose homes at the corners of Bull and Jones streets were among the intellectual centres of ante-bellum Georgia. Money has now become the great factor in the fad of collecting, but with Tefft and Smets it was not so much lavish expenditure of money as rare taste and a wide knowledge of art, history and literature, a genuine love in their pursuits of antique and modern books of more than ordinary merit, and the search for historic papers, signatures and engravings.

There was a wide appreciation of the intrinsic value of the Smets collection and a desire that it be preserved in its entirety to serve the public. Soon after his death a movement began to have the State take it over. The matter was brought to the attention of the legislators in April, 1863, and they directed Governor Brown to confer with the executors of the Smets estate as "to the terms on which his extensive and valuable library may be purchased by the State, and to report the terms at the next session of the General Assembly."

Smets Residence   **Tefft Residence**

Homes of Two Leaders of Savannah Culture Three-quarters of a Century Ago.

The Journals of the General Assembly do not show any report or further action in this connection, which is not surprising in view of the disturbed conditions resulting from the invasion of the State.

Mr. Smets' library was taken to New York and sold in 1867 for $10,000, said to have been far less than it would have brought in Savannah, although the financial havoc wrought by the war was still sadly omnipresent in the South. An amusing story is told in this connection of A. T. Stewart, the "merchant prince." Those in charge of the sale naturally presumed that with great wealth had come the desire on the part of Stewart to play the part of the bibliophile, or at least become the seeming patron of literature by the accumulation of books accredited as of unusual interest and value. The Smets collection was accordingly brought to his attention and he requested that a catalog be sent to him. This was done. Hearing nothing further from him some one ventured to again direct attention to the opportunity to enrich his library at the sale. To the astonishment and amusement of those handling the books there came back from the canny Scotchman the reply:

"The books are entirely too old to suit me."

Evidently the merchant prince looked upon the treasures the Savannah lover of books had gathered from the marts of the world as though they were merely so much second-hand merchandise, out of place in his vast emporium or palatial home. Yet, had he but known it, the treasures he so ignorantly rejected would have brought to his estate, in the fullness of time, a vastly greater increment of profit than the bulk of his investments, skilfully made though they were. What would not the multi-millionaire bibliophiles of to-day bid in competition for the rare items of this Savannah library which was sold for a fraction of its value? In it were manuscripts of the 9th to the 14th century, including curious parchment deeds of the 12th century. Black letter books of the 16th century of extreme rarity stood on

the shelves of Smets' library with actual impressions from
the presses of Gutenberg, Fust and Schoffer, the immortal
triumvirate of Mayence printers, and close by them volumes
from the press of William Caxton, father of printing in
England. Egyptian papyrus, three thousand and more years
old, contested in interest with manuscripts of Horace Wal-
pole, Laurence Sterne, Addison and others. From the rich
stores of despoiled monasteries there had come to this collection parchment missals, illuminated with numerous
paintings in miniature, in their original bindings, over which
the mediaeval monks had labored with love and a keen sense
of the truly beautiful and enduring. The oldest manuscript
had been executed in the 9th century, a copy of a work by
Pope Gregory in the 6th century. Such were a few of the
wonders of a library to which visitors of culture sought admission as the most interesting thing Savannah had to of-
fer for their inspection and delight. No wonder an unknown
local lover of art and literature, bewailing its departure, said
of the Smets collection: "Its loss to Savannah must be reck-
oned among the calamities of the war—a misfortune which
can be borne the more cheerfully, however, when it is reflected that this library has at least escaped the ravages of
an invading army which destroyed so many other monu-
ments of wealth and culture in the South."

Smets was a director of the Bank of the State of
Georgia, of which, as stated, Tefft was cashier. He was
librarian of the Georgia Historical Society in 1843 and its
treasurer 1855-1862, holding that office at his death.
There were other Savannah professional and business
men who had tastes in common with them, making
a group of connoisseurs such as one would find
in few of the smaller cities of the country at that time.
It was fortunate, one feels, that Tefft did not, in a moment
of unreasoning anger, accept the challenge from the irate
Turner, or Savannah might have been deprived of one who
was a most valuable citizen over a long period of years, a
leader in its higher cultural life as well as an exponent of
the sterling integrity of its men of business affairs. His

unceasing interest was a great factor in the development of the Georgia Historical Society and to him Savannah is indebted for much of the wealth of historical matter gathered at Hodgson Hall. It is interesting to recall that the long life of the Society, eighty-four years, from 1839 to 1923, is spanned by two of its officials, Mr. Tefft and the present librarian, Mr. William Harden, who assumed that position in 1866. During "The War Between the States," the activities of the Society lapsed. Mr. Harden's service of fifty-seven years is probably a record unequalled by any other American librarian.

Commodore Josiah Tattnall
Who, While in the Old Navy, Challenged Any British Officer in Chilian Waters,
But Gallantly Came to the Rescue of the British in the Battle of
the Pei-Ho River

CHAPTER XII.

THE TATTNALLS, CONGRESSMAN AND COMMODORE

EDWARD F. TATTNALL'S CHALLENGE TO A SPANISH OFFI-
CER—WOUNDED IN ARM IN DUEL SERVES ON A COURT
OF HONOR—ACTS AS SECOND FOR JOHN RANDOLPH OF
ROANOKE IN HIS MEETING WITH HENRY CLAY—
JOSIAH TATTNALL WOUNDS OFFENSIVE BRITISH OF-
FICER—CALLS AN ENGLISH SECOND TO SHARP AC-
COUNT FOR HIS ACTS—TOGETHER THE BROTHERS LIE
UNDER THE OAKS OF THEIR BOYHOOD HOME, BONA-
VENTURE.

DISTINGUISHED as a lawyer and public man, another
Savannahian of this period occupies a unique place in
the annals of duelling as the second in one of the most remarkable meetings under the code between two men of the
highest prominence in national affairs, the meeting in which
the principals were Henry Clay, then Secretary of State, and
John Randolph of Roanoke, that most unique of Virginians.
Reference is made to Col. Edward Fenwick Tattnall, son of
Governor Josiah Tattnall, and brother of the famous Commodore Tattnall.

Tattnall, who was born at the plantation home of the
family, Bonaventure, near Savannah, in 1788, partook by inheritance of brilliant and sterling characteristics of his family. As a young man he displayed unusual ability at the
bar and the possession of qualities of a genial, courageous
and high-principled manhood that drew wide attention to
him as one of Georgia's gifted and prominent sons.

Soon after the second war with Great Britain began,
Tattnall received an appointment as captain in the 43d Regiment, United States Army, and was stationed on the St.
Mary's river. When the British forces invaded Georgia in
December, 1814, he was located at Point Peter. In one of his
letters written from Savannah at that time, Ebenezer Jackson, an officer of the Revolution, who had removed from

Massachusetts and settled on Whitemarsh Island, told of the
bravery of Capt. Tattnall in an engagement with the enemy.
Said he:

"The British landed on Cumberland Island and afterwards took Point Peter and St. Mary's. The garrison, which
consisted of one hundred and fifty regulars, made good their
retreat after a handsome affair in which Edward F. Tattnall
commanded a charge, in which he displayed the most intrepid conduct. He seized the gun of a wounded man of his
command and shot dead the British officer who commanded
the force opposed to him. At the same time Captain Tattnall was wounded in the arm severely. He was, however,
brought off."

It was through Capt. Tattnall that there came to Savannah its first news of the great American victory at New
Orleans, he having received it through a British bomb ship
that put in at St. Mary's. Through him also came the information that the British forces would next probably be used
against Savannah, leading to feverish preparations here for
their reception. Only the news of the signing of the treaty
of peace checked the design of Admiral Cockburn and other
British commanders to try issues with the hastily gathered
forces that defended this city.

Whilst Capt. Tattnall was at Point Peter the Spanish
officer on Amelia Island gave a ball to the merchants and
their families. The place attracted to it at that time many
persons on account of the facilities which it offered for carrying on trade, says Governor Gilmer, to whom we are indebted for this incident in the life of the Savannahian. "The
officers at Point Peter were invited. The ball was opened
offensively to the Spanish commandant by the omission to
place his wife at the head of the first dance. Spanish soldiers were ordered into the ball room, accoutred with their
full complement of arms, and commanded to disperse the
company. The utmost alarm prevailed among the ladies and
their husbands. Some hid in one place and some in another.
Capt. Tattnall and Lieut. Holt defended themselves as they
could, whilst they made for the seashore, where they had
left the boat, in which they passed the strait from Point

Tomb of Edward Fenwick Tattnall
John Randolph's Second in His Famous Duel With Henry Clay
(Monument to His Memory Erected by Savannah Volunteer Guards)

Peter, with a squad of four soldiers. With these soldiers they returned to the ball room, drove the Spanish officer and his men from the house, collected the affrighted company, and attempted to resume the dancing, but the spirit of jollity was gone and the party dispersed.

"On the next morning Capt. Tattnall sent a challenge to the Spanish commander. Upon his declining to fight he made a representation of his conduct to the Governor of Florida, who put his inferior into chains and sent him to Old Spain to be tried for cowardice."

Resuming the practice of law in Savannah, Tattnall, when twenty-eight years of age, became Solicitor General of the Eastern Circuit, holding the office a term. He then resumed the practice of his profession and represented the county in the General Assembly. At this time he fought one duel, at least, doubtless an issue of the acrimonious politics of the day, when the Clark-Crawford feud dominated the public life of the state. With whom he fought no printed record appears to tell.

In his sketch of Robert Rutherford, in "The Bench and Bar of Georgia," Miller prints a letter from Major Joel Crawford, in which he tells of Seaborn Jones, afterwards Congressman, challenging Gen. John Scott, of the state militia. Scott announced his willingness to fight with broadswords, a weapon uncommon to Georgia duellists.

Jones was disinclined to meet Scott with such weapons and Rutherford, his brother-in-law, assumed to relieve him of the duty.

Going to Gen. Scott Rutherford said: "Gen. Scott, you must fight Jones with pistols or adopt me as the swordsman," and gave him one hour in which to decide.

According to Crawford's account, Scott or his friends got busy in bringing about an armistice and a court of honor. By the latter the difficulty was peaceably adjusted.

"Col. Edward F. Tattnall, then with his arm in a sling from just fighting a duel," was one of the court," wrote Crawford, and added, "All the court, I think, were of the legislature."

In 1820 Tattnall was a candidate for a seat in Congress. At that time the representatives at Washington were not elected by districts, as now, but all of the voters balloted for their preferences among the candidates, the seven highest winning.

The popularity of Tattnall throughout the state is shown in the fact that he ran second only to John Forsyth, and far distanced the others in the race.

He was an earnest and eloquent advocate of the principles of his party and a most forceful speaker in opposition to the tariff policy of Clay and his associates. His formal speeches and running debates in the House show his thorough grasp of the subject and the fact that he was a formidable opponent to those who were espousing the "American tariff system."

Tattnall served in the 17th, 18th and 19th Congresses, 1821-27. It was in 1825 that the unexpected call came to him to act as second for John Randolph, a duty in which he acquitted himself, as in all the affairs of life, in the most admirable manner.

All know of the political bitterness that existed between the great Kentuckian and the erratic though brilliant Virginian. Attacks in the newspapers on Randolph were imputed by him to President John Quincy Adams and his Secretary of State. The opportunity came to flay them in the debate in the Senate on the sending of representatives from the United States to the Pan-American Congress at Panama. This was a pet project of Clay's and Adams claimed the presidential prerogative to send special ministers from this country without senatorial approval. Randolph denied such a right and attacked it.

In the course of his satirical and ofttimes bitter remarks, Randolph indulged in that ferocious allusion to Adams and Clay as "The coalition of Blifil and Black George —the combination, unheard of till now, of the Puritan with the blackleg."

Clay was furious. Only a short time before he had condemned duelling as a relic of barbarism. Now he challenged Randolph without delay.

The Virginia Senator accepted the challenge and selected the Savannahian as his second. Tattnall had fought one or more duels, had acted in a court of honor, was versed in the code, was a gentleman of the highest standing.

Gen. Jesup acted as Clay's second. In calling on Randolph the general remarked that no one had the right to question Randolph out of the Senate for anything he said in debate in that body, unless he, Randolph, voluntarily chose to waive his privileges as a senator.

Never, Randolph replied, would he shield himself under such a subterfuge as pleading his privileges as a senator of Virginia, and stated that he held himself amenable to Secretary Clay.

But for his relationship to Mrs. Randolph Senator Benton, of Missouri, would have been called in as second. To Benton Randolph confided his intention not to fire at Clay.

Tattnall was in ill-health at the time, practically confined to his room, but he came at once to his friend and arranged with Gen. Jesup the terms of the meeting.

"A duel in the circle in which Randolph belonged," wrote Senator Benton, in his "Thirty Years View of the United States Senate," was an affair of honor, and high honor, according to its code, must pervade every part of it."

For a week Jesup and Tattnall sought to arrange an accommodation, but to no purpose. On April 8, the parties met on the bank of the Potomac, within the state of Virginia. "If he fell," said Benton, "Randolph chose Virginia soil as the ground to receive his blood."

"There was a statute of Virginia against duelling within her limits, but, as he merely went out to receive a fire without returning it, Randolph deemed that no fighting, and consequently no breach of her statute."

The day before the duel, Senator Benton called on Clay. Mrs. Clay was present and her sleeping child was in the room. Referring to this visit when he met Randolph the morning of the duel, the Virginian quietly remarked: "I shall do nothing to disturb the sleep of the child, or the repose of the mother."

On the eve of the meeting Tattnall came to see his principal. Accompanying him was Gen. James Hamilton, of South Carolina. The Savannahian had been told that Randolph was determined not to fire at Clay. The second was opposed to any such procedure.

"Mr. Randolph," said Tattnall to him, "I am told you are determined not to return Mr. Clay's fire. I must say to you, if I am only to go out to see you shot down you must find some other friend."

General Hamilton told of this in a letter to a friend after the affair. After some conversation the South Carolinian induced Tattnall to allow Randolph to take his own course. Randolph said smilingly, "Well, Tattnall, 1 promise you one thing, if I see the devil in Clay's eyes, and that with malice prepense he means to take my life, I will change my mind," a remark, Hamilton said, intended to propitiate the anxiety of the Savannahian.

At his bank Randolph secured nine pieces of gold. In the event of his death these were to be given three each to Tattnall, Benton and Hamilton, to make seals to wear in remembrance of their Virginia friend.

The count was to be quick after receiving the word "Fire." As Randolph had no intention of firing, the short interval between "fire" and "stop" meant nothing to him. With Clay it was otherwise. Unaccustomed to the pistol, as he was, he expressed the fear that he could not fire within the brief time limit.

Gen. Jesup mentioned this to Col. Tattnall.

"If you insist upon it," replied the Savannahian, "the time must be prolonged, but I should very much regret it."

Fortunately Clay did not insist, nor his second, and the original agreement was adhered to.

Col. Tattnall won the choice of position, which gave to Gen. Jesup the delivery of the word.

Randolph asked Jesup to repeat the words, as he would speak them. While he was doing this Randolph's pistol went off, the muzzle to the ground. Instantly he turned to the Savannahian: "I protested against that hair trigger," said he.

Col. Tattnall took the blame to himself for having himself sprung the hair, says Benton.

Another pistol was furnished. On the first exchange of shots, Randolph's bullet struck a stump behind Clay, while Clay's bullet knocked up the earth behind Randolph.

Efforts at mediation failed.

As Benton told of the duel, "Clay said, with that wave of the hand with which he was accustomed to put away a trifle, 'This is child's play,' and required another fire. Mr. Randolph also demanded another fire."

Randolph, Benton says, regretted that he had fired at Clay. He had been vexed by the accidental discharge of his pistol with its possibilities of misconstruction, and by a statement Tattnall had made to him that it had been proposed to give out the words more deliberately, so as to prolong the time for taking aim. This information, Randolph said in a quick note to Benton, led to the thought that Clay had determined "by the use of a long preparatory caution by words, to get time to kill me. May I not, then, disable him? Yes, if I please."

But Tattnall had been misinformed, and so Randolph was laboring under a misapprehension. Randolph, however, had aimed low, he stated to Benton, so as to avoid any chance of killing Clay.

"I would not have seen him fall mortally, or even doubtfully, wounded, for all the land that is watered by the King of Floods and all tributary streams," said the Virginian as he returned to his position and again faced the Kentuckian.

Clay's second bullet passed through Randolph's coat, very near his hip. Randolph raised his pistol in the air and discharged it.

"I do not fire at you, Mr. Clay," said he, and advanced and offered his hand.

As Clay met him and grasped his hand, Randolph said with a smile: "You owe me a coat, Mr. Clay," and Clay replied, "I am glad the debt is no greater."

The parties left the field, as Benton said, "with lighter hearts."

At supper that night, when Randolph, Tattnall, Benton and Hamilton gathered, Randolph took the nine gold pieces from his pocket.

"Gentlemen," said he, "Clay's bad shot shan't rob you of your seals. I am going to London and will have them made for you," which he did.

And so it was that two Savannahians acted as seconds in two of the most noted duels in American history—Pendleton for Alexander Hamilton in his meeting with Aaron Burr, and Tattnall for John Randolph of Roanoke in his meeting with the great Henry Clay.

Carl Schurz, in his life of Henry Clay, makes the pertinent comment:

"Randolph's pistol had failed to prove that Clay was a 'blackguard' and Clay's pistol had also failed to prove that Randolph was a 'calumniator'; but according to the mysterious process of reasoning which makes the pistol the arbiter of honor, the honor of each was satisfied."

As mentioned, Congressman Tattnall was the older brother of Commodore Josiah Tattnall, hero of the dramatic Pei-Ho river incident with its "Blood is thicker than water" explanation of his valorous aid for the British in their extremity. Both men were of the same unflinchingly courageous type of manhood, never encroaching on the rights of others and permitting no violations of their own sense of dignity and honor. In the old navy duels were almost a matter of course, so it is not surprising that one is found to the Commodore's credit, nor that he stood ready at all times to defend his country's honor as well as his own, when men of another flag became offensive. Jones tells of two incidents of this kind in his "Life and Services of Commodore Tattnall," growing out of the employment of a number of former British naval officers with the Chilian navy, then preparing to invade Peru, still a dependency of Spain. This was in 1818. The American victories over the British ships in the war but recently ended still rankled in the breasts of the English officers and seamen and their feelings gave rise to violent expressions. As Jones puts it:

"Despite his early English education, and the affection he cherished for his English relatives, Lieutenant Tattnall would not, with his love of country and her flag, brook the slightest reflection upon the conduct of the young Republic or her adherents during the late contest upon sea or land. The language and conduct of one of Lord Cochrane's officers proving offensive in this regard, a challenge ensued, which resulted in a quick duel with pistols, Tattnall's antagonist retiring from the field with a bullet in his shoulder."

Some months later the Macedonian, on which Tattnall was an officer, was once more in the port of Valparaiso. There was a recurrence of the former situation. The American officers refrained as much as possible from going ashore because of the disagreeable tendencies of the English officers in the improvised Chilian navy. One night, though, the Savannahian accompanied Midshipman Richard Pinckney, of South Carolina, and some others to a party at a hotel. A number of the English officers were among the guests. In a heated argument Pinckney denounced Lord Cochrane, a personal quarrel ensued with an Englishman, Pinckney challenged him and an immediate meeting was agreed upon.

"Armed with heavy ship's pistols and swords," says Jones, "the principals accompanied by their seconds proceeded to the sea beach. The moon was at full and the night was cloudless. Hundreds had assembled to witness the meeting. Pinckney having given the challenge, his antagonist named the distance, ten paces. It was arranged that the principals should wheel and fire.

"The requisites being all adjusted, the principals took their positions. At that critical moment one of the English officer's seconds advanced and stated that as his friend had heard that Pinckney was a dead shot he declined fighting at ten paces, but would fight at five paces.

"Pinckney's friends insisted that the duel should proceed upon the terms as agreed upon, and in accordance with which the principals had already been posted. To this the friends of the Englishman stoutly objected, and, amid the growing confusion, there appeared no alternative save an acquiescence in the murderous proposition.

"At this juncture Lieutenant Tattnall walked up to the Englishman's second who had interrupted the proceedings and said to him:

" 'You are a coward and a scoundrel, and have made all this difficulty. Now you shall first fight me at five paces.'

"This settled the controversy. The fellow backed down, asked Tattnall's pardon, and said his friend would fight Mr. Pinckney at the distance of ten paces as named.

"The duel proceeded. Several shots were exchanged. The clothing of both principals was cut and the Englishman wounded. The ammunition being exhausted, and the police threatening interference, a reconciliation was brought about."

But for a time it looked as though the Savannahian would not leave Chili without either having a dead or wounded Englishman to his credit, or himself being marked up as a victim of the code. Other English officers indulged in comments that were far from pleasing to the Georgia officer. So, to bring it to a head, the message went from Tattnall to the antagonistic Britons that "If his course had in anywise displeased them he would be most happy to fight them of all grades, from the cockpit to the cabin door." And to let the Chilians understand their position properly, when a corvette ran up the American flag under the British one day there was a boat load of brawny American tars under Tattnall's orders alongside in a few minutes and the American flag was soon at the topmast.

Yet this was the same gallant American who, in 1859, forty-one years later, came to the rescue of the disabled British ships in their dire distress on the Pei-Ho river and won the plaudits of his own countrymen and the English thereby. It falls to the lot of few men to have their names immortalized by connection with a phrase that promises never to die. That was the rare fortune of Tattnall. Whenever one hears the expression, "Blood is thicker than water," memory reverts to the Savannahian who used it on that memorable occasion.

There was a sharp wrench of the heart strings when the call of Georgia caused a severance of the ties that bound

Tattnall to the old navy. For a half century he had served under its flag in many seas and in many dangerous lines of duty. During two wars, those of 1812 and with Mexico, he had battled under the Stars and Stripes against his country's enemies. Numerous and dear were the personal associations that had come in the course of those many years of fellowship with the brave seamen gathered from all parts of the common land. But Tattnall, an old man of sixty-six, even though hale and hearty, took his place unhesitatingly with the South, placed himself unreservedly at her disposal, and rendered her the same gallant, faithful and unselfish service he had given to the nation before the sectional separation had come.

Referring to this the morning after Tattnall's death, Editor Thompson, of the "News," said: "In an interview with the leaders of the Confederate movement the Commodore expressed his decided aversion to such a contingency as a collision of arms between the North and the South, and declared that he would not for the world fire the first gun which was to precipitate the war. In the event of a collision, however, he said that his sword was at the service of his State."

Tattnall was governed by the same thought that inspired R. W. Habersham, then the United States District Attorney, to give as his toast at the dinner on St. Patrick's Day, 1827, this sentiment:

"My native State of Georgia. If the mother who has nurtured us be wrong, we are bound to side with her; and if she be right, we should deserve contempt if we took part against her."

This sentiment, in one form or another, came to the front whenever Georgia's vital interests seemed to clash in those early days with the authority of the Federal union.

Edward F. Tattnall died in 1832 and was buried in Bonaventure, where a monument erected to his memory by the Savannah Volunteer Guards, of which he had been the commander for a number of years, was unveiled on Washington's Birthday, in 1834. Gov. Gilmer, who had served in Congress with Tattnall, said of him: "His spirit was the essence of chivalry. He preferred death to the

Tomb of Commodore Josiah Tattnall
Hero of Three Wars, of "Blood Is Thicker Than Water" Fame

slightest coloring of dishonor. He risked his life, and was near losing it several times, that he might be considered above wrongdoing."

The inscription on the high obelisk over his grave tells of the deep regard of his comrades of the Guards:

SACRED
To the Memory of
EDWARD FENWICK TATTNALL
who died in Savannah
on the 21st day of November, 1832
aged 44 years.
This Monument was
Erected by the Savannah
Volunteer Guards, which Corps
he for a period of Years Commanded, as
a tribute of affection for his qualities
as a Man, a Soldier and a Patriot.
Munera parva quidem sed magnum
testanter amoren

His more famous brother, whose services in both the old American and the Confederate navies made him one of the most distinguished Georgians of his day, died in Savannah in 1871, at the age of seventy-six. A eulogist in the "Republican" wrote:

"His remains repose in the ancestral acres of Bonaventure by the side of his chivalrous brother. He will sleep under the shade of those immemorial oaks, planted by his remote progenitors. Those noble old trees, renowned so long for natural beauty, will acquire henceforth a new significance and a richer glory. Spared by the storms, saved by holy dedication from human desecration, cherished and cultured by the rains and the dews of Heaven, they shall now fulfill their destiny when, with new dignity and glory and majesty they stand the faithful, unswerving, watchful sentinels who guard all the approaches to the tomb of Tattnall."

On the surface of the tomb three laurel wreaths enclose the dates which tell of the wars in which he served his country: 1812, 1847, 1861, with an extended sword connecting them. On the sides of the tomb are these inscriptions:

COMMODORE JOSIAH TATTNALL, U. S. & C. S. N.
BORN NEAR THIS SPOT NOV. 9th, 1795. DIED JUNE 14th, 1871.

Erected by Admiring Friends
To the Memory of a Grand Manhood and an Exalted
Character Without Fear and Without Reproach.

To few Georgians, or to any others, has it been given after well spent lives that added new lustre to the fair fame of their native city, to rest beneath the great trees of the old home where their boyhood had been passed. No tombs in Bonaventure should awaken a greater interest or revive prouder memories among Savannahians than those of the two Tattnalls.

CHAPTER XIII.

THE SAVANNAH ANTI-DUELLING ASSOCIATION

PROMINENT CITIZENS UNITED IN MOVEMENT TO CHECK
THE INCREASING PRACTICE OF DUELLING BY EDUCA-
TION OF PUBLIC SENTIMENT AND THE INVOKING OF
THE LAW WHEN REQUIRED—COMMITTEE ON CONCIL-
IATION A FEATURE OF THE ASSOCIATION'S WORK—ITS
ANNIVERSARY ORATORS—OUTCOME OF DIFFICULTIES
BETWEEN MILLEN AND POOLER, KERR AND GUERARD,
BLANE AND McKENZIE, ROSSIGNOL AND GUERARD,
BOURKE AND ARNOLD—KILLING OF STARKE BY MINIS,
AND STILES BY MORRISON—BENJAMIN EDWARD
STILES TURNS DOWN CHALLENGE FROM JOSEPH FAY
—HOW FORMER JUDGE LAW, ACTIVE IN THE ASSOCIA-
TION'S WORK, STOOD READY IN LATER YEARS TO
RESENT AN INSULT ON THE FIELD OF HONOR.

A BLOW, an intimation of dishonesty, a reflection on
veracity, a sharp difference of opinion on a political
issue, an accusation of cheating at cards, an insinuation of
unchastity on the part of a woman—these and other offences of less magnitude constituted the provocations that
justified challenges.

So frequent had become the duels in Savannah, and so
rampant the spirit that encouraged and prompted hostile
meetings as a means of settling personal disputes, even
though the actual fatalities were rare, that a determined
and concerted effort was felt to be necessary in order to
educate public opinion against duelling, and gradually lead
to the abandonment of the practice of resorting to the pistol
or rifle when politics or other cause of estrangement changed
erstwhile friends into temporary enemies. To this end a
meeting of citizens was held in the Long Room of the City
Exchange on December 26, 1826. Perhaps the Christmas
spirit of "Peace on earth, good will to men" may have played
its part in bringing about the gathering.

A number of clergymen and prominent men of affairs
attended. Dr. George Jones, who was probably mainly in-

George Jones
President Savannah Anti-Duelling Association, 1827-38; Judge Superior Court,
1804-08; United States Senator, 1807.
(From Oil Painting by Rembrandt Peale in DeRenne Library, Wormsloe.)

strumental in calling the meeting, was chosen as chairman, and Joseph Cumming as secretary. The constitution of the recently organized Charleston Anti-Duelling Association was read and it was resolved that the chairman should call another meeting of all interested citizens on January 1. The advertisement for this meeting said:

"It is presumed that there will be but one opinion as to the propriety and necessity of such an association and therefore a full attendance is expected."

The second meeting was largely attended. Judge William Davies was called to the chair, Rev. S. B. Howe, pastor of the Independent Presbyterian Church, delivered an address on the general subject of duelling and moved the formation of an association for "the purpose of restraining and, if possible, suppressing the practice of duelling." This was seconded by Mr. William B. Bulloch and adopted, and to draft the constitution the following committee was appointed: Rev. S. B. Howe, Rev. Abiel Carter, of Christ Church, Rev. Henry O. Wyer, of the First Baptist Church, Dr. James B. Read, William B. Bulloch, Anthony Barclay, Thomas Young, William Law.

The constitution as adopted set forth that the subscribers "considered the practice of duelling as a violation of all law, both human and divine, as hostile to the peace and good order of society, and as destructive to the happiness of domestic life, and being desirous of checking and if possible suppressing so serious an evil, do agree to associate together for the purpose as the Savannah Anti-Duelling Association."

It was further provided, as probably the most important feature of the work laid out for the Association, that a committee of seven should be appointed which "should endeavor by seasonable and friendly interposition, with or without the aid of the civil magistracy, as may seem to them most expedient, to prevent the occurrence of any contemplated or appointed duel, of which they may have information or well founded apprehensions, to procure from time to time the publication of any such essays or papers against duelling as they may deem calculated to operate for the correction of the error of the prevalent opinion on the subject, and in general to adopt all prudent, honorable and legal measures for lessening as much as possible the frequency of the practice in this community, and gradually effecting its entire suppression."

All members of the Association were to give to its standing committee any information or intimation of duels which came to them. By mediation it was hoped to bring about amicable adjustments. If that failed, then recourse was evidently to be had to the law to prevent meetings, if possible.

Essays against duelling were to be printed in the local papers, and, as a matter of fact, several were printed, painting in glowing language the evils resulting from the custom, and pointing out wherein duelling violated the laws of God and of the State. The annual meeting was to be held on the second Tuesday in January of each year, at which time a suitable address was to be delivered by an orator selected the year before. As the orator for the first annual gathering, Anthony Barclay, prominent as a merchant and literateur, was selected.

On January 9 a third meeting was held at which officers were elected for the Association, as follows:

President, Dr. George Jones.

Vice-presidents, Wm. B. Bulloch, William Davies.

Secretary and Treasurer, C. W. Rockwell, merchant and bank president, who removed North and was appointed United States Commissioner of Customs by President Taylor.

Standing Committee, Anthony Barclay, A. B. Fannin, William Law, Alexander Telfair, Benjamin Edward Stiles, Richard F. Williams, Joseph Cumming.

This staff of officers made a highly representative group of the best Savannahians of that day.

No one ever stood higher in the community than he who was chosen to head the Association, and who apparently continued its president throughout its life. Dr. George Jones, son of the patriotic Dr. Noble Wymberly Jones, had a long life of public usefulness. He was a member of the Georgia Constitutional Convention of 1798. He served as an alderman of the city in 1793-94, 1802-03, 1814-15, and as mayor in 1812-14. In 1804, although not a lawyer, so much confidence was felt in his strong common sense and high sense of justice between man and man, that he was appointed Judge of the Superior Court and served with entire satisfaction to the public for four years. In 1807 he filled for a few months an unexpired term in the United States Senate. A noble type of unselfish manhood, his interest in the Anti-Duelling Association arose from a strong conviction of the curse the custom had been to his State, and he was unceasing in his efforts to broaden and strengthen the influence of the Association. Deeply concerned in the injuries wrought by intoxicants, he also became president of the Savannah Temperance Association.

At the first anniversary meeting held in January, 1828, a prize of $50, or a gold medal, was offered for the best essay on duelling. A committee was appointed to pass on the essays submitted, composed of John Cumming, James M. Wayne, Richard W. Habersham, William Law, Matthew Hall McAllister. The prize was to be awarded at the next annual meeting and Matthew Hall McAllister was selected as the orator for that occasion. McAllister was winning recognition as a lawyer and public speaker and as a man of broad culture. His oration in 1829 was evidently replete with historical allusions and dealt with the subject in a most forceful way. The editor of "The Georgian" honored him with a special comment: He could not agree with McAllister, the editor said, "in reference to his strictures upon the remarks made by the biographer of Charles V, relative to duelling, and must still continue to think that the vice of duelling now sought to be suppressed is a relic of chivalry, though moldering and decayed; that the spirit of chivalry in it was probably corrupted, like every other channel of thought or of feeling, through the influence of Italian morals, which then ruled the court, the camp and the grove throughout the whole of Europe, engendering deceit, exciting a feverish thirst for revenge, and creating a strong disposition toward the coarsest licentiousness everywhere."

The Chatham Artillery attended this anniversary meeting in a body, "dressed in their new and splendid uniforms."

The gold medal for the best essay was awarded to William Jay, of Bedford, N. Y. William Law was selected to deliver the third anniversary address.

Whether it was due to the influence of the Anti-Duelling Association is not clear, but it is quite apparent that for several years after its organization there was a lull in the hostile meetings. It may have been the fear of prosecution brought about by the Association, or perhaps the invoking of the good graces of its standing committee as a medium of conciliation, or both combined, that checked the headstrong in their eagerness to meet each other on the field of honor. To its efforts, too, may have been due the action of the legislature in passing the act signed by Gov. John Forsyth, on December 19, 1828, requiring that all civil and military officers appointed on and after July 1, 1829, should take an oath that they had not, since that date, been engaged in a duel, either directly or indirectly, as principal or second, nor given a challenge, or knowingly carried or delivered a challenge or message purporting to be a challenge, either verbally or in writing.

The awakening of public opinion through the Association doubtless had a salutary influence for a time, but like all other reforming agencies its energies slackened with the passage of the years, its influence ebbed, and finally it passed from the stage of action. The last advertisement of its annual meeting apparently is that for 1837, but it continued its existence for some years after. It had served a good purpose during its brief life, but the period that immediately followed its decease seems to have been marked by a recrudescence of duelling, with a swamping of the carefully nurtured adverse opinion to the custom, and a reaction that seems to indicate that there had been a chafing at the bit of repression during the years of the Association's curbing restraints. Its anniversary orators were all men of the highest position in the professional, business and social life of Savannah. They were:

1828.   Anthony Barclay, prominent merchant, British consul, and recognized as one of the classical scholars of the city.

1829. Matthew Hall McAllister, prominent at the Georgia bar and in State Democratic politics until he removed to California, where he was appointed Federal judge by President Pierce. He was mayor of Savannah in 1837-39, resigning from that office. A pen sketch of McAllister, published in the Columbus Sentinel, in 1838, described him in this fashion: "A man apparently about thirty-five years of age, stout and athletic in his person, with a countenance that could not be mistaken for its expression of candor, magnanimity and benevolence. His hair is a light auburn and worn in the style of a studioso, fresh from the halls of old Cambridge. His face appears beardless. As an orator he is graceful, fiery, fascinating, and in all things quite Shakesperean. As a speaker he is fluent, persuasive, forcible, and being a ripe scholar his ideas are clothed in language chaste, rich and copious."

1830. William Law, who had been Solicitor-General 1817-21, and succeeding to the Judgeship of the Superior Court on the death of Judge Davies in 1829 served until 1834. Until his death he was one of the leaders of the Savannah bar.

1831. Joseph Cumming, a leading merchant of his time and founder of the First Presbyterian Church, Justice of the Superior Court and for some years President of the Marine Fire Insurance Bank.

1832. George B. Cumming, brother of Joseph, successful merchant, and prominent in the Independent Presbyterian Church.

1833. William Henry Stiles, Solicitor-General 1833-36, Congressman 1843-45, minister to Austria and author of a "History of Austria." It was said of him, "As an orator he was noted for his faultless rhetoric and education, and as a gentleman for a grace and polish of manners not to be excelled." Judge Clark wrote of him: "He was master of a soft, melodious and magnetic voice. His speeches were all finished orations, and fell delightfully upon the ear and understanding."

1834. William H. Williams, principal of the Chatham Academy, and a man of scholarly attainments.

1835.   Robert M. Charlton, Judge of the Superior Court
1835-37, United States Senator 1852-53, well known Georgia author of his day.   Of him Judge Richard H. Clark
wrote: "He was a lawyer and judge of the first ability, but
great as that was he exceeded it in the perfection of his
private and personal character."

1836.   S. T. Chapman, of the Chatham Academy.

1837.   Rev. J. L. Jones, pastor of the First Presbyterian
Church, then located on Broughton street.

The type of men who consented to deliver the annual
philippics against duelling, their high standing in the community as leaders of opinion and as directing forces in its
public activities, shows the aroused conscience of thinking
men at a time when duelling was claiming its many victims
throughout the country.

Dr. John Cumming—first president of the Savannah
Branch of the United States Bank—was elected vice-president in 1830 to fill the vacancy caused by the death of Judge
Davies.   William Bee became secretary and treasurer in
1834.   In that year Patrick Houstoun became chairman of
the standing committee, he and Joseph W. Jackson taking
the places on the committee of Alexander Telfair and Joseph
Cumming.

Some years after the Association ceased its activities
its re-written records were placed with the Georgia Historical Society.   In the course of time they were forgotten,
buried among the lumber that always accumulates.   It was
only recently that in the cleaning up of the books and ar-
chives at Hodgson Hall the dusty old volume was brought
to light, making available information not found in the
newspapers of the period during which the Association labored.   From the minutes it appear that the Anti-Duelling
Association had hardly begun its noble mission of good will
to men when its altruistic offices were effective in prevent-
ing a meeting between two well known Savannahians,
George Millen and Robert W. Pooler.   This was in May,
1827.   The procedure adopted by the Standing Committee
is well shown in the report of its secretary, C. W. Rockwell,
in a copy of the letter sent in its name to Mr. Pooler:

"It has been intimated that there exists a difference between yourself and Mr. George Millen, which it is apprehended may lead to serious results. As members of that committee, Joseph Cumming, Anthony Barclay and Alexander Telfair, Esqs., beg leave to propose to you that any differences which may exist be submitted to an amicable reference—to gentlemen either in or out of this Society, in whose integrity and honor you may have entire confidence. The committee will be happy to hear from you in reply as soon as your convenience will admit, and by their direction your communication will not be opened unless there be one also from Mr. Millen. They will meet promptly at six o'clock this afternoon, when it will be very desirable to have your reply. We believe you will receive this in the spirit which dictates it, and not as an officious interference."

The principals to this affair required a pledge that no legal steps would be taken by the Association, either by prosecution or otherwise, before they would consider its offices. The committee so pledged and Joseph Cumming and William Law were appointed to wait on the friends or seconds, S. Philbrick and Col. M. Myers, and obtain their consent to refer all differences to gentlemen of their selection. As a result the arbitration of the trouble was placed in the hands of W. C. Daniell and William Bee, neither of whom was then a member of the Anti-Duelling Association, and by them an amicable settlement was reached. This was the first feather in the cap of the Association and it was with a peculiar satisfaction that in its first annual report the Standing Committee advised its members that "No duel has been fought in this vicinity since the Association's formation and the committee have reason to believe that this is partly owing to the influence of the Association." Again, in the second annual report, that for 1828, the committee likewise reported that there had been no duel fought between Savannahians.

The meagre minutes of the next three years, 1829, 1830 and 1831, throw no light on the duelling situation, except the inference, from the absence of specific statements, that there were no meetings under the code, or that the Association's work was quietly and effectively done and it

was not deemed necessary to make a permanent record of
it. In August, 1832, though, the Standing Committee moved
to adjust a trouble between James Kerr and Mr. Guerard,
who had chosen as their seconds William McKay and A.
Drysdale, and "were about to settle a dispute by an appeal
to deadly weapons." This affair was "adjusted between
the seconds in an amicable manner." In another trouble
between two citizens, though, the committee signally failed
as a mediating influence, through no fault of its own, and
one of the most notable tragedies of that period ensued.

This was also in August, 1832. Information was given
to the secretary that "An affair of honor existed between
James Jones Stark and Dr. Philip Minis," with Charles
Spalding acting as the friend of the latter and Thomas M.
Wayne as the friend of Stark. Letters were sent by the
secretary at once to each of the seconds, tendering the services of the Standing Committee and urging an arbitration
of the differences. Unfortunately Mr. Spalding did not receive the letter which was left at his residence. As the
minutes set forth, "About an hour after the sending of these
letters, Mr. Stark was attacked and slain with a pistol at
the City Hotel, on the Bay, by Dr. Minis. It is said that Mr.
Stark was in the act of sending a reply to the committee's
letter when some circumstance drew him into the bar room
where he met his antagonist." "This record is made," continued the report, "lest it should ever be enquired, where
was the Anti-Duelling Association and its Standing Committee on this occasion?"

"The Georgian" gave a very meagre reference to the
tragedy: "A most melancholy occurrence transpired in this
city on Friday last (August 10). James Jones Starke, of
Glynn county, formerly of Savannah, was shot at the City
Hotel, by Dr. Philip Minis, through the breast, and almost
instantaneously expired. This is, indeed, a most unfortunate circumstance, which has cast a gloom over the whole
community, as both parties are extensively connected in
this city."

In those days a favorite amusement of the leading
young men of the city was playing quoits. A "Coit Club,"
as it was called, embraced many citizens of prominence, and

Old City Hotel on Bay Street
Famous For Its Wines and Whiskies Eighty Odd Years Ago; Here Several
Duels Had Their Origin in Quarrels

at its grounds on the outskirts of the city they gathered for their sport. It was here that the difficulty occurred between Starke and Minis that led to the shooting of the former. Prior to this there had been antagonism existing between the two men, which only needed intensifying to furnish the climax of a challenge. The additional provocation came in a personal allusion by Starke, resented by Minis as insulting. With no apology forthcoming there was a quick drift toward a duel, which was only prevented by the unfortunate meeting between the young men and a resumption of the difficulty in a public place.

The City Hotel at that time was a famous little hostelry, given a most enviable reputation throughout this section by the skilful management of Capt. Wiltberger who, as a packet captain had learned to cater to the wealthy planters and other travelers and had been induced by their assurances of support to quit the water and become a Boniface. Its cellars held the finest vintages of Europe and its whiskies and brandies were of unexcelled qualities. Its bar was the rendezvous of the leading young men of the city and of all the country between Savannah and the Florida line. It was a day when all drank and the Savannah Temperance Society, headed by men of influence, sought merely to restrain an intemperate use of intoxicants. One can readily perceive that the atmosphere of this gathering place of the young bloods of the town was well calculated to quickly inflame the angered feelings of men already intent on a hostile meeting. No record has come down of what passed between the principals, or what part others took in the rencounter, but the eventual acquittal of Dr. Minis seemed to prove that he had either acted on the defensive or had provocation sufficient to justify his action.

Dr. Minis was arrested and indicted. The trial which came off in January, 1833, was a famous one in the annals of Chatham. Some of the most prominent attorneys of the Savannah and Charleston bars were employed in the prosecution and defence. The State was represented by Col. Joseph W. Jackson, Solicitor General; Col. Seaborn Jones, of Columbus; Charles S. Henry and Joseph L. Shaffer, Esqs. "The defence," the "Georgian" stated, "was ably conducted by George W. Owens, John C. Nicholls, Richard R. Cuyler, John Millen and Robert M. Charlton, Esqs., of this city, and James L. Petigru and Solomon Cohen, Esqs., of South Carolina." The trial extended over six days, and "was closed with a lucid and impartial charge to the jury from Judge Charles Dougherty, of the Western Circuit. The jury returned into court after being absent two hours, and rendered a verdict of 'Not Guilty'."

The disqualification of Judge William Law and the bringing here of Judge Dougherty to try the case may have been due to Judge Law's connection with the Anti-Duelling Association and the part he had been called on to play as a member of its Standing Committee in seeking to reconcile various parties and prevent duels.

In 1833 the Association's committee on mediation had a prospective meeting between Surgeon Blane and Lieut. McKenzie, of the United States army, brought to its attention. "The committee did not interfere as several gentlemen were taking all the measures which circumstances required." The difficulty was adjusted without exchange of shots. This year, too, in September, the committee apparently for the first time resorted to the authorities to back its determined efforts to prevent duelling in Chatham "having been bound to keep the peace there," came from that state to Savannah to settle their differences with duelling pistols. Letters preceded them, urging that steps be taken to prevent the meeting. "The committee had warrants issued for them and placed in the hands of the sheriff, but the principals were kept concealed and no arrests could be made." "The next day a number of gentlemen interfered, the warrants were suspended, and a friendly settlement ended the matter." The Anti-Duelling Association properly felt that it had maintained its position before the community and that the delay caused by its action had given others the opportunity to intervene successfully.

Even as late as forty years after this, Carolinians coming to Savannah to arrange for duels were checked by threats of arrest or the actual issuance of warrants. As a rule, though, from 1820 to 1860, citizens of the lower part

Tybee's Old Martello Tower
Within Whose Shadow the Sands Soaked Up the Blood of Brave Carolinians
Who Fought Their Duels There
(Martello Tower, Erected About 1820. Removed 1913.)

of that state, seeking the opportunity outside of its borders to fight under the code, rowed across the river and met on Tybee Island. The sand of this island beach, close by the lighthouse or the old Martello tower, soaked up the blood of many wounded Carolinians in the long period during which the code held dominion over men's minds. It was no uncommon thing for boats to draw up at the upper end of the island and discharge their human cargoes of principals, seconds, surgeons and friends. A few minutes walk brought them to the long stretch of beach that at that time extended far out into the ocean, the beach of to-day, old citizens say, being but a shadow of what it was a half century ago. There, with no fear of disturbance, the twenty or thirty paces were stepped off, the principals placed in position, and the shots exchanged that were necessary to preserve a sense of personal dignity and honor. The keeper of the light house was the sole Georgia witness of many encounters of this sort. If wounded, the unfortunate duellist was given attention as he lay on the beach, and then placed comfortably as possible in his boat, and the negro slaves pulled lustily away at the oars to return him to home and loved ones. If killed, as doubtless some were, although the records of these meetings are not to be had in Savannah, the stiffening corpse was a pitiable object as it lay covered in the bottom of the boat, gazed at by sorrowing friends on the long journey across the water to the shore from whence he had come an hour or two before in the full vigor of glorious manhood. Georgia did not prosecute these visitors from a sister state, nor even seek their extradition. As for Savannahians, Tybee Island was too inconvenient of access and the memories of living men, and the written or printed records, make scant allusions to meetings there. Sometime before the war Col. William R. Pritchard and Mr. Stoney met behind the Martello Tower, a picturesque feature of the island removed some years ago, and fired at each other one time in a final adjustment of some personal difficulty. The bullet grazed Stoney's leg, it is said, a mere flesh wound, and his adversary escaped without injury. It was always much easier to row across to Screven Ferry, S. C., or to visit one of the plantations near the city, than to take the long trip to Tybee, so no stories of Savannah duels cluster around the long stretch of sand from Lazaretto creek to the Inlet.

In 1834 there was but one duel and that, the report showed, was without serious injury to the parties. It was "so silently conducted that the Standing Committee had not an opportunity to take the customary measures." Three affairs of honor, though, came to its attention in 1835, in one of which, one of the saddest in the story of duelling in Savannah, a young man of prominence met his death. This was the meeting between James Morrison and Samuel Stiles on July 7. Thomas Bourke was second for Morrison, while Stiles' brother acted in that capacity for him. The news of the proposed duel came to Secretary Bee at night. It was impossible for him to get the Standing Committee together at once to exert its influence so he assumed the initiative and swore out warrants for the principals and made arrangements for the committee to act later. Morrison and Stiles were arrested and held to bail. "The chairman of the Standing Committee assisted by Judge Law, Major Fannin, John W. Anderson and the secretary used every effort to reconcile the parties and prevent the duel, but all in vain." "The seconds would listen to no proposals, not even admit that they were acting as such." Of the resulting tragedy Secretary Bee wrote in his report:

"On Tuesday morning, the 7th July, these deluded young men, with all the feelings which false notions of honor and their own bad passions could excite, and in disregard of all laws, whether human or divine, crossed the Savannah river and fought on the South Carolina shore. Stiles was shot through the body at the first fire and died on Wednesday morning, the 8th July."

In the trouble between Charles Rossignol and G. Guerard, soon after, the committee "happily accomplished its purpose." Three months later, in October, it once more exerted itself successfully, this time to prevent two of the city's leading men, Thomas Bourke and Dr. Richard D. Arnold, from exchanging shots. The minutes set forth the adjustment of this affair of honor in this fashion:

"Savannah, October 1, 1836.

"The Standing Committee being informed some days since that a challenge to fight a Duel had been given by Mr. Thomas Bourke and accepted by Dr. Richard D. Arnold; after many fruitless personal efforts to reconcile the parties, resolved to address an official letter to the seconds, requesting their consent to entrust the affair to the decision of disinterested gentlemen, not members of the Association. This resolution was carried into effect, but did not answer the desired end. The committee then resolved to make one more effort to prevent A FASHIONABLE MURDER, and having obtained the co-operation of Messers. George Schley, W. T. Williams and James Hunter, again urged a reconciliation upon the seconds, who finally agreed to leave the matter with friends of their own selection. This was done, and the quarrel was settled in a manner honorable to both parties."

In 1836, the minutes tell us, there "was no duel fought in the vicinity of this place." In 1837, "not one instance of a duel had occurred within the jurisdiction of this Association, nor any case requiring its interposition, plainly setting forth the fact that this degrading relic of barbarism has fallen into disrepute and almost into disuse." With this year the minutes cease but subsequent years showed that the secretary's happiness in prophesying the downfall of the code was premature and without foundation. The Association itself was quite evidently losing its force and its standing. It seemed to find it impossible to secure an orator after this year, its attendance and membership dwindled, and apparently it soon became almost moribund. For ten years, though, it had served a useful purpose and perhaps saved several lives by its interposition in prospective duels as well as by its agitation against the practice.

Included in the membership of the Association during its life were over sixty men of local prominence, including Daniel E. Adams, George W. Anderson, Richard D. Arnold, William M. Baker, Anthony Barclay, Timothy Barnard, William Bee, Horace Blair, B. Bourquin, E. Bourquin, R. C. Brown, James S. Bulloch, William B. Bulloch, Rev. Benjamin Burroughs, Rev. Abiel Carter, S. T. Chapman, Moses Cleland, George W. Coe, William Crabtree, Jr., George B. Cumming, Dr. John Cumming, Joseph Cumming, Judge William Davies, Raymond P. Demere, Jacob D'Lamotta, Abram B. Fannin, Elias Fort, Joseph George, Robert Habersham, Richard Habersham, Martin Hathaway, William Hotchkin, Rev. Samuel B. Howe, Patrick Houstoun, Joseph W. Jackson, Dr. George Jones, William King, R. King, Dwight Lathrop, Judge William Law, A. O'Lyon, Matthew Hall McAllister, Joseph S. Pelot, Almond Price, Dr. James Bond Read, J. B. Richmond, Charles W. Rockwell, Charles Rossignol, Jacob Shaffer, Frances Sorrell, Archibald Smith, William H. Smith, Benjamin Edward Stiles, William H. Stiles, Joseph Stokes, Alexander Telfair, James M. Wayne, George White, Richard F. Williams, Stephen L. Williams, William H. Williams, Rev. H. O. Wyer, Thomas Young. Robert Barnwell, of Beaufort, S. C., was also a member.

Before the Anti-Duelling Association ceased its efforts to suppress duelling by the force of an awakened adverse public opinion, one of the leaders of its Standing Committee, Benjamin Edwards Stiles, had his principles put to a severe test. This was in 1844, at a time when political opinions in Savannah were strongly aroused and the town was divided into two hostile camps of almost equal strength. President John Tyler had appointed Gen. Edward Harden Collector of the Port, but the impression got abroad, perhaps designedly, that he would not accept the office, although the appointment had been confirmed by the Senate. Mr. Stiles began circulating a petition for the appointment of William B. Bulloch as Collector and sought among others the signatures of Joseph Fay and his partner, Edward Padelford. A letter appeared in the "Republican" attacking Stiles as "Seeking to forward his ends by injuring the Hon. J. M. Berrien." The editor of the "Republican" refused to furnish the name of the author unless Mr. Stiles "Intended to prosecute or procure personal satisfaction." Stiles replied that he was well known to be a member of the Anti-Duelling Association, and "he had never been governed by the laws of etiquette but by his own dictates of right and wrong," and "what his action would be would depend on circumstances." Fay's name was furnished and an acrimonious

correspondence resulted, a final letter being written by Fay
on board the vessel on which he was leaving for the North.
On his return to the city Stiles assaulted him at South Broad
and Bull streets, using a cane. Fay grasped the cane, others
interfered, and Fay sent Stiles a challenge which Stiles "felt
constrained to refuse."

"He cannot drive me from the principles which I profess into that school of honor which supposes that an improper or base act can be cancelled by the flash of a pistol
or the glitter of a sword," wrote the Anti-Duelling commit-
teeman. "Mr. Fay makes upon my character a wanton and
slanderous attack and then refers me for reparation to the
law or a duel. . . . . He has appealed to the public, and
there I am content to leave the matter, holding in my hands
the proof of the falsity of his charge and the propriety of
my own conduct. I cheerfully submit to that tribunal the
decision of the question raised, whether my opposition upon
principle to duelling should deprive me of the right to chastise insolence or to defend my character or person when
assailed."

Fay charged that Stiles was shielding himself behind
his position as a member of the Anti-Duelling Association.
"The surprise which should properly arise will be that he,
professing the principles under which he now shelters himself, could so far forget their obligations as to make an
attack upon a defenceless man, and so quickly recollect them
when necessary to shield him from the consequences of such
ungallant and unworthy conduct. . . . . I pronounce
his position to be that of a poltroon and the refuge of a
coward."

The correspondence, together with a number of cor-
roboratory letters from citizens, was published, but no further
personal assaults and no duel resulted. Stiles stood fast
to his position in antagonism to the "Code Duello."

Judge Law took a great interest in the Association and
its work. He served on its committee of conciliation for ten
years. He was popular with the people and admired for his
sterling character. The Grand Jury, in 1830, in referring
to his election, stated that "No choice of the legislature
could have been more acceptable to the people, as none could

have afforded a surer guarantee that justice would be ably, promptly and impartially administered."

There is no incident in the story of duelling, though, which shows more clearly its unmistakable hold on the popular mind, or its appeal to the individual whose sense of propriety had been grossly violated, than that of many years later when Law, no longer a judge but a highly honored member of society and of the bar, had recourse to it. No other incident likewise shows more strikingly the pressure of opinion forcing an offending party to make an honorable amende for his misconduct.

In this instance Judge Law felt called upon to resent an affront upon his professional and personal character made in the court room in the hearing of a case. Law was a man of purity of life and a keen sense of honor, and much loved by the lawyers as a class for his uprightness, sincerity and unvarying courtesy. One day an attorney gratuitously intimated that Law was unfair in his conduct of a case, somewhat offensive inferences being easily drawn from his comments. Those were days when mere angry recriminations could not satisfy the sense of injury from a reflection upon one's official or private character. Law, after court adjourned, called on the offender for an absolute apology, in failure of which he would require him to meet him on the duelling ground. The lawyer at first was obdurate and declined to withdraw his remarks in open court as demanded, so the challenge was passed and accepted. The duel was to be fought on Monday. On Sunday Law, who was an elder in his church, attended services and partook of communion. Monday he was ready for the exchange of shots that might mean his death. But the other members of the bar, outraged by the conduct of the offending lawyer, intimated so plainly to him that his refusal to apologize and thereby force the former judge to a duel would mean professional and social ostracism, that the culprit changed his attitude and when court convened begged Law's pardon and withdrew his offensive strictures. Law accepted the apology and it is said never thereafter showed the slightest animosity toward the lawyer in question.

Years later there was another stirring episode in the life of this noted Savannahian.

It was at the time when the North and the South were preparing for civil warfare. The secession movement in Georgia had been strongly combatted. In Savannah the old Union party had been very powerful in the days when South Carolina was leading the first secession movement and had remained a factor of prominence in the political life of the community for many years thereafter. Those in favor of breaking the ties that bound the sections together and establishing a separate Southern confederacy were in the great majority and the spirit of enthusiasm for the new cause was swelling daily. The State had not yet withdrawn formally from the constitutional compact of the Union when a great gathering of the citizens of Savannah was held to consider the situation and determine its action. The meeting was called at the Masonic Hall, at the northeast corner of Bull and Broughton streets, afterwards for many years the home of the Oglethorpe Club, and now occupied by the Savannah Board of Trade. Hundreds crowded into the spacious hall, while thousands filled the streets surrounding the building. From the stage within and the veranda without the orators —and Savannah then did not lack men of high eloquence— awakened tumultuous applause by their pictures of the South's grievances and of the brilliant future that awaited it in a Confederacy solely of its own creation and control. It was a secession audience in the main, but it was felt and known that there were yet many who grieved over the seeming necessity of dissolving the Union for which their forefathers had fought, and who perhaps were not yet convinced that it was inevitable. At such a crisis an appeal from one who had been a pronounced Union man, and who enjoyed the esteem and confidence of all, was calculated to weigh the balances solidly in favor of secession, and the venerable Judge Law was called upon to speak in favor of the resolutions endorsing the adoption of a secession ordinance by the State convention.

Miss Adelaide Wilson has told of the historic incident with so much forceful charm that it may well be repeated in her language:

"Introduced by Francis S. Bartow, he came to the front of the platform, his white hair and feeble step contrasting strangely with the stamp of intense purpose in every lineament of his face and the fire of his eye. In few words he sketched the wrongs of his section, and the unavailing effort that had been made to right them, and then, concluding:

" 'Therefore,' he said, with a sweep of his arm, that smote upon the hearts of his hearers like the grasp of a hand upon the strings of a harp,—'Therefore, as a Southern man, I give to these resolutions my absolute and unqualified approval.'

"The effect upon the meeting was electrical; in an instant every man was on his feet, every hat in the air, while a great shout went up that was like the roar of a tornado. Some sprang to the windows crying to the crowd in the street, 'Judge Law has indorsed the resolutions,' and then cheer answered to cheer from those within to those without, until exhaustion brought comparative quiet. The resolutions were carried by acclamation."

One is loth to turn away from these old Savannah worthies of a half century ago. Judge Law looms in another momentous incident before the curtain fell upon his earthly career. It was in 1866. An Act of Congress provided, in effect, that before Southern lawyers could resume practice in the Federal courts, or be admitted to practice therein, they must by the most searching oaths, purge themselves of kinship with the cause of their section in the war recently closed. To Judge Law fell the duty of resisting such a barrier to men of honor resuming their professional activities. He sought on motion to be permitted to continue practice in the United States Court at Savannah, in which he had practiced forty-nine years, without taking the lawyer's test oath, as it was called. In defense of his right to do so he made a notable argument before Judge Erskine, pointing out that he had taken the oath of allegiance to the Union under the amnesty proclamation of President Johnson, that this carried a full pardon with it, that the test oath was an ex post facto law inflicting pains and penalties illegally and in violation of the Federal constitution, and that it was therefore void. Ex-Governor Joseph E. Brown appeared with him and also dissected the offending law in its relation to the constitution.

Henry S. Fitch, United States District Attorney, vigorously opposed the motion. Even though he assailed the right of Judge Law to practice without taking the test oath, he did not refrain from paying him a tribute that to-day recalls the high position he held in the esteem of all who knew him. Said he:

"The pro-movent in this instance is one of those rare old gentlemen who through all the trials and vicissitudes of half a century of professional labor has, wherever known, commanded admiration for his legal lore and honor for his private virtues."

Fitch's argument was characterized by Judge Erskine as of unusual scholarship and brilliancy, but the judge held, nevertheless, that the Act imposing the oath was repugnant to the Constitution of the United States, and under his opinion Judge Law was not required to take and subscribe the oath. Not long after, in a similar case from another State, the United States Supreme Court likewise decreed the obnoxious statute unconstitutional.

To Judge Law belongs the honor of assuming an unflinching attitude of stalwart opposition to the test oath and of willingness to incur the penalties of an unalterable refusal to obey the drastic provisions of a statute passed by the extreme radicals in Congress to degrade and punish the lawyers of the South.

The ante-bellum period is sometimes referred to as "The Giant Days of Georgia." New occasions and new duties show forth the same crop of virile men. Haloed by distance, the generations that have passed from the scene of action may seem greater in the attributes of glorious manhood, but if we recall the spirit and the scenes of 1917-18 we may glimpse that a half century from now the feeling with reference to Savannah men and women of this generation will be the same with which we now look upon those who illustrated Georgia in the eras that have become the province of the historian.

CHAPTER XIV.

AN ASSORTMENT OF DUELS, ODD AND OTHERWISE

TRAGEDIAN MACREADY SHOCKED BY HIS EXPERIENCE
IN SAVANNAH—FATAL DUEL FOUGHT AT FORT
PULASKI—CAROLINIANS EXCHANGE SHOTS ON
HUTCHINSON'S ISLAND—ONE CHALLENGER'S COUR-
AGE WILTED ON FACING BUCKSHOT—PATTERSON
KILLS BARNARD—GRIFFIN-RUSSELL DUEL—AN IRATE
SOCIETY MAN CHALLENGES AN ENTIRE BOARD OF
GOVERNORS—NOBLESSE OBLIGE!

THE author of a little book published at Baltimore, in
1847, entitled "The Code of Honor, or the Thirty-nine
Articles," who dubbed himself a "Southron," after mentioning the penalties prescribed by statute in some of the states,
sagely added: "These penalties are never inflicted. Such
laws are mere brutum fulmen. They are evaded or trampled
upon by the very legislators who framed them. And were
they even carried into effect, which popular feeling would
render somewhat impracticable, duelling would not be prevented, because the practice of duelling is supported and
encouraged by public sentiment, and because that man who
declines a fair and honorable challenge is branded as a
'coward'."

This "Southron" also, while deprecating duelling and
its abuse, held that "The duel is a sharp but salutary rem-
edy for rude and offensive conduct, and its most inveterate
opponents must admit that wherever encouraged it has produced at least a marked courtesy and polish of manners.
Duelling, like war, is the necessary consequence of offence,
and when the cause shall have ceased the effect will no longer have existence."

Three years before this was written, W. C. Macready,
the noted English tragedian, while visiting Savannah, had
a peculiar example of the fact that public sentiment sustained duelling and coerced public officials into quiescence,
if not actual co-operation with those violating the law, as

WILLIAM CHARLES MACREADY, (1843)
(From "The Diaries of Macready" by permission G. P. Putnam's Sons)

had been the complaints of grand juries two and three decades before.

Macready spent several days in Savannah, playing to large houses. The weather was wretched, he was not well, his nerves were doubtless unstrung. It was in such a condition that on January 25, 1844, after packing for the journey to New Orleans, he came into contact with the extraneous circumstances of a duel. He tells of it fully in his reminiscences:

"Walked down below the bluff, and saw the places of business, etc.; I admired the novel appearance of the street upon the face of the bluff, planted as it is with trees, and looking over an extent of low land, river and sea. Was accosted by a rough person, who gave his name, Nichols, whom I heard say—to the observation that 'Crowds were hurrying down below'—'They need not be in such a hurry, the duel is not to be till twelve.'

"I turned round and looked with amazement in his face.

" 'How do you do, sir?' he answered to my surprised and shocked gaze.

"Did you say a duel was to be fought?"

" 'Oh, yes; just over the water, but not before twelve.'

" 'And can such a thing be publicly known and no attempt on the part of the legal authorities to interfere?'

" 'O, Lord, no, they dursn't; they've too many friends about them for any number of officers that could be got together to have any chance with them.'

" 'And are the crowds going down to see them fight?'

" 'No; they go to wait for the news—it's across the river they fight.'

" 'Do they fight with pistols?'

" 'I don't know; either pistols or rifles—but they generally fight with rifles in this part of the country.'

" 'Um.'

" 'They are two gentlemen of the bar here. It was a quarrel in court; one said, 'The lie was stamped on the other's face,' so there was a challenge. I suppose you don't do such a thing as take a glass of wine in the morning?'

" 'Oh, no, never.'

" 'Well, it's our way; just come in and see the reading room; it's the best room in the South; come, it's just here.'

"I complied with the importunity of my new acquaintance, who informed all about himself, but my stomach felt sick with horror at the cold blooded preparation for murder with which he acquainted me."

Not a word was printed in the Savannah papers about this duel. It has been commonly accepted that it was fought between Henry R. Jackson, afterwards the noted soldier, poet and diplomat, and Solomon Cohen, one of the leaders of the local bar. Evidently neither was wounded.

Macready appears to have been an irritable personage, with an exalted impression of himself. His bete noire was the average American hotel man. To Macready an inn keeper was an inn keeper—and nothing else. The "glad hand" variety of Boniface did not sit any better on his stomach than the duelling stories with which Nichols regaled him. In his diary, under date of January 21, he wrote:

"It grew dark after we passed the lighthouse and the merchant ships lying at anchor before the river's mouth. There were burning woods in different parts along the banks, and we went on our dark way between narrow banks till we reached the window lights of Savannah. Costas met me at the boat; he accompanied me to the Pulaski House. The landlord, Captain Wiltberger (I had a true instinct at the name) was standing at the door, and a stiff-necked, old piece of fat importance I found him; he could not give me my meals in my room, then I could not stay; then he led me to several rooms, all indifferent, and finally I took a double bedded room."

Showing his antipathy to the American variety of hotel proprietors, Macready later in his diary wrote: "It is curious what important persons the landlords generally are; they receive you much more like hosts that are going to give you shelter and entertainment than as inn keepers who are served and obliged by the preference of your custom."

As an antidote to the unpleasant impression one receives from the tragedian's comments, a quotation from the "Morning News" on the death in 1853 of Capt. Peter Wiltberger, probably the most popular hotel man Savannah ever had, may be apropos: "His death will awaken in the memories of many the courteous and gentlemanly attentions of which they were the recipients whilst sojourning beneath the shelter of his hospitable roof. All the relations of life were maintained by him in a manner to command the respect of all who knew him."

The "Republican" of September 9, 1852, contained a brief statement of a duel fought on Hutchinson's island the previous morning "by two gentlemen from Beaufort, Mess. Whaley and Jenkins." In the Charleston "Courier" I found a more detailed account: "We have been politely furnished with the following correct version of the affair of honor between Col. E. M. Whaley and E. E. Jenkins, Esq., of this state. The parties met at Major Starke's plantation, opposite Savannah, and after a single exchange of shots the challenging party, in response to a demand of the other side whether they were satisfied declared they were, and there the matter ended, but without a reconciliation having been effected."

In October, 1855, a duel was fought at Fort Pulaski between John Chaplin, of South Carolina, ex-lieutenant in the United States navy, and his brother-in-law, Dr. Kirk, of Savannah. Three shots were exchanged. On the last fire Dr. Kirk was killed. Chaplin was slightly wounded in the foot. The statement was made that Chaplin fired his first shot in the air, but Dr. Kirk refused to acknowledge this gracious act with a reconciliation and forfeited his life.

Another ante-bellum story, and perhaps apocryphal, is that of the young man with poor eyesight who became involved in a dispute at the old City Hotel, on the Bay near Whitaker, for many years Savannah's leading hotel for the planters and other visitors. Its bar was the gathering place for the convivially inclined, and there the best of liquors, domestic and imported, satisfied the palates of the most critical of connoisseurs. More than one duel that ended without bloodshed, as well as one in which a man was winged, was hatched behind the brick walls of the famous old hostelry, now decadent and given over to varied businesses. In this particular instance, as the tale goes, the aggressor was a man inclined to be bulldozing in his tendencies, while the aggrieved was less pugnacious but, as developments showed, of really truer grit.

Whatever the origin of the quarrel it forced the man with defective vision into a duel. He had resented the others man's offensive attitude and remarks and was challenged to combat. He was quick to announce the acceptance and his terms:

"I am entitled to be placed upon an equal footing with you as regards ability to see," said he. "At ten or twenty paces I would be at a serious and unfair disadvantage. Here is a table convenient. I will sit on one side, you on the other. Each will have his pistol in readiness for use. You will hold one end of a handkerchief with the left hand, I the other end. At the signal from the second pistols will be raised and fired."

"That is not a duel, that is murder," declared his opponent.

"With my eyesight it would be murder on your part for me to meet you otherwise," was the calm reply. "I am ready; are you?"

Friends interposed, proper apology came from the offender—and the man with the defective eyes received more respectful consideration thereafter.

Even in Savannah men sometimes despoiled the homes of other men. One can only wonder why in such an event the husband whose honor had been outraged should give to the seducer the opportunity to take his life in addition to the great wrong he had already done him. Yet there were rare instances here, as elsewhere in the South, where that course was followed, and in one notable case the husband carried to his grave a bullet received from the pistol of the wrecker of his home and happiness, the latter escaping with his life but also to carry a bullet in his hip as an ever present reminder of the sin which forced him to the duelling ground. At this late day the mantle of charity may well be permitted to fall upon them all.

Then there are instances, still told with amusement by men grown venerable, of angered citizens who dilly-dallied with their notes until the public made a joke of their prospective meeting and fairly laughed the would-be, but not overly-zealous, combatants away from the field, and of other instances where men deliberately refused a challenge in the days when duelling had more or less fallen into disrepute in Savannah and so helped to put a few more nails into the coffin of the obsolete custom.

Curious, indeed, are some of the stories one finds, either in traditions among the "oldest inhabitants," or embalmed in the cold print of forgotten newspapers, or in family letters, concerning affairs of honor between 1850 and 1870, in which neither participant suffered injury. Sometimes these affairs grew out of family differences, whereas almost inevitably the earlier meetings seem to have been the outgrowth, directly or indirectly, of impassioned politics, or business misunderstandings. The local newspapers continued to ignore the meetings as a rule, or simply made a passing comment, of which the following from the "Morning News" of October 21, 1868, is a fair sample:

"An Affair of Honor: It is commonly reported among persons who are acquainted with the parties that a little difficulty between two young men of this city is to be settled to-day at Screven Ferry, S. C., in accordance with the Code of Honor."

The old fire department was the source of many difficulties, growing out of the jealousies between the companies and internal criticisms and disputes, but there is only one recorded instance where a duel ensued. This emanated from a sharp exchange of personalities, at a meeting of the Oglethorpe Fire Company, between John A. Griffin and R. Wayne Russell. Some of the comments of Griffin were bitterly resented by Russell as a reflection on the character of his father. Nothing that friends could do lessened the bitterness, a sharp correspondence ensued, and a challenge from Russell was promptly accepted by Griffin. The "News and Herald" told of the affair as follows:

"The place, on the Carolina side, opposite Screven's Ferry, the time yesterday (May 21, 1868) at 6 o'clock; the weapons, Colt's 4½ inch revolvers; the distance, ten paces. Mr. Robert Lewis acted for Mr. Griffin, and Mr. Benjamin Sheftall for Mr. Russell. Early yesterday morning the principals and their friends proceeded to the scene of combat, but an officer getting wind of the affair made an attempt to arrest the parties; they, however, succeeded in getting away in a boat, but the pistols and a case of surgical instruments were captured by the officer.

"They reached the ground about 8 o'clock, and preparations were entered upon. Other weapons were obtained, and there being no possible chance of a settlement of the difficulty, excepting upon terms which could not be agreed to, the arrangements for the fight were completed, and the parties principal, their seconds, and Drs. Myers and Rogers, took their posts. Mr. Russell drew the choice of position, Mr. Griffin having the word, which being given both fired simultaneously, doing no damage. Mr. Griffin called for another shot, but the seconds upon consultation coming to the conclusion that the honor of both principals was sufficiently vindicated, proposed a settlement, which was agreed to, and the contending parties shook hands and with the crowd returned to the city. Thus fortunately closed the bloodless duel."

The statement is made that the principals wore the long linen "dusters," in common use at that time, and that the bullets went through them, but several inches from their bodies—perhaps just close enough to promote the peace efforts of the seconds.

Duels and rumors of duels continued to excite the public mind for some years after the cessation of civil warfare and the return of the people to the ordinary vocations of peace. Where there was one meeting, with or without bloodshed, there were several difficulties with actual or prospective challenges that were amicably adjusted. On one occasion, too, there was a duel arranged and all the preliminaries carried out that had a farcical, where a most tragical ending might have been looked for. This was in the latter part of 1869, and for a few brief hours the town was stirred by wild reports as to what had taken place. Instead of "Pistols for two and a coffin for one" there was every likelihood. if this duel had gone to its full conclusion, of coffins and graves for two. Looking at the meeting through the intervening half a century and more it tickles the risibilities almost as much as the famous duel in which Bob Acres so distinguished himself. The report in the "Morning News" is humorous enough in its quiet suggestiveness to have been written by Thompson, author of "Major Jones' Courtship," who was then the editor of that paper. It was as follows:

"The gentlemen had a personal difficulty, and a challenge was passed and formally accepted. At a very early hour yesterday morning two boats were seen to cut through the heavy mists which had settled on the river, on their way to the old duelling ground, on the Carolina side. They arrived upon the ground about four o'clock a. m. and after searching for a fitting spot found one where without the dread of magistrates they could settle their difficulty. The weapons selected by the challengee were double-barreled shotguns loaded with fifteen buckshots, distance twenty paces, the parties to wheel and fire at the word. At 5½ o'clock the antagonists were placed by their respective seconds and the loaded weapons handed to them.

"The challenged party had doffed his coat, bound his head, and was in position as though he meant business, and while waiting for the words 'Are you ready' was astonished to find that the challenger had thrown down his gun, stating at the same time that 'He would not fire on his antagonist.' This unanticipated event naturally excited the indignation of the challenged party who, supremely disgusted at the turn affairs had taken, with his friend and physician returned to the city after administering a sound reprimand to the challenger."

Double-barreled shotguns, loaded with fifteen buckshot, at sixty feet! No wonder the challenger grew tender-hearted and refused to fire on his antagonist. And imagine the relief of the challenged party who had selected such weapons when he found that instead of fifteen buckshot coming his way the gun in the other's hands had been thrown to the ground. What subtle touches the writer gave to the near-duel in the "indignation" and "supreme disgust" and "sound reprimand." And how unfortunate that it was a day in the history of Savannah journalism when names were as frequently omitted as they were published. The challenger's last moment prudence reminds one of Judge Dooly's famous remark after his encounter with Judge Tait: "I would rather fill a dozen newspapers than one coffin."

To an earlier period belong other duels about which information is scarce, unreliable, and mainly traditionary, diligent search failing to bring to light written or printed records thereof. In one of these local affairs of honor the principals were John Barnard, of the well known family of Wilmington Island, and William Patterson, also a large planter of some prominence. This meeting is said to have been at the Screven Ferry ground. The origin of the difficulty between the two men is not known. The terms of the duel, it is a matter of family detail, provided that the two men should stand twenty paces apart, with their backs toward each other. At the word from the second they were to wheel and fire.

Barnard, repute has it, was an excellent shot, while Patterson was an indifferent marksman. The odds were presumably in favor of the former. But the race is not always to the swift—nor the duel to the sure-shot.

When the signal came Patterson proved the quicker on the trigger. Before he had completely faced his antagonist the bullet from his pistol speeded across the short space between them and found its target. It was a chance shot but a true one. Another grave in the family burial plot at their island home marked the resting place of John Barnard. The claim was made that Patterson had fired prematurely, that he should have waited until fully facing Barnard. But the fact that the result of the duel was accepted by the public attested that he had acted within the conditions prescribed for the meeting.

Then there are the Arnold-Mongin duel and others, the very haziest memories of which remain—not tangible enough to hazard an account, duels in which there were no casualties, and in one or more of which family skeletons even to-day have a visible tremor when a bare reference is made to the provocative causes. Buried in Laurel Grove and Bonaventure are all of those who might speak with the voice of authority concerning these meetings.

Most interesting of all is the story of the duel that threatened wholesale slaughter and concluded as a comedy farcical enough for the most humorous skit of the burlesque stage. Don Quixote, in his most extravagant illusion, never imagined anything more deliciously absurd than this.

The memory of ante-bellum duelling still lingered and the sense of personal honor and affronts to it was still acute in many. Among those who retained this feeling in a somewhat exaggerated form was a former South Carolinian who had already played his part in a duel, not fatal but in which, it is said, he had winged his opponent. He had been a member of the Soiree Club and when its great annual function arrived invited a visiting Carolina young lady to accompany him to it, either oblivious or indifferent to the fact that for non-payment of dues, or some other minor reason, his name had been stricken from the roll.

Arriving at the hall where the dance was being held he met the cold announcement that he was not eligible for admission. It was a situation of extreme strain. A friend relieved the young lady of embarrassment by escorting her within while the irate escort freely expressed his views, denounced the Board of Governors and then and there verbally challenged them, individually and collectively, to deadly combat.

The following morning the challenges were sent in a more formal manner to the five governors. The tempestuous Carolinian sought to fight them one after the other. The governors were amazed at the brain storm they had provoked and sought in vain to assuage his wrath. Nothing remained but to accept. Probably by concerted action each challenged man selected a different weapon, so that the list ran something like this: Rifle, pistol, sword, shotgun, sabre. The day was selected and in view of the number involved arrangements were made for a special train of two coaches to run some distance down the old Gulf road to a suitable place.

The story got out, as rumors of all such meetings will and, doubtless without opposition from the challenged parties, steps were taken to prevent the progressive duels. Early in the morning the house in which the belligerent lived, and in which he and his second and physician, and probably one or more friends, were gathered, was invaded by the Chief of Police with several of his force in citizens clothes, and the entire party were notified that they were under arrest and must furnish peace bonds.

The challenger was outraged.

"You are a gentleman," shouted he to the chief; "would you interfere with an affair of honor?"

The chief merely smiled. "I am obeying the instructions of the Mayor," was his reply. "The other parties to this unfortunate affair will all be required likewise to give bond."

Protests were useless, no matter how vociferously made. Everyone connected with the affair gave security to keep the peace and before long cordial relations were re-established. But the most wonderful duelling incident in the history of Savannah had been spoiled by the interference of the law's minions.

There are several accounts, all reminiscential, none published, of this incident. I have given the one that appears the most authentic—absurd though it may seem to-day.

References have been made to public posting where an invitation to the field of honor had been declined or ignored. As illustrating the method of standing by the posting of an adversary and awaiting developments, I will cite an instance of the early days of the Confederacy.

It was in March, 1861. Military companies were being rapidly organized. Drilling was the order of the hour. Every day the parade ground was occupied by the men who had responded to the call of the South and were preparing for the bitter years of war ahead. Hardly a moment from dawn until night that companies were not maneuvering on its broad acres or practicing the manual of arms, their work witnessed and commented on by the assembled admiring youth of the city. It was during one of these periods of training that Francis L. Gue alleged that he had been insulted by Edgar L. Guerard. Being in uniform and under the restraint of discipline, he did not resent it at the time but the next day hunted up Guerard and demanded an explanation of his remark. There was scant satisfaction forthcoming. Guerard's reply was:

"I see that you want a fight with me and if you do you can have it."

Angered by this Gue struck Guerard and a fisticuff ensued, with the latter apparently worsted in the combat.

Speedily Mr. Fraser, as the friend selected for Mr. Guerard, called on Gue with a demand for satisfaction, for what Guerard claimed was an "unprovoked assault." Apparently Guerard had meant by his words to Gue that he would meet him on the duelling ground, whereas Gue interpreted them to be an invitation to a fist fight then and there.

Dr. Banks acting for Gue, carried the reply from that party:

"I am right on this issue and will not fight a duel on it. If you wish further satisfaction you can come and take it."

Finding his challenge repudiated Guerard posted Gue on the gate to the postoffice. There by his card of denunciation Guerard stood for three hours awaiting developments. If Gue or any friend had attempted to tear down the offensive placard, those who know say, a shooting encounter would have ensued without waiting for the formalities of the code.

But the long vigil by Guerard was unnecessary. Gue ignored the posting and stood pat on his announcement that if Guerard wanted satisfaction he could come and get it whenever he pleased.

In this, as in other cases, the conduct of the parties impugned the bravery of neither. A few months after this trouble Gue appears as captain-elect of the Republican Blues, but his active service must have been brief as in October, 1861, he was elected an Alderman, serving in the City Council for eight continuous years. During the war he was chairman of the military committee of that body and was active in the sinking of vessels and other impediments in the river channel. He also served as aide-de-camp to Brig. Gen. H. W. Mercer, commanding the military district of Georgia in 1863, when an attack on this city by the Federals was feared. Gue came to Savannah from St. Augustine and was quite popular.

Guerard served bravely in the war, with the rank of captain, and was the subject of highly favorable comments from his superior officers for his effective work in the quartermaster's department. In his report on the fight at Olustee, in February, 1864, for instance, Gen. G. P. Harrison said of him: "I would ask particular attention to the gallantry of Capt. E. L. Guerard, acting brigadier quartermaster. His services, together with the gallantry and promptness of Lieut. H. P. Clark, my aide-de-camp, was of the greatest importance during the whole engagement and particularly after the remainder of my staff had gallantly fallen and been borne from the field." After the war Guerard settled in South Carolina where he died.

Too many duels were taking place at the time of the clash between these two men. News reports from over the South showed a disposition among officers in the newly formed forces to resort to the code and the feeling grew that the headstrong and hot headed might better give their blood to their country than shed it in the satisfaction of personal wrongs, imaginary or otherwise. Probably mutual friends, with this in mind, obviated further trouble after Guerard's posting at the postoffice, where Savannahians of every class could read his denunciation of Gue for treating his challenge with contempt.

As emphasizing the fact that even after a challenge had been passed and accepted, and the parties were actually on the way to the duelling ground, the amenities of gentlemen were not to be lightly laid aside, there is extant a letter written by a Savannahian of prominence before the war between the States, who had become involved in a personal difficulty with another well known public man. In it he stated that on his way to the meeting place his carriage broke down. While in this embarrassing predicament another carriage came by in which sat the gentleman with whom he was to fight the duel.

Without the slightest hesitation this party expressed his regret at the inconvenience to which his antagonist was subjected and requested that he permit him to leave his servant to help with the carriage, and that the gentleman take a seat with him in his conveyance and proceed with him to the house of a mutual friend.

The invitation was accepted. Arriving at the home where the second gentleman had arranged to spend the night the other prospective duellist was invited to remain. Politics, the cause of the difficulty between them, was barred from conversation. They ate supper together and were escorted to the same room where they slept, but in different beds. In the morning they performed their ablutions in the same bowl, breakfasted together, and bowed formally in parting, the damaged carriage having in the meantime arrived.

At the duelling ground three shots were exchanged but neither was wounded. They then shook hands and parted friends.

Noblesse oblige!

CHAPTER XV.

A MOCK DUEL THAT COST AN EYE.

THE "KNOW NOTHING" MOVEMENT BROUGHT A CLASH IN
LIBERTY COUNTY THAT CLOSED IN A WILMINGTON
ISLAND REHEARSAL—A DUEL OF WORDS IN NEWS-
PAPERS THAT THREATENED A TRIO OF DUELS WITH
BULLETS.

OCCASIONALLY, through the publication of the correspondence in the public prints, or by a research in
public documents or among private letters, it is possible to
follow the entire course of a personal affair that either resulted in the tragedy of a duel or a peaceful, and sometimes
ludicrous, denouement. This was signally the case in the
affair in the fall of 1855 that threatened at one time to result in several duels between prominent citizens of Liberty
county, all well known in Savannah, and in the progress of
which difficulty an intense interest was felt in this city.

It was at the period when the great political duel was
on between the American, or "Know Nothing" party, and the
Democratic party. Feeling ran very high in Georgia, and
nowhere more so than in Chatham, Liberty and other
counties of the First district. Families were divided, communities were torn asunder, antagonisms were created that
lasted until the war between the states drowned them in the
blood shed over its greater issues.

The number of foreign born in the section was comparatively insignificant. Outside of Savannah they must
have been a very meagre fraction of the population. But
that fact did not prevent the politicians who were maneuvering the American party from instituting its lodges and
gaining a large membership. The members were oath bound
and the abandonment of the party principles and support
by anyone who had formally united with it brought severe
denunciation. It was just such an incident as this that
provoked the trouble which threatened for a time to make
Liberty county the scene of a series of meetings on the "field
of honor."

Dr. E. H. Hart had withdrawn from "Know Nothing"
Lodge No. 202. His action was resented and brought a card

from James D. McConnell, denouncing him, in the "Savannah Republican." The two men, up to that time, had been associated in terms of ordinary intimacy and friendship, and were well known in Liberty and near-by counties. Offended by the publication, Dr. Hart, through A. Maybank Jones, invited McConnell to an interview with him. McConnell met them, accompanied by W. A. Fleming. A personal encounter followed, in which McConnell, said to have been much inferior in physical condition, was worsted.

At this time began the proceedings looking to a duel. Dr. Hart, through Jones, challenged McConnell, "To meet him on the field of equality." McConnell promptly refused on the ground that Hart was not a gentleman, and added that "in affairs of this kind the second is responsible for the principal, and especially in this case do I hold him (Jones) responsible before the public." He then applied the opprobrious word "Coward" to Jones. Jones then issued a challenge, inviting McConnell to a "hostile interview." This brought forth a reply from McConnell, through his friend, W. L. Walthour, in which McConnell pointed out Jones had asked for "a hostile interview." McConnell claimed the right, as the challenged party, to "a choice of mode of combat," while Jones' challenge, he held meant "a fisticuff."

Jones' reply was tart. He did not consider his letter a challenge. "I intended it only as an occasion for finding and chastising you promptly," said he. "I particularly avoided sending a challenge in deference to the expressed opinion of my friend and his well known sentiment in opposition to the custom of duelling." Jones then formally "demanded redress in the field of honor and in such mode as honorable gentlemen adopt for redressing their grievances."

One might think that this would have brought out the duelling pistols and the surgeons, but not so. McConnell replied that Jones had put himself in the same class as Dr. Hart, and could not be considered a gentleman. "But to a challenge from your new friend, or any friend who is a gentleman, I will accede. Your conduct has put it out of my power to recognize you."

While McConnell did not give his authority for his stand as regards Hart and Jones, it was probably based on Article 9 of the "Code of Honor" published at Baltimore in 1847:

"Should both parties be gentlemen, recognizing the propriety of the duel, they may not have recourse to fisticuffs or cudgels, which, though an obvious and natural mode of determining difficulties, is one properly at a discount among men of honor." Hart having assaulted him and Jones having invited him to "a fisticuff," McConnell put them both outside the pale.

But back comes Jones with a summary of the events up to this time. "Hart begins to chastise him; McConnell evades a full chastisement on the score of physical inferiority; Hart challenges him to meet on the field of equality; McConnell refused at the time and says in a letter afterwards he (Hart) is not a gentleman, but holds his friend or second responsible; Hart's friend (Jones), thus recognized, proposes two fields to McConnell—one for corporal chastisement, the other for mortal combat, just which would suit him; McConnell says I can't fight the second of Hart, for he is no gentleman, but I will accede to a challenge from his second. The natural inquiry is, when would this secondary courage come up to the sticking point." "I dismiss this man now and leave him to wear the epithet with which the laws of honor and brave men and spirited ladies will, I know, gracefully crown him."

Henry Hart Jones, who had carried the challenge to McConnell from his brother, A. Maybank Jones, then seems to have discussed challenging McConnell through the medium of the Jones' brother-in-law, Joseph A. Anderson, W. L. Walthour continuing to represent McConnell.

Of course McConnell had to have another inning before the public. In his final card he sets forth that "When he (A. M. Jones) knew that I would recognize him, he dared not challenge me; after I refused him recognition he boldly challenged me. The public has seen how he acted as a second; his infirmity seems to have been shared by his brother and brother-in-law. I expected to find among the trio one brave and honorable enough to do the fighting, but I was disappointed. Let me suggest for them that if they cannot fight for themselves they should get one who can fight for them, and let the newspapers alone." "Disgrace is now stamped upon A. M. Jones, and his friends are compelled to fight for him, or wear it with him."

The stigma of cowardice thus put on the two Jones brothers and Anderson could not be ignored. A. Maybank Jones had become more vitriolic in reviewing the affair. McConnell had brought into his last card the names of three friends, Capt. P. W. Fleming, A. S. Quarterman and G. T. Handley, in a way that seemed to be an endorsement by them of various statements published by him in a card in which McConnell declared "A. M. Jones, on the evidence of these gentlemen, is now before the public in the capacity of a liar." Jones now pointed out that Capt. Fleming in a statement had shown that McConnell had received a challenge from Dr. Hart. "As for Mess. Quarterman and Handley, I found they were both persons of honor and courage. When the amende honorable, or satisfaction in a mortal combat, was demanded, they obeyed the voice of justice and honor, and granted the former by a full retraction of their unjust insinuations. Mr. McConnell has been challenged both by Dr. Hart and myself; by the one in a peremptory verbal manner, by the other in a formal written challenge. They are both still to be considered operative; neither ever having been withdrawn. Mr. McConnell refuses to accept them upon the singular but convenient plea that we are not gentlemen. He knew when urging such a subterfuge that it was all the prompting of cowardice, an evasion that would not meet the approbation of the community. But to place the matter beyond doubt, where our relative positions are not known, and the grounds of this artifice are not suspected, and also to remove whatever scruples his own conscience may entertain, we submit the enjoined expression of opinion of a number of the first gentlemen of our county."

"We take pleasure in certifying that in point of honor, courage and respectability, Dr. E. H. Hart and Mr. A. M. Jones are perfect gentlemen and stand upon a full equality with gentlemen of our community. (Signed) W. P. M. Ashley, P. W. Fleming, George W. Walthour, John A. Thomas, R. Cay, Joseph Quarterman, J. P. Stevens, G. W. Dunham, Wm. Maxwell, Abial Winn, B. A. Busby, W. S. Baker, B. W. Allen, W. Winn, Thomas Mallard, E. J. Delegal."

This put the issue squarely up to McConnell. In the meantime the trouble between Jones and Quarterman and Handley had become acute, so that there was a prospect of three duels on Jones' hands. This was obviated by the mediation of friends, resulting in the publication of this card:

"We, the undersigned, mutual friends of Messrs. A. S. Quarterman, A. M. Jones and George T. Handley, knowing their difficulty having come to a crisis which would lead to mortal combat, have thrown ourselves between the parties, as mediators in the matter, have investigated the case, and have the pleasure of saying the whole difficulty has been settled honorably and satisfactorily to the parties, as by the following agreement. (Signed) P. W. Fleming, George W. Walthour."

In the agreement referred to, Augustus S. Quarterman and G. T. Handley stated that in the certificate given by them to McConnell it was not their "intention to endorse his charges against Mr. A. M. Jones as a coward and liar." They regretted any impression made on the public mind "in regard to the courage and veracity of Mr. Jones" "as it was not our intention to convey that idea."

Two months had been consumed in all this correspondence. The time had come for the duel of words to cease, for leaden bullets to take the place of paper pellets. Public opinion demanded an arbitrament in another field than that of the newspaper columns. Maybanks Jones challenged McConnell and selected William Brailsford, of McIntosh county, as his second. But not a word is found thenceforth in the Savannah papers concerning the affair. And thereby hangs one of the most unique developments in any duel that was ever planned, the details of which have come down during nearly three-quarters of a century through the families of interested parties.

Seeing that a meeting had become inevitable, McConnell, who was expert neither with the pistol nor the rifle, began to practice. Col. W. R. Pritchard, of Savannah, became his mentor, and the practice took place on Wilmington island. There one Sunday afternoon a mock duel was arranged between McConnell and John R. Norton, with Col. Pritchard as master of ceremonies. Duelling pistols were used and a lot of blank cartridges were taken down. Col. Pritchard desired to get McConnell accustomed to firing the pistol while being fired at. Several shots were satisfactorily exchanged and McConnell was developing ability in controlling his nerves and taking careful aim.

"Now," said Col. Pritchard, after reloading the weapons, and addressing Norton, "I want you to fire point blank at McConnell's head. Aim right between the eyes. I want him to get used to the flash of the pistol in his face. Are you ready, gentlemen? Aim! Fire!"

There was a simultaneous explosion and McConnell fell to the ground as though dead.

"Fine," said the colonel. "You did well, that time. We'll try it again."

The supposition, of course, was that McConnell had dropped in play. But when he failed to get up the others rushed to see what was the matter. They found him unconscious, with blood oozing from over one eye, where a bullet had entered. In some way a loaded cartridge had become mixed with the blanks.

Doctors visiting the island were summoned, shook their heads, refused to probe, and gave the unfortunate man over to death. For three days and nights Col. Pritchard sat by his side. Then McConnell's eyes opened with a look of recognition.

"Colonel," said he faintly, "That bullet went through my head. I feel it back of my ear."

Examination showed this to be the case. The bullet had been deflected and was easily removed from its lodgment. McConnell recovered. The accident, though, cooled off everyone and all talk of a duel, or series of duels, ended.

McConnell lost an eye as a result of the mock duel. Many years after the civil war a gentleman visited West Point. Chatting with the superintendent he asked if any cadets were there from Georgia. He was told the names of the boys from this state, among them that of Pritchard, of Savannah. Requesting to meet him, young Pritchard was brought to the office.

"I am glad to see you, young man," said the visitor, over one of whose eyes was a green cloth. "I knew your grandfather well. Unwittingly he cost me this eye."

It was James D. McConnell.

CHAPTER XVI

THE PEN IS MIGHTIER THAN THE BULLET.

EDITORS SQUABBLED BUT SELDOM FOUGHT—HOW THE DIF-
FICULTY BETWEEN BULLOCH AND CHAPMAN WAS
ADJUSTED BY ARBITRATORS SELECTED BY THEIR
SECONDS—MAYOR WAYNE'S LITTLE TIFF WITH A
NATIVE AMERICAN PROPAGANDIST—HAMILTON AND
SNEED ADJUSTED THEIR DIFFICULTY ON THE FIELD
OF HONOR—TRIBULATIONS OF CARPETBAG EDITOR
HAYES—NEGRO POLITICIANS FIGHT DUEL WITH BUCK-
SHOT—TABER SHOT AND KILLED BY MAGRATH IN
FAMOUS CAROLINA MEETING—HOW AN AUGUSTA
EDITOR GOT BULLETS IN HIS THIGHS—EDITOR DAW-
SON'S WORK IN SUPPRESSING DUELLING IN SOUTH
CAROLINA.

THE bitterness of politics engendered a personal bitterness between old-time editors which is happily missing
to-day. In the decades that immediately preceded the war
with the North political differences were the source of personal differences that quite frequently led the parties engaged in editorial combats to the verge of the duelling
ground, and occasionally forced the wielders of the vitriolic
pens to face each other with pistols.

During the battle over nullification as championed by
Calhoun, with many ardent disciples in Georgia who pointed
to stirring incidents in this State's history as establishing
its sympathy with the same principles in former years, the
Savannah editors were more than usually bitter in their
personalities.

The "Republican" championed the extreme States
Rights theories of the South Carolina leaders, while the
"Georgian" espoused States Rights within the Union and
followed the leadership of Andrew Jackson. Toward election
day, when the latter party won a signal triumph, the bitterness increased in intensity. The denunciation of one political
editor by another, these few lines from the "Georgian"
furnish a fair sample:

"The editor of the 'Republican' is a hired, pitiful sland-
erer, picked up from the dunghill, an outcast of creation
brought to Georgia that he may compete with gentlemen."

The columns of the Georgia newspapers teemed with
letters assailing the political record and creeds of the candidates. That such weeks of growing excitement and bitterness could have passed without sufficient offense being given
to bring about one or more duels is hardly possible. If so,
the scribes of the press were not included among the antagonists who crossed the ferry to South Carolina. They fought
with pen and ink. Unfortunately, too, they failed to record
the hostile meetings of those whose brains were influenced
by their passionate exhortations.

There was ample fuel in the political atmosphere of
Savannah from 1830 to 1840 to keep a steady pilgrimage
boating across the river. With hundreds of men their
political beliefs were so woven into the warp and woof of
their daily existence as to make their advocacy of them a
matter of life and death. Undoubtedly some of them exchanged more than verbal shots, but the local historians
failed to chronicle their meetings.

It was a super-heated campaign of months, that early
fight between the Union men and the secessionists. In those
days the representatives in Congress were still elected by
the State at large, instead of by districts, and two popular
Savannahians, James Moore Wayne and George W. Owens,
were candidates on the Union ticket and were victorious in
October, 1834, so that Chatham had two members-elect of
the House at Washington. Matthew Hall McAllister ran
for the State Senate, with Wm. W. Gordon, John Millen and
George Shick for the House, while on the States Rights
ticket the opposing candidates were Dr. James P. Screven,
Timothy Barnard, Joseph W. Jackson and Edward Houstoun.
The States Rights ticket was swamped at the polls.

Of course the Union party had its campaign song. It
was a day when the voters loved to sing the merits of their
candidates. So some local bard wrote a song patterned after
Burns' "A man's a man for a' that." This is how he ex-
tolled the merits of the Savannah opponents of the Calhoun
ideas:

> There's Georgie Owens, of Chatham dear,
> A lawyer sound, and a' that;
> We'll fix him where his judgment clear
> Will rank him high, and a' that.
>
> Another pillar, noble Wayne,
> Fair Georgia's hope, and a' that;
> Whose fame remains without a stain,
> So pure and free, and a' that.
>
> McAllister was born to grace
> A Senate grave and a' that;
> A star so bright would soon efface
> The cloud so dark, and a' that.
>
> There's Willie Gordon, who, we ken,
> Is fearless, free and a' that;
> We'll send him with three gallant men
> To guard our rights and a' that.

When the returns came what more fitting place could there be to celebrate the glorious victory than the decks of the good ship "Constitution" then lying in port. Thither the "Union and States Rights Association of Chatham" marched, beneath the Stars and Stripes, with the band playing "The Star Spangled Banner." As the scowling "States Rights Nullificationists" watched them there came a salute of twenty-four guns from the deck of the ship, one for each state in the Union, not excluding South Carolina, and then from the Bay an answering salute of twenty-four guns. Down on the deck of the "Constitution," beneath the gay decorations of flags and bunting, the Union leaders gathered, and there Robert M. Charlton read an ode written by him for the occasion, the last lines of which stirred the crowd to a renewed outburst of enthusiasm and the wild waving of flags:

> "We swear that till our life shall end,
> Whilst one remains of all our band,
> With utmost vigor to defend
> Our Flag, OUR UNION, and Our Land!
> May He, to whom all spirits bow,
> Record, and bless this holy vow."

There was a fervor to their politics in those days in Savannah akin to that which comes in religious awakenings, when men allow their emotions to sweep them from their usual apathy and full vent is given to the feelings that surge within their breasts. Some Savannahians have the impression that local politics are marked by too much bitterness to-day. If they study the politics of Chatham before the last two decades, back to the very inception of the independence of the country, they will realize that present politics are of the milk-and-water variety.

Reference has been made to the fact that two Savannahians were elected Congressmen in the 1834 contest. Before the new Congress convened, President Jackson, on January 14, 1835, appointed Wayne to the United States Supreme Court. He had already served three terms in Congress. By his acceptance of this appointment Savannah lost one of its representatives in the House of 1835-36.

Judge Wayne's devotion to the Union was no newly fledged sentiment, nor was it of a transient nature. It was a deep-seated conviction that neither time nor changing political conditions could weaken. His sympathies were with the Union during the war, although his affection for Savannah and Georgia remained. He continued on the United States Supreme Court bench until his death, July 5, 1867, a period of thirty-two years. Hampton L. Carson points out, in his "History of the Supreme Court," that Judge Wayne was the last member of the Supreme Court as constituted under Chief Justice Marshall, "a fact which was one of the felicities of his career, and while it was the remarkable fortune of President Jackson to fill a majority of the seats upon the bench of the Supreme Court by appointment to vacancies occurring during his term, it was the lot of Mr. Justice Wayne to be the last survivor of these appointees." "At the outbreak of the Civil War his sympathy and efforts were all with the cause of the Union, and his opinions indicate his fidelity to the Constitution, as interpreted by the principles of Marshall. He lived to see the triumph of his views and the restoration of peace under conditions which promised to be permanent."

Judge Wayne's son, Henry C. Wayne, though, cast his lot with his native state, and is well remembered as the adjutant and inspector-general of Georgia under Governor Brown. After the war Judge Wayne was instrumental in securing pardons for several of his old Georgia friends, among them General Edward J. Harden, Judge of the Confederate Court for the District of Georgia, a well-known Savannahian, father of the present William Harden, and also for former Senator Benjamin Hill. The latter failing to acknowledge the pardon, Judge Wayne, in seeming distress of mind over the ignoring of the executive clemency and his part in securing it, wrote to Judge Harden, and a tardy letter from Hill to Washington made the proper amende to his old Savannah friend.

Succeeding political battles were fought just as bitterly, with personalities verging toward viciousness, and "Courts of Honor" were more than once called in to adjust personal differences that had provoked challenges. Notable among such instances was the difficulty in the fall of 1844 between William H. Bulloch, editor of the "Georgian," and S. T. Chapman, editor of the "Republican." It was the year of the great struggle between the Democratic and Whig parties, headed by Polk and Clay. Seldom in its history has Chatham County been so closely divided in the political allegiance of its voters. The eyes of Georgia were centered on the battle here. Already the slogan was, "As Chatham goes, so goes Georgia." Great rallies of the contending parties were held, intense enthusiasm prevailed in each camp, and as the election of November drew near the bitterness between editorial writers, speakers, and the rank and file generally, grew more and more intense. Editorial comments became more personal in their nature toward the close of the campaign. The thin veneer of courtesy was brushed aside, and finally the short, nasty words of "liar" and "coward" disfigured the editorial columns. Editor Bulloch sent a challenge by Dr. Richard D. Arnold to Editor Chapman, who accepted and named Robert R. Scott as his second.

The seconds carefully considered the situation and decided to call in Robert Habersham and George Schley as arbitrators in an endeavor to amicably adjust the differences of the editors and prevent the exchange of shots. The arbitrators did their work carefully and conscientiously, and their published conclusions, accepted by the principals, are somewhat of a model. They decided that the "Criticism of the 'Republican' (the Whig organ), although chafing in its tendency, did not call for or render proper the personal bearing of the reply of the 'Georgian'; that this reply was not so offensive as to justify the imputations contained in the 'Republican's' retort; that the subsequent articles on both sides assumed an asperity which we cannot consider justifiable, and we particularly designate the underscoring of the word 'Gentleman', and the charges of lying and cowardice, which we are confident emanated solely from the intemperance of contest, resulting more from the peculiar public position of the parties than from the convictions of their judgment.

"We, therefore, believing that there was no proper ground for the inception and harsh progress of this quarrel, consider and award that the particular expressions which we have designated, and all others personal in their character, shall be deemed by the parties as recalled and all personal unkindness as remitted.

"We trust that we shall be excused, as the friends of the parties (although it be a supererogation) for concluding with a recommendation to them, that in future personalities will not be allowed to mingle themselves in the discussions which literary or political topics may claim from them as editors—they add no force to the arguments and give no pleasure to right-minded readers."

A few days later Chatham went Democratic, for Polk and Dallas, the vote being 835 to 816 for the Whigs. Editor Bulloch called for "One Hundred Guns for Old Chatham" "Redeemed from Whiggery," and a Democratic rooster crowed lustily over a dead coon. A monster demonstration was held by the Democrats, joined in by the unterrified of adjacent counties and near-by Carolina. To this came perhaps the last surviving officer of the Revolutionary army that had sought to recover Savannah from the British in the memorable siege and attack of 1779—Colonel Tarleton Brown, a "Life-long Democrat," who was received with prolonged cheers as he rode in the procession.

Flushed with their victory, the Democrats refused a proposition that political lines be forgotten and a ticket be elected for Mayor and Aldermen of a bi-partisan or non-partisan character. This was the first election in which

the people voted directly for their Mayor, the aldermen previously having chosen the chief executive of the city from
their number. Dr. Richard Wayne was at once nominated
by the Democrats for Mayor, and elected. During the brief
campaign he became involved in a dispute with William
King that but for some reason not now apparent might have
brought a duel. Mayor-elect Wayne referred to it in his
comments: "It was our common misfortune that King's
peculiar position precluded him from the ordinary means
of redress." What the "peculiar position" was that prevented recourse to the code does not appear, but Dr. Wayne
went on to say: "He has learned that no position can protect the author of falsehood from exposure, though the
punishment may be escaped."

King had been arousing and organizing the sentiment
against those of foreign birth. His close to this affair is a
gem in its way, one of the most concise and dispassionate
verbal salutes at the close of any trouble of this sort to be
found:

"He has gained his office. I have saved my character.
If he has a clear conscience and is satisfied, so am I. Let
us add no greater insult to the public by annoying it with
our communications."

After the many columns of letters that had been inflicted upon the newspaper readers in the Bulloch-Chapman
affair, one can hear the audible "Amens" as the readers of
the "Georgian" and the "Republican" read this final card.

In the campaign of the next year (1845) the Whigs
triumphed and Dr. Wayne was defeated in his fight for re-
election to the mayoralty by Dr. Henry K. Burroughs.
Mayor Wayne became involved in an acrimonious dispute
with the editor of the "Republican," but there was no resort to the code. The Whigs for years had their headquarters in the Lyceum Hall, at the southwest corner of Broughton and Bull streets, while the Democratic headquarters
were at the southwest corner of Broughton and Barnard.
Sallying from their respective castles for parades, the contending political elements at times crossed paths with resulting collisions that meant cracked heads and bloody
noses. This particular election day was marked by much

disorder and bullying at the polls, one party being doubtless as guilty as the other in its violent tactics. In a fracas within the court house Dr. Wayne was assailed by several bitter Whigs running amuck through that building. At the expense of his arm, the Mayor protected his head from blows from clubs. A bone was broken in his arm and one of his fingers fractured. Wayne and Arnold and Daniell and Burroughs were a quartette of "Before-the-War" physicians who took an active, one might truthfully say pugnacious or bellicose, part in Savannah politics. Between them they held the mayoralty sixteen years. Three other doctors, Jones, Screven and Waring, were also honored with the mayoralty, and local history records that as Savannah's chief executives the doctors were as active in the performance of their duties, as efficient, and as satisfactory in the results achieved, as those business men and lawyers who held the office.

The excellent advice of the arbitrators in 1844, accepted though it was at the time and printed for the public information, could not long restrain the rival Savannah editors. Hardly a year passed before there were further sharp exchanges of offensive personalities between Bulloch and Chapman, and the former is found referring to Chapman as having "descended to the low and dirty work of traducing character," coupled with the suggestion that the editor of the "Republican" should "with his kindred reptiles crawl and die." Chapman was not less severe in his strictures, but as their editorial pleasantries avoided such expressions as "liar" and "coward" they managed to pull through the campaign without a challenge.

That was a famous battle, that Georgia fight for the governorship between the Whigs and Democrats in 1845. Savannah had the honor of furnishing the Democratic candidate, Matthew Hall McAllister having been enthusiastically nominated in the State convention. Opposed to him was George W. Crawford, then closing his first term as Governor. Political lines were too tensely drawn to permit of Savannah rallying unitedly around McAllister as a native Savannahian, a brilliant son, whose life had been spent in and devoted to the city. He was fought as vigorously and as viciously as though he were not "to the manner born."

Local political organizations were formed then, as in some former campaigns, along lines of racial origin. The foreign-born elements and their children aligned themselves with the Democratic forces. To enthuse and encourage them, and create a spirit that would hold them steadfast in their allegiance, beautiful banners were made by Democratic women and presented with much formality. The Germans and Poles, united in one body, bore in their parades a banner of satin with the eagle of America surmounted by thirteen stars, emblems of the old thirteen states. The eagle bore aloft in its beak a scroll with the honored names of DeKalb, Steuben and Pulaski. The Irish had another distinctive banner with the harp. The old Democratic-Republican party for some years carried as its main banner one of white satin with a golden fringe. On one side, encircled with a green wreath, was the title of the Association, and on the reverse the arms of Georgia enclosed by the motto, "The Union of the People for the Sake of the Union." Near riots came when the opposition sought to wrest the banner of Democracy from its strong-armed carrier. It was a day when brawn was needed in politics much more than in the puerile present.

McAllister was doubtless the first Georgian to bear the proud title of "War Horse of Chatham." On political banners he was fondly inscribed as such, and from one end of the State to the other the expression was used in praise of his stalwart devotion to his party. But the Whigs aimed the shaft of "kid glove" at him. Throughout the country districts he was dubbed an "aristocrat." Nowhere was the governorship more heatedly contested than in his home county. So close was the strength of the parties that he carried Chatham by but fifteen majority, McAllister 715, Crawford 700. Polk had defeated Clay here by nineteen votes. Welded together by both principle and prejudice, it was difficult to break the ranks of the Democratic or Whig parties in other than purely local contests.

In the state at large, Crawford triumphed. A Savannah correspondent of the Charleston "Patriot" said of McAllister that he was defeated "simply because he was a native of the city of Savannah," and the Savannah papers reprinted the comment without dissent. Perhaps Georgia had already begun to look upon Savannah as an outsider, and the "State of Chatham" was coming under the ban of political ostracism when high offices were the prizes.

The Whig party in Chatham at that time was almost a "Native American" party. The "Georgian" tacitly admitted this in its editorial the day after the election, congratulating Chatham on its endorsement of McAllister:

"Thanks to the Sons of the Emerald Isle, who have disdained the presents offered to tempt their political honesty;

"Thanks to the noble Germans;

"Thanks to the gallant Frenchmen;

"Thanks to all, native or adopted, who have placed Chatham in her proper position."

The Democracy sent Joseph W. Jackson, J. W. Anderson and John E. Ward to the Legislature at this time. When their legislative duties were concluded a mass meeting of citizens, irrespective of party, was held, at which each legislator gave an accounting of his stewardship directly to the people, and replied to questions as to his course while in the Assembly. This was done at other times, too—a plan which might be re-adopted with much advantage to both legislators and constituents today.

The local alignment of the hostile partisans of a somewhat later period, Whigs, Native Americans, Democrats, was clear and unmistakable. Feeling ran high at all times and satire, denunciation and abuse were not spared by the ofttimes embittered journalists. Candidates for office, regardless of standing, seem to have been pilloried as objects of contumely, if one is to accept as a correct portraiture of conditions the comments of Editor Thompson, of the "Morning News," when Seward, Democrat, and Bartow, Whig, ran for Congress in this district in 1853:

"Alas! Who will be able to recognize them when the canvass is over? He that will believe one-tenth of all the meanness, the deceit, the downright villainy, which will be laid to the charge of each candidate by the press which opposes him, will be disgusted with human nature. If they are pelted with one-half the filth, the slander, the detraction, the serious charges of dishonest purposes under which the two candidates for governor (Johnson and Jenkins) have been compelled to await the issue, their friends will be hardly able to recognize them, they will hardly believe their own senses, and admit the fact of their own existence. Messrs. Seward and Bartow may consider themselves in the stocks until the election is over, there to be pelted."

The public had apparently not modified its attitude toward candidates, nor the press curbed its virulence, when Samuel Prioleau Hamilton became associated with the "Georgian and Journal" three years after this campaign. It was the period of the dissolution of the Whig party, before its members passed into one or the other branches of the Democratic party, or temporarily espoused the false issues of the American party in the vain hope of defeating their old-time enemies. Hamilton was the son of General James Hamilton, the nullification governor of South Carolina and advocate of armed resistance to Jackson's enforcement of the tariff of 1828. He is described as a young, one-armed man, full of fire and determination, aggressive in tone and very pronounced in his opinions. The "Georgian" had merged its identity with the "Evening Journal" in May, 1856, under the name of the "Georgian and Journal" labeled as the "Organ of the Democratic party," and was edited by R. B. Hilton, assisted by Hamilton and Isaac S. Clark. The "News" welcomed Hamilton to the Savannah fraternity as "a young gentleman of talent, a ready writer, and a zealous supporter of Democratic principles," and, it might have added, by heredity and education of the extreme "Southern States Rights" variety. It was not long before he became involved in a dispute with Editor J. R. Sneed, of the "Republican," the old Whig organ. The dispute speedily became sufficiently acute and offensive, in Hamilton's opinion, to justify a challenge from him.

Sneed had come to Savannah in August, 1855, from Washington, in Wilkes county, and had quickly become an active factor in the local politics, his journal being conservative in tone, or, as Lee expressed it, "opposed to secession as unjustified by any grievance then in existence." The "Georgian" had been very bitter in its strictures both on the Whigs and the Union Democrats, many of the former having taken refuge under the latter banner. Montgomery Cummings bore the challenge from the sanctum of the "Georgian" to that of the "Republican." The prominence of the two editors in this section of the state aroused unusual interest in the prospective mortal combat and on the day the duel was to be fought little else save its outcome was talked of in Savannah.

The old ground in Carolina had been selected and the parties were making their way from the ferry landing to the spot where the shots were to be exchanged, when Cummings casually remarked to W. R. Pritchard, who represented Sneed:

"It is a shame for these two men to fight, especially after a willingness has been expressed to withdraw the challenge."

"Withdraw the challenge!" said Col. Pritchard in surprise. "This is the first I have heard of it. Do you say with authority that your principal is willing to withdraw the challenge?"

"A letter looking to withdrawal was unquestionably prepared, and, I believe, sent," said Cummings.

"Under such circumstances it would certainly be a shame for either of them to lose his life," commented Pritchard.

Two friends accompanying the would-be duelists were called in for conference. Under the code the seconds had the right, even the duty, to intervene if they believed an amicable settlement could be, and should be, reached.

The result of the conference was a satisfactory adjustment of the affair. It appeared that the party to whom was entrusted the delivery of the note withdrawing the challenge had unfortunately looked upon the wine when it was red in the goblet. He had fallen by the wayside with the note forgotten.

Instead of the Savannah papers the next morning conveying to the world the intelligence that one or the other, or both, of the editors, had fallen on the field of honor, they contained the following card:

Screven's Ferry, So. Ca.,
November 11, 1856.

In an affair of honor pending between Mr. J. R. Sneed and Mr. S. P. Hamilton, we, the undersigned, selected friends, express our gratification that we have been enabled to make an adjustment of the difficulty between the gentlemen, which is honorable and satisfactory to both parties.

JOHN RICHARDSON,
JOHN M. B. LOVELL.

What the agreement was is not known. At the expiration of the month, though, Hamilton retired from his editorial connection with the "Georgian and Journal," and was succeeded by Albert R. Lamar, who became associated with R. B. Hilton as part proprietor and assistant editor. Hamilton had but a brief connection with Georgia journalism. He continued to live in Savannah, married and died here. The "Georgian and Journal" itself passed out of existence three years later, after a life, on the part of the "Georgian," extending over forty-one years, marked by a full average of political strife.

When native editors, in sympathy with the South, its traditions and its institutions, fell out as a result of their political and personal strictures, or were called to account by a citizen outside of the editorial fraternity for comments regarded as offensive, what could be expected when a rank outsider, who had traveled in the wake of Sherman's army as a newspaper representative, seized a Savannah newspaper and became the editorial exponent and protagonist of the Northern viewpoint of the war and its results.

James E. Hayes landed in Savannah on December 29, 1864. He had been war correspondent of the New York Tribune but evidently decided that the local field was more enticing, less dangerous, and probably more remunerative, and under army auspices took possession of the office and plant of the "Savannah Republican," without compensation to its owners, and continued its publication as an organ of the radicals. From then until his sudden death on September 16, 1868, he was almost continually involved in troubles, sometimes of a most serious nature. In 1867, Solomon Cohen, who had been the Democratic or Conservative candi-

date for Congress, had him prosecuted in the Superior
Court for criminal libel and the jury found him guilty. He
appealed and doubtless death nol prossed the case. In this
case Judge Fleming delivered an interesting charge, holding
that "A candidate for public favor puts his character and
competency on issue and any true information in regard to
either would not be libelous, unless the occasion was used
for wicked and malicious purposes. If the election was over,
though, the lawful occasion did not exist, for it is of candidates, and not of persons who had been candidates, that
the law gives this permission. That the candidacy (of Mr.
Cohen) had been recent does not affect the matter, for if
this were so what a wide door would it throw open for the
indulgence of spleen and malice on the part of disappointed
partisans. The liberty of speech and the freedom of the
press are not invaded when persons are held liable for what
they say or publish."

Hayes' troubles as editor were not confined to Southern
men. Even his own radical friends, blacks and whites, had
their dissensions with him, and either maligned him in print
or made physical assaults upon him. The notorious Bradley, a negro ex-convict from New York, who had become
the dangerous leader of his people and a menace to the community, became his bitter foe. Hayes threatened to shoot
him and it is amusing to note the comment of the "News
and Herald" thereon:

"We regret when one of our profession permits himself
to dispute with a negro, and more particularly when he
threatens to kill the negro and then fails to do so."

While Solomon Cohen would not acknowledge Hayes
socially sufficiently to challenge him for slander, a young
Savannahian called the editor to sharp account when Hayes
permitted himself to reflect in the "Republican" on his veracity. This was Frank D. Lee, who had entered the Confederate service in 1861, as a boy of seventeen, and served
throughout the war. Lee believed that he might provoke
the carpetbag editor into a duel, but he was mistaken in his
man. This was Lee's last card:

"John E. Hayes having impugned the honor and bravery of the writer, he takes this opportunity of daring him
to make good his accusations by meeting the writer in open

and honorable conflict at any time and place he may designate."

Although Lee had previously advertised him as an all-round, wilful, malicious and cowardly liar, Hayes ignored the cartel, apparently. But in the four months that intervened before his death he brought additional troubles by shifting toward the Conservative side in political matters. The white radical leaders, the Hopkinses, assaulted him, the negro Bradley encouraged the idea of his assassination, and his path was a veritable briar patch of the sharpest thorns. Some of the negroes had been induced, either from intelligent comprehension of the benefits their race would receive by co-operation with Southern whites, or by promises of reward, to espouse the Conservative side in politics and a number of them are said to have voted for Gen. John B. Gordon for governor and Henry S. Fitch for Congress, the Conservative candidates at the 1868 election. Negro Conservative Clubs were organized. A negro named Jackson Brand, who had been violently connected with the radical element, professed conversion and came into one of these clubs, connected with which was another negro, Eugene Morehead. Two negroes aspiring for leadership meant trouble. Morehead claimed he caught Brand coming from the house of Hopkins late at night and charged him with treachery. After a fisticuff a duel was arranged, and with all due form and ceremony, accompanied by seconds and friends, but not surgeons, the pair sought South Carolina soil. Double-barrel guns, loaded with sixteen buckshot were used, at forty-five feet. Brand received a number of the shot in each hip and fell to the ground grievously wounded, but urged his second to hold him up while he exchanged shots again with Morehead. The second had too much regard for his own hide to desire its perforation and refused. Brand died soon after reaching Savannah. The "News" commented that "Everything was conducted properly, but their neglect in not providing a surgeon was most criminal." Morehead was not molested.

These incidents illustrate the conditions under which Savannah labored during the years that immediately followed the war, leading up to the later "Ogeechee riots," and disturbances at the polls, and the final overthrow of the radicals locally and in the State, and the restoration of clean government and white supremacy. When Hayes died the property of the "Republican" was sold at public outcry and bought in by John R. Sneed, its former proprietor and editor, who resumed its publication. It was in this year (1868) that Capt. S. Yates Levy was forced by the military powers to relinquish his editorship of the "Advertiser," of which mention has been made.

As far as can be ascertained, these were the only Savannah editors whose duels ever ran beyond the verbal stage, acrimonious though their newspaper disputes often were. They were fire eaters with pens for swords and threw ink instead of drawing blood. The editorial pages of the Savannah papers, in common with those throughout the country, in the last four decades, have fortunately abandoned the offensive element of personal vituperation. The old-style bludgeoning editor, like the custom of duelling, has long since gone to his final resting place, never to return. Instead of so much rancorous airing of personal political views, current news marks the journals that bulk so much larger in size and prosperity to-day. It is the reporter, and not the editorial writer, whose work builds up the subscription list of the twentieth century newspaper.

While connected with Savannah only through the great interest they awakened among all classes at this time when political turbulence ran amuck in Georgia, there are two duels in which editors well known in this city were involved that may not inappropriately be inserted here. In both of them the responsibility of the editor for permitting the use of his columns for personal political attacks became the issue. In one instance the editor accepted it and filled an untimely grave as a result. In the other the editor denied it and declined to accept a challenge, throwing upon the writer of the offending articles the acceptance or rejection of the demand for personal satisfaction from the man whose ruffled sensibilities could be mollified only through the medium of the duelling pistols. In the former case South Carolinians were the principals, in the latter Georgians

To all the duels fought by Savannahians in a half century hardly as much space was given by the local papers as to the meeting in which Editor William R. Taber, Jr., of the

Charleston "Mercury" met his death. This grew out of the
Congressional race in the fall of 1856, in which Judge A. G.
Magrath was a candidate. Young Edward Rhett, Jr., attacked the Judge anonymously in the "Mercury" Until that
time the relations between the Magraths and the editors of
the "Mercury" are said not to have been strained. In the
absence of Judge Magrath his brother, Edward, took upon
himself the protection of the Judge's honor and challenged
not one but both of the editors of the "Mercury." Rhett
avowed himself the author of the articles and stood willing
to accept a challenge from Judge Magrath, but to no purpose. Judge Magrath hastened a messenger to Charleston
to prevent, if possible, the meeting between his brother and
the editors, but he arrived too late. Nothing shows more
clearly the disinclination to interfere in such affairs than the
report of this friend to the Judge:

"The time, place and circumstances of the proposed duel
were known throughout the city. Magistrates knew them,
the conservators of the peace knew them, pious men and
even clergymen were as well acquainted with the facts as the
parties interested."

But not a hand was raised to prevent the duel.

Editor Taber's attitude in accepting the challenge was
that he was championing the hard-won liberty of the press.
Magrath's letter of challenge he regarded as an assault on
the freedom of newspapers as the medium for the open consideration of the views and acts of men in public life, and
especially of candidates for high place. Magrath, on the
other hand, held that while an editor is free to publish what-
soever he will, he must take the consequences of so doing.
Taber was, in effect, called upon not only to apologize for
publishing the utterances of his correspondent and to dis-
claim them, but to also avow that he did not believe them.
The entire burden of the anonymous expressions was thus
thrown upon the editor, even though the author assumed
responsibility for them himself.

The correspondence was sharp. Accepting the challenge, Taber said: "You assume to represent the honor
and manhood of your brother, an avowed candidate for the

highest office in our gift, and by your interference reduce his honor and manhood to a vicarious existence. I do not admit that when a candidate by his own consent he can avoid the proper, necessary responsibilities of his position as a candidate. If a judge, he is no less a candidate. He cannot legitimately put his character in commission and maintain his honor by proxy. If he can resign his seat to go to congress, he can resign it, if necessary, to vindicate his honor. He has no right to be a candidate if he ceases to be a man. It is a refuge without honor and without character. But truth shall not be muzzled, though he be a judge, and the liberty of the press shall be maintained, even against the vicarious champion of his manhood and the intrusive representative of his honor. This much for your warrant to represent your brother and insult me."

Efforts were made after the first and second exchange of shots to adjust the trouble, but without avail. A form of settlement was prepared but rejected by Taber and his second. Everything seems to have hinged on the use of the word "retract" required of Taber as to the Rhett publications. "Mild and harmless as it may seem," held his second, "it was too palpable that it amounted not only to an identification of Mr. Taber with the whole responsibility for these articles, but as a disclaimer of and apology for them. It would have been a stultification of him as an editor and a humiliation of him as a man."

Those were punctilious times, and because of Magrath's insistence on the word "retract" instead of the word "regret," Taber died. The editor was convinced that a great principle was at stake and that if he fell, he fell a martyr to the glorious cause of the liberty of the press. On the third exchange of shots he was killed.

John Heart, associate editor of the "Mercury," was on hand with his second and notified Magrath of his presence and willingness to proceed with the duel.

"I am ready to answer your demand for satisfaction," said he, as they bore away the body of his co-laborer on the "Mercury."

Magrath conferred with his second and answered that he had no further demands to make and retired from the field.

Young Rhett was also near the field, ready to meet any demand that might be made upon him if Judge Magrath appeared.

Judge Magrath immediately withdrew from the congressional race. He subsequently became the last of South Carolina's governors under the Confederacy.

Many and bitter were the comments on this affair. The view of many was undoubtedly expressed by the editor of the "Central Presbyterian," when he wrote:

"A duel settles no principles, elects no truth, vindicates no innocence, proves no man brave. Why should the 'The Code' be called a 'Code of Honor,' which violates the laws of God and Man?"

It was another Rhett, U. S. Senator Barnwell Rhett, who gave a high exhibition of Christian manhood, when, being the subject of offensive remarks by Senator Clements, of Alabama, and urged to challenge him, he replied: "My second reason for not calling the senator from Alabama into the field is of a still higher and more controlling nature. For twenty years I have been a member of the Church of Christ. The Senator knows it; everybody knows it. I cannot and I will not dishonor my religious profession. I frankly admit that I fear God more than I fear man. True courage is best evidenced by the firm maintenance of our principles amidst all temptations and trials."

In the Georgia editorial duel the circumstances were different and the result was not fatal to either of the participants. This was in October, 1851. The Augusta "Chronicle" had contained articles reflecting upon the political course of Editor James M. Smythe, of the "Constitutionalist and Republican," an "Independent Whig," or Clay organ, established by Smythe in 1848, he having previously been associate editor of the "Chronicle." Evidently there was no love between the editors for Smythe, instead of sending a cartel to the author of the letters, challenged Editor Jones, of the "Chronicle." Jones had a sufficiently clear vision to see that if he became a physical target for leaden bullets in return for the paper pellets shot by all the correspondents of the "Chronicle," his life was apt to be snuffed out at any moment. He declined the challenge. Then Smythe turned to Mr. Thomas, the author of the articles which had so exasperated him. Mr. Thomas accepted. They met at Vienna, S. C., and, the newspaper reports say, fired three shots at each other. The editor was the only sufferer. Bullets went through his thighs. But the wounds were not serious and he was soon enabled to bathe his enemies in vitriol again, and to demonstrate that in the hands of a truly valiant editor the pen is mightier than the old smooth bore duelling pistol. This duel, like that at Charleston, brought widespread comment. They both may have played their part in persuading Savannah editors not to resort to the field of honor to adjust their differences but preferentially to continue to bomb each other from the safety of their editorial tripods. Considering their fiery invectives, the duels between Georgia journalists seem entirely disproportionate to those among the politicians as a class.

It is interesting to note that the "Constitutionalist" was merged in the "Chronicle" in 1877.

Many years later another Charleston newspaper man, governed by religious principles, not only refused to accept challenges but labored so zealously and so continuously to stir the public conscience to the need for legal suppression of duelling, backed by a sentiment that would not tolerate ignoring of the statute, that Pope Leo XIII conferred on him the title of Knight of the Order of St. Gregory in recognition of his meritorious labors and their final success. This editor was Capt. F. W. Dawson, of the "News and Courier," known to so many Savannahians as one of the noblest spirits of Southern journalism of his day, courageous, conscientious, serving the public with high ideals. It was a strange stroke of fate, indeed, that sent the chivalrous soul of this editorial antagonist of the duel into eternity as a result of his defense of a woman's honor. Capt. Dawson was slain by a man accused of wronging a young woman of the editor's household. Under the old custom, that he had so persis-

tently and so successfully fought to destroy, a challenge
and a duel would, in all probability, have ensued from the
wrongdoing of another, a duel from which Capt. Dawson
might have merged the victor and unscathed. But recourse
to the code had been finally suppressed through Capt. Dawson's own efforts, even had it not been that as a devout
Catholic the editor bowed to the judgment of his church
and the ban it had placed on duelling. Many will recall the
reception of the news in Savannah, on March 12, 1889, of the
killing of Capt. Dawson, he being known and admired by
many in this city. The "Morning News" said of him: "He
possessed in an eminent degree the courage and honor of
the Southern gentleman of the old school, and was imbued
with the hopes and ambitions of the Southern people of
today."

When the brilliant Gonzales later lay dead in Columbia,
slain by a politician whom he had assailed in his journal,
more than one editor in that state echoed the sentiment that
in destroying the duel Capt. Dawson had temporarily produced a worse condition. Gonzales, himself, in describing
the rise of Ben Tillman, of "pitchfork" fame, declared that
had not the duel been outlawed as the result of the efforts
of "an editor of foreign birth and whose church proscribed
it," Tillman would probably never have reached the United
States Senate, as he could not have continued to run amuck,
but would have been called to account for his public utterances, challenged, and either forced, as Gonzales apparently
believed, to retract and apologize, or been slain in a meeting
of honor by one of those whose characters he had attacked
and whose influence he was seeking to destroy by unlimited
and ceaseless abuse. Gonzales was doomed to fall a victim to
the pistol, not on the field of honor which had been barred
from his state, but on a main street of South Carolina's
capital.

This has been a digression from Savannah duels and
duellists, but these incidents show that the spirit which
once ruled here survived to a much later period across the
river, politics in Georgia subsiding forty years ago to a lamb-
like tameness compared with the virulent variety that flourished until quite recently in South Carolina.

CHAPTER XVII

WITH RIFLES AT TWENTY-FIVE PACES.

DISPUTE OVER GAME OF BILLIARDS AT CLUB LEAD TO
DEATH OF TOM DANIELL AT THE OLD SCREVEN FERRY
GROUND—A WEEK LATER HENDRICKS SHOT THROUGH
THE HEART AT THE SAME SPOT—AN OUTBURST OF
POPULAR DISAPPROVAL THAT SOON WANED—
SCREVEN FERRY A DUELLING GROUND FOR SEVENTY
YEARS.

DURING the decade before the secession of Georgia the
upper floor of the building at the southwest corner of
Bull and Congress streets was the home of the Chatham
Club. There the young bloods of the city met at nights
to drink and chat and play pool and billiards or cards—poker
was a favorite game then, as now, with many.

It was a period here, as elsewhere, when drinking was
almost the invariable rule among men, and in the heat of
wine or whisky young men's irascibilities were aggravated
and friendships were seriously estranged at times. More
than one prospective duel resulted from contentious disputes
at the old club rooms, only to be settled by the intervention
of elders, or the cooling influence of the next day's sobriety.
In some instances, though, the results were more tragical,
and one particular meeting that developed from the clash of
two erstwhile friends was the topic of widespread talk for
years thereafter.

One night a party of well-known young men, scions of
prominent families of the city, had an encounter at the club
over a billiard game. The details have passed beyond the
ken of men's memories, but the death records of the city
are a sad witness to the resulting fatality.

Stewart Elliott and Tom Daniell were the players. The
table was surrounded by friends. A dispute arose. Flushed
with anger and alcohol, Daniell seized a glass of wine from
which he had been drinking and dashed the contents into

Elliott's face, at the same time applying an insulting epithet. The spectators prevented immediate hostilities. The insult was one that could not be ignored or satisfied except by a complete apology or recourse to the duelling ground across the river.

Elliott was willing to accept a reasonable apology. Daniell's friends urged him to accept the opportunity to withdraw his utterances and have his action pardoned. With some men the appeals might have gathered strength from the fact that Elliott was admittedly an expert shot, but Daniell preferred to ignore the danger which was so evident to his family and friends. The challenge from Elliott was accepted.

Two or three mornings after the encounter at the club two little parties made their way through the cut and over the back river into Carolina, the "No man's land," so far as the laws against duelling were concerned.

One can imagine the little procession slowly wending its way from the ferry landing along the old corduroy, dirt-covered road through the Carolina lowlands, through a section of country better cultivated then than now, with the rice fields on either side, at that time of the year a drab and sombre painting in browns and yellows, a picture of the desolation that is the aftermath of the golden crop and the prelude to the spring resurrection of green promise. Perhaps a bunch of negro slaves working on the dikes and ditches in preparation for the coming spring planting ceased their labors to watch them pass, knowing intuitively that two more white men were to settle a difference near by, and then, perchance, waiting with eager interest for the cracks of the weapons coming faintly through the quiet morning air.

There could be no levity on a walk like that, a walk the memory of which would linger for untold years and be among the thrillingly interesting reminiscences of old age. Only the principals and their seconds and one or two intimate friends of each principal, and a surgeon or two with their black bags of instruments and bandages and stimulants.

The sharp breath of the morn fans their faces. The twitter of birds in the brush is the only sound that breaks upon their thoughts. The sunshine that illumines the roadway and the zest that comes from the bracing air of midwinter stimulate the hope of life and suggest its sweetness. But the stern faces of the men reflect naught of the placidness which surrounds them. Passions and hatreds and fear of public sentiment are the driving forces that urge them on.

The spot for the duel is not far from the river. All too soon the little distance has been covered. The broad flat top of an embankment is selected and arrangements proceed.

As the principals and their friends grouped together, Elliott turned to his second, son of a prominent Carolina family.

"I don't want to kill Tom Daniell," said he. "I am willing to accept any reasonable amende from him."

The suggestion for such an amicable adjustment goes again to Daniell, but he is obdurate.

Perhaps the idea occurred to him from his antagonist's overtures that Elliott was really afraid.

While Daniell and his advisers are conversing, Elliott has taken what occurred to him as a more practical step toward peace, a striking illustration of his skill in marksmanship.

As the story goes, picking up a heavy clod of earth and tying a string about it, he requested his second to suspend it from a low tree near by.

"I will try out my rifle," said he loudly, but in an indifferent way, and then in a lower tone to his second, "I will cut the cord with the bullet so Daniell and his second can see what I can do with this weapon."

Raising the rifle to his shoulder, Elliott, almost without aim, severed the string.

Daniell's second brought back word to Elliott's second that the proposed adjustment of the difficulty was not agreeable. It was afterwards told that Daniell's sharp answer had been: "Damn it! He must fight."

And the sight of the severed cord, swinging in the light morning breeze, had no effect unless it had been that of aggravating the hot tempered Savannahian like an insult or threat.

The subsequent preliminaries were brief. Stepping off twenty-five paces is a matter of a moment or two—a mere seventy-five feet over which the bullets must speed on their deadly mission. The rifles are examined by the seconds as a matter of form. Too well they know they are in perfect order. Then the cartridges are glanced at and each second has placed the one for his principal in his rifle.

There is a pause, and each second, feeling as he does its utter futility, asks his principal once more if an adjustment of this difference with his opponent is not possible. It is a sop to their own consciences, this last step toward a reconciliation.

"What shall I do?" Elliott is said to have asked his second.

"You must shoot to kill, or he will certainly kill you," is the reply.

The principals take their positions facing each other, rifles held loosely in hand. How close they must have seemed to each other. The friends and surgeons have taken their places at one side. The seconds have assumed their proper places. It is like the stage setting for a drama, a picturesque grouping where other men in other years have faced each other, pistols or rifles in hand; where still other men are to similarly meet in coming days.

One might think the very soil into which had already soaked the life blood of the impetuous would cry out against further sacrifice.

Perhaps the sighing of the wind, as it swayed the browned marsh grass and the scattered clumps of rice straw that had escaped the reapers, is nature's vain protest.

To one of the seconds has come the doubtful honor of giving the signal. If of sensitive temperaments the tension to duellists, to seconds, to all the onlookers of the tragedy, must have been excruciatingly intense.

"Are you ready, gentlemen?"

How sharp and painful must the words have fallen on all ears.

Death, hovering near, draws closer.

The rifles are brought to the duellists' shoulders. Not a quiver of eyelid, not a tremor of muscle, speaks of fear.

The little party on the side line grips itself in a suspense that is almost mental anguish. Their bodies are tense, their ears are strained.

"Fire! One, two, three. Stop!"

Did one fire before the other?

No one can tell.

The reports seem like one. But before the first word has died upon the second's lips, one of the duellists has sprung a foot in the air, his rifle has fallen to one side, and his body has pitched backward to the ground.

Tom Daniell is dead, bullet-pierced through the heart.

Through the long lapse of years has come from eye-witnesses the sad story of the home coming.

Slowly the corpse-burdened boat made its way across the river to the East Broad street dock. The news had gone swiftly before. In the crowd that assembled was the young man's father, Dr. Wm. C. Daniell, one of the most prominent physicians of his day, a former mayor of the city.

All fell back as he went forward with a friend or two to receive the body of his boy.

"His face was as fixed as stone," many years afterward said one who was present. "Not a tear was shed."

But beneath the mask of passivity there hid the agony of the soul from the eye of the curious.

Curtained by that mask was a heart crying to its Maker, like David of old, "Absalom, my son! my son!"

It may have been that when Tom Daniell left home that February morning his father had a premonition that death would ensue. It is hardly possible that he was not aware of the preparations for the duel. Such meetings were commonly known by too many for information not to reach members of the families immediately concerned. It was not possible, under the rules of the code, for the father to accompany his son. All that he could do was to await in anxiety for the outcome.

Five years before this young Daniell had fought another duel—perhaps that may not have been even the first, for he is described as headstrong and impetuous, as a young man of intense friendships and intense antagonisms, quick to take offence and slow to forget. This previous meeting had been with Dr. Charles Ganahl, another well-known Savannahian, prominently identified with the local military and with his profession, and active in local Democratic politics, serving as health officer in 1850 and as an alderman in 1853-54. He and Dr. Wildman had a private hospital on Indian street.

What brought about the trouble between him and Daniell in 1852 is not now ascertainable. It may have been about politics, or it may have been the result of a military dispute. Daniell was first lieutenant of the DeKalb Rifles in 1850 and Ganahl was captain in 1850-52. Both had been active in the organization of that company, but Daniell's lieutenancy was of brief duration. All that is known of their duel is that two shots were exchanged between them, that neither found its mark, and that then an amicable settlement of their differences was reached.

But the fact that Daniell was willing to fight, that he was not prone to apologies and adjustments before an exchange of shots, and that he was aggressively inclined at a period when there was much to provoke angry dispute, must have prepared his friends in a measure for the snuffing out of his life in 1857.

His father, Dr. Daniell, was a man of very strong traits of character, said to have been almost fierce at times in the intensity of his convictions, a trait which passed to his son, those who knew them said, and even found vent in the practice of his profession. It was a period when bilious fever made serious inroads on the people of Savannah. Dr. Daniell used "red pepper tea" to a much greater extent than others as a stimulant, so much so that he became known among the other physicians as "Old Doctor Capsicum." He was one of the Nestors of the medical profession here and regarded as one of the ablest practitioners. He had been quite a power in local politics, an alderman in 1818, 1821-24, and mayor in 1824-26. It was in his administration that the first great step toward the promotion of the health of Savannah came in legislation prohibiting wet rice culture within two miles of the city. Other progressive measures showed the vision of the man and his devotion to his town. He was among those who left the city with the Confederate forces under Gen. Hardee, but returning he lived several years longer, dying on December 30, 1868.

It is a commentary on the newspaper attitude toward duels at that time, or to the editorial willingness to spare relatives and friends from the harrowing details, that the killing of Daniell was told in a few lines in the "Morning News" of the day following:

"FATAL DUEL: A hostile meeting took place yesterday at Screven's Ferry, on the Carolina side of the river, between D. Stewart Elliott, Esq., and Thomas S. Daniell, Esq. The weapons used were rifles—distance twenty-five paces. On the first round Daniell was killed."

The following day the body was borne to Laurel Grove Cemetery. In the cemetery record book appears the simple statement: "Thomas S. Daniell, aged 30 years, February 16, 1857; (buried) February 17. Brought dead from South Carolina."

Elliott never ceased to deplore the death of Daniell. Some now living of his close friends tell how he confided to those who knew him intimately that after Daniell fell the horror of the killing came with frightful force upon him.

To his last day the memory of the quarrel and its fatal ending hung like a perpetual shadow over Elliott's life. Yet there was no doubt in his mind, or the minds of his friends, that if he had not slain Daniell in all probability his own life would have been forfeited.

Was it the law of suggestion that lead to the use of rifles in the next duel, and that but a week later? Investigation does not show that it was the rule to resort to that weapon. Yet seven days after the bullet from Elliott's rifle

found its mark in Daniell's heart a bullet from another
rifle sped on equally as fatal a mission, and perhaps on the
same plot of ground another young man lay stretched a
victim to the code duello.　In this instance the newspaper
account was more circumstantial, but gave no inkling as
to the nature of the grievance, or which was the challenger.
The difference between the journalism before the Civil War
and that of the present time is in nowise more strikingly
illustrated than in the perfunctory baldness of the item, bare
of display headings, with an utter indifference to their natural desire to know the whys and the wherefores, that told
the readers of the "News" of this tragedy.

The Rough and Loosely Constructed Landing
at Screven Ferry, S. C.

"DUEL:　A meeting took place yesterday noon (February 23, 1857) near Screven's Ferry, on the Carolina side of
the river, between O. S. Kimbrough and Mr. Jacob E. Hendricks, both of Columbus, Ga.　The weapons used were rifles
at thirty paces.　On the second fire Mr. Hendricks was
shot, the ball striking above the hip and entering the abdomen, inflicting what is feared to be a mortal wound.　At a
late hour last night he was still alive, but very little hope is
entertained of his recovery."

Hendricks died from his wound the next morning.　The
records of the Laurel Grove Cemetery give his age as 33

years, and his place of nativity as Savannah, residence on Gordon street, Calhoun ward. He was buried from the house of Mr. A. A. Solomons, "opposite the Pulaski monument."

Probably never before in the history of the city had two young men been slain in such a tragic way within a week. For many days the two duels and their endings were on men's tongues throughout the state. They gave an impetus for a time to the demand that duelling be suppressed by the power of public opinion, but it was a temporary outburst of opposition to the custom, void of effectiveness. South Carolinians believed even more ardently than Georgians in recourse to the code of final arbitrament of personal disputes. No indictments were ever returned, or apparently asked for, in that commonwealth for Georgians who sought the famous duelling ground near Screven's Ferry. More than one case of "wounded honor" was yet to be satisfied there, under the pressure of a challenge backed by the social endorsement of the custom, before the war with the North came to absorb men's thoughts and energies and sacrifices, and eventually bring new conditions which tabooed the duel as a means of adjusting personal differences and put the stigma of actual crime upon what for generations had been condoned by society, if not commended, despite the statute classing a fatal outcome as murder.

The immediate vicinity of Screven's Ferry has changed for the worse since the years when it was one of the South's most notable duelling grounds. In the early years of the last century the causeway led through the rice plantation of Major John Screven, one of the most productive and most profitable on the Savannah River, its large harvests being marketed here. On his death the plantation came to his son, Dr. James P. Screven, at one time mayor of Savannah. Why, and exactly when, this was selected as one of the most available and most acceptable spots for the final disposition of affairs of honor no one can tell. Its history in this connection reaches back to the early years of the last century and its story as a duelling ground probably covers the seven decades from 1800 to 1870. The gradual decay of the rice growing industry after the abolition of slavery lead to the final

The Lonesome Road That Leads Over Marsh Lands from the Old Ferry Landing in South Carolina.

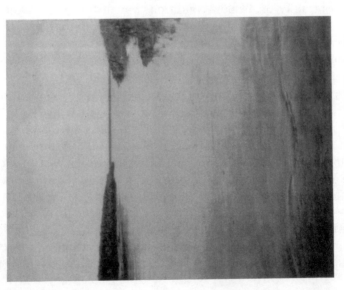

The Cut from the Savannah to the Back River and to Sereven's Ferry, S. C.

abandonment of the plantation and the low-lying fields are now a jungle of marsh grass, the ditches filled with rushes and weeds, the flood gates rotted away. Nature has almost obliterated the productive handiwork of man. A brick chimney that catches the eye a few hundred feet from the river marks where a rice barn and cabin once stood. On this bit of high made land more than one duel took place. Other parties utilized one of the broad main embankments, and still other affairs were quickly disposed of on the roadway that leads from the ferry. There was no danger of being disturbed. The travel by the ferry was light and of a neighborhood type in the main. Closeness to the river made it easier to handle the dead or wounded on the return trip to the city. Automobilists now drive over the shelled road from the landing, indifferent to the fact that in bygone years on this narrow stretch of highway, and on either side of it, duelling parties gathered from time to time. A desolate, sun-burned, lonesome stretch of road it is, not a habitation in sight for miles. Tourists are eager to pass over it, to the flat boat and across the swift running stream. There is nothing to awaken their interest, to pique their imaginations, to picture to them even in a shadowy way the dramatic hold the spot has on those who know its past.

CHAPTER XVIII

SAVANNAH'S LAST FATAL DUEL, IN 1870

A BOAT RACE AND ITS TRAGIC RESULT—SPLENDID NERVE
OF LUDLOW COHEN WHO FELL MORTALLY WOUNDED
ON THE FIFTH EXCHANGE OF SHOTS WITH "OLD DICK"
AIKEN—JUDGE GIBSON'S COMMENT AND WHAT THE
CODE HELD AS TO CONTINUED EXCHANGE OF SHOTS.

THE last fatal duel between Savannahians was that in which Ludlow Cohen fell from a bullet from a pistol of Richardson F. ("Dick") Aiken. This was in 1870. Both were men of recognized courage. Aiken was about sixty years of age, a rice planter from near Darien, a frequent visitor to Savannah, a lover of the water and owner of one or more fast sailing pleasure boats. In Savannah his only associates were the lovers of sport. That was the period when aquatic sports flourished here. Cohen was in his early 30's, of the firm of Wilkins & Cohen, dealers in fertilizers. He had come from "over home," as Charleston was even then dubbed, and was popular not only with the young element of sportsmen but with all who became acquainted with him. Like Aiken, he was the owner of a fast sailing boat. A half century ago the Savannah owner of a yacht felt the same keen interest and pride in its good points and performances that the owner of a race horse did, constantly extolling his boat's merits, and was ever open to a challenge.

It was out of this jealousy of the racing qualities of their boats that this duel came. One day the two men and a number of companions of similar tastes were gathered at the house of John Anderson, at Beaulieu, afterwards the Lester place on the point. There was a good racing breeze and a test of the boats of Aiken and Cohen was suggested and agreed upon. Aiken's son was placed in charge of the stake boat, stationed a mile or two from the starting point, and the race began with the usual zest. Cohen's yacht lead and turned the stake boat a considerable distance ahead of Aiken's. The breeze then died out and the contest degenerated into a drifting match back to Beaulieu.

Gathered at the Anderson house the merits of the boats were the topic of conversation among the group of young men who remained for social intercourse. It was suggested that as Aiken's boat had seemed to be gaining on Cohen's boat, another race between the two should be arranged to determine which was the better craft.

"I will not race with Aiken again," said Cohen. "He is not a gentleman."

"What do you mean by that?" demanded B. B. Ferrill, a close friend of Aiken's, who had made the suggestion that the race be run over, and who is still remembered by many Savannahians as "Benny" Ferrill.

"I mean what I said," replied Cohen. "His son moved the stake boat forward in order to give his father an advantage of shorter distance. I will not race with a man who would profit by such a move as that."

Ferrill is described as quickly resenting this, as he had suggested the second race.

"If you do not retract what you have said," came his sharp rejoinder, "I will tell your comments to Aiken immediately."

"I have nothing to retract," was Cohen's final remark as he turned away, and nothing could convince him that he was in error in his suspicion as to improper practice in the race.

True to his threat, Ferrill at once sought Aiken, who was still in the Anderson house, and informed him of Cohen's words.

Dictated by Aiken, Ferrill penned a peremptory challenge to Cohen and delivered it at once.

It demanded a full retraction and apology, and in lieu of that an immediate meeting with such weapons as Cohen might select.

Cohen declined to consider the suggestion of friends that he withdraw his offensive remarks. The fact that he was a poor shot and that Aiken had had much greater experience in the use of firearms did not deter him from the meeting.

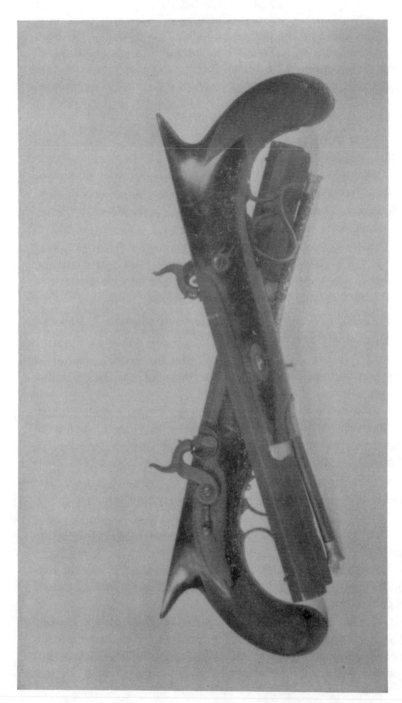

Pistols Used in Savannah's Last Fatal Duel Between Cohen and Aiken; Made in London Over a Century Ago, They Figured in Several Affairs of Honor. (Owned by A. G. Guerard, Savannah.)

The regular duelling pistols were selected as weapons. Several friends refused to act as seconds and urged a settlement of the trouble. Capt. David Waldhauer, of the Georgia Hussars, a one-arm veteran of the Civil War, became Cohen's second, while Ferrill acted in that capacity for his friend Aiken.

Late that afternoon, Thursday, August 18, the two parties left the city. Aiken and his friends spent the night at the McAlpin place, the Hermitage, while Cohen and his friends slept at the adjoining Brampton, the plantation of Dr. J. B. Read. Dr. William Duncan and Dr. Thomas J. Charlton accompanied them as surgeons.

At daybreak on Friday morning the duellists met at the place selected, on the Brampton plantation, about four miles from the city, near a little cluster of trees, on the left-hand side of the Augusta road.

Twelve paces had been decided upon as the distance and were at once stepped off, and the seconds went through the usual preliminaries.

Captain Waldhauer, having lost his right arm at Gettysburg, was unable to load the pistol for Cohen, and that duty was performed by Dwight Roberts, the only living witness today of the duel. The pistols were the old style smooth bore, the calibre being a one-fourth ounce ball.

It was the freshness of the early dawn. The dew was still on the grass and shrubbery, the birds were singing their matins, butterflies fluttered about them, the varied insect life of the woods and fields was astir, nature was just awakening from its night's rest.

The darkness had been one of little slumber for the principals and those accompanying them, and while the sun was dissipating the mists that still obscured a part of the landscape it could not rob the two groups, that faced each other with cold and formal salutations, of a sombreness which seemed to foreshadow the tragedy that lay within the womb of the next half hour.

The seconds drew for positions, and to Cohen fell the choice. He selected the east, with the sun's glints falling over his shoulders and lighting and warming up the little

stretch of ground, half sand and half grass, that lay between him and the man who felt that only in the shedding
of Cohen's blood could be washed out the stigma that had
been attached to him in the young man's intemperate utterances.

No efforts at reconciliation were made, it being apparent from the attitude of the two men that nothing could
be accomplished in that direction.

Four shots were exchanged, without either of the duellists being hit. Under the ordinary procedure, after each
exchange of shots, the seconds were supposed to seek an
amicable adjustment, or an expression from the challenging
party that he was satisfied. For some reason this appears
not to have been done.

For the fifth time the pistols were loaded and the two
men confronted each other with the same grim determination that had marked them from the beginning.

It was evident from the spirit of the principals that
the exchange of shots would continue until one or both of
them fell wounded.

Just before they took their positions for the last time
one of Cohen's friends said to him:

"Aiken will try to kill you. You must keep cool. Are
you nervous?"

Cohen laughed.

"Nervous? Not a bit," and with a careless swing he
threw the pistol into the air and caught it by the end of the
barrel as it came down, and once more calmly faced his
adversary.

Again came the usual question, and again the two nod-
ded their heads that they were ready.

Again came the word, "Fire! One, two, three. Stop!"

But the admonition not to fire, if either man had failed
to do so at the signal, was unnecessary.

As quickly as the word "Fire" came, Cohen had pulled
his trigger. His fifth bullet failed of its mark.

Aiken's aim was better than his preceding efforts to
lodge a bullet in his living target. The report of the pistol

came distinctly after that of Cohen's, and the bullet from it entered Cohen's right side, passing through the abdomen, cutting the intestines.

Cohen's right arm dropped to his side, the empty pistol fell from his grasp, and the unfortunate young man sank to the ground.

Instantly the surgeons came to his aid. Their examination showed that the wound was in all likelihood fatal. Placing him in a carriage they brought Cohen quickly to the city to his residence. Other surgeons were called in, but he was beyond human aid. Shortly before 3 o'clock that afternoon he breathed his last.

There has come down a story that Aiken was really a good shot, that he could have wounded or killed Cohen in one of the first exchanges of bullets, but refrained from doing so in the belief that his antagonist would express a willingness to apologize or retract, and that he only took more careful aim on the fifth round from a recognition of the fact that Cohen's persistence in shooting might eventuate in his own death.

The facts do not sustain this tradition.

Aiken and his friends came to the city and Aiken delivered himself to Justice Isaac M. March, who held him in bond of $5,000. Coroner Harden later gathered a jury to investigate the killing.

The surgeons were called upon to testify.

"Was the shot that proved fatal given in self-defense?" was asked of Dr. Charlton.

"It was," he replied. "Mr. Cohen fired first and it was after he fired that he received the fatal wound."

Dr. Duncan and Mr. Roberts confirmed this. Mr. Roberts added: "I think there would have been another exchange of shots if Mr. Cohen had not been wounded."

The jury's deliberations were brief. Its verdict was:

"We find that the deceased came to his death from a gunshot wound received at the hands of Richard F. Aiken, whilst fighting a duel, contrary to the laws of Georgia."

Savannah Duelling Pistol Case of the Days When Affairs of Honor Were Frequent.

For a time it seemed as though an example might be made of Aiken. The coroner discharged his jury, stating that the case would be brought to the attention of the grand jury. Aiken was released by Judge Schley on $20,000 bond. Apparently that was the end of the matter. The newspapers gave more details than of previous duels, but the present-day instinct to cover tragedies fully was absent, and much of the information herewith presented was obtained from other sources. In its brief account of the hearing the "Morning News" said:

"The questions involved are nice legal ones, and as the unfortunate affair has attracted much attention, there will doubtless be a crowd to listen to the arguments involved in the case." And it further informed its readers that "It was currently reported that Governor Bullock had telegraphed, upon hearing that a duel had been fought with fatal results, to arrest all parties engaged in the affair of honor."

Perhaps that was a move to awaken sympathy for the living duellist, interference by Bullock in a Chatham affair not being relished here. But there was not a word of editorial protest against duelling as a practice, not an expression of disapprobation by the journals of public opinion.

If the grand jury considered the duel, it refused to bring in an indictment.

The pistols used in this affair are now the property of Mr. A. G. Guerard. As far as known, they are the only pistols extant in Savannah used in a duel with a fatal ending. The Anderson house, where the trouble brewed, was burned to the ground on December 26, 1877.

The killing of Cohen caused much excitement. Those who recall it tell of the feeling which swept the community and the sentiment it awakened against recourse to the code to settle personal difficulties.

Cohen had become quite popular during his residence in Savannah. He was a young man of high principles and drew many friends to him. That his life should have been snuffed out, in violation of law, in response to an old code of honor that many thinking men looked upon with disapproval, if not horror, awakened hostile criticism that did not entirely die out after the proverbial ten days' sensation.

There were more meetings of this nature afterwards, in which no one was wounded, but the era of duelling for Savannahians was nearly over.

Its tragedies ceased when Cohen's life blood gushed out on the sands of Brampton.

It is related that Judge R. T. Gibson, who had been City Treasurer several years before this, and was conversant with various affairs of honor, was at the old Habersham office on the Bay when told of the details of the duel.

"My God!" said he, when informed it was on the fifth exchange of shots that Cohen received his mortal wound. "Five shots! Did they not know that one, or at the most two shots, amply satisfies a man's honor?"

And the old man was right to a certain extent. It all depended on how serious Aiken considered Cohen's statement to be that "He was not a gentleman."

An old writer on duelling held that if more than two shots were exchanged, it was evidence of a malevolent desire to slay, or of an ignorance in the use of weapons that brought the custom into disrepute.

Governor John Lyde Wilson, of South Carolina, the noted authority on duelling, in his Code published in 1838, said to have been the first prepared in this country, and which became the accepted standard in the South Atlantic section, pointed out that after an exchange of shots, neither party being hit, "It is the duty of the second of the challengee to approach the second of the challenger, and say: 'Our friends have exchanged shots; are you satisfied, or is there any cause why this contest should be continued?'

"If the meeting be of no serious cause of complaint, where the party complaining has in no way been deeply injured, or grossly insulted," Governor Wilson went on to say, "the second of the party challenging should reply: 'The point of honor being settled, there can, I conceive, be no objection to a reconciliation, and I propose that our principals meet in middle ground, shake hands and be friends.'

"If this be acceded to by the seconds of the challengee, the second of the party challenging says: 'We have agreed that the present duel shall cease, the honor of each of you is preserved, and you will meet in middle ground, shake hands, and be reconciled.'

"If the insult be of a serious character, it will be the duty of the second of the challenger to say, in reply to the second of the challengee, 'We have been deeply wronged, and if you are not disposed to repair the injury, the contest must continue.' And if the challengee offers nothing in way of reparation, the fight continues until one or the other of the principals is hit."

Aiken and his second may have considered Cohen's accusation of unfair practice in the race as coming under the last provision of the code.

A number of Cohen's friends accompanied the body to his former home, Charleston, S. C. The Charleston "Courier," of August 22, 1870, said:

"Obsequies of Mr. Ludlow Cohen: The remains of this gentleman who fell in a duel on Friday last, in Savannah, Ga., were brought to the city on Saturday, and carried to the residence of his uncle, D. D. DeLeon, Esq., corner of Wentworth and Smith streets. The funeral took place yesterday at the house and continued at the cemetery, Coming street, according to his faith, and were concluded by the lodge of which he was a member. The deceased was well known here as a young gentleman of high tone and character."

CHAPTER XIX

SOME SAVANNAH COURTS OF HONOR

HOW THEY INTERVENED AND BROUGHT PEACE BETWEEN
IRATE INDIVIDUALS BENT ON HOSTILE MEETINGS—
THE DAVENPORT-LATHROP AND JOHNSTON-WETTER
MEETINGS—PROVISIONS OF THE STATE CODE RELA-
TIVE TO DUELLING—NEWSPAPER RIDICULE OF BOM-
BASTIC AGGRESSORS—THE "ROARING LION" OF LIB-
ERTY AND WAY—TROUBLE BETWEEN HONE AND
DAVIDSON, WARING AND ANDERSON, WARING AND
LEVY—HOW THE DANCY-OWENS AFFAIR WAS HAN-
DLED—HAYES AND HUNTER CHECKED BY WARRANT.
THE TOMPKINS-RUCKER TROUBLE ADJUSTED ON THE
FIELD—SAVANNAH REPRESENTED AT THE LAST DUEL
BETWEEN GEORGIANS, THE CALHOUN-WILLIAMSON
MEETING.

AFTER the meeting between Cohen and Aiken the pre-
war public mentality as far as duelling goes seems to
have begun to undergo a persistent change, and whatever
elements of approval of the practice still lingered disappeared after a few years.

In this early post-bellum period was the bloodless duel
between Benjamin R. Davenport and James W. Lathrop, Jr.
Tradition has it that this duel grew out of a quarrel at a
military dance over a trivial cause. Both of the young men
were officers in the Johnston Light Infantry, of which S.
Yates Levy, once a well-known figure in Savannah's legal
and literary circles, was captain. Levy was recognized as an
authority on the "Code" and figured in an advisory capacity
in several affairs of honor, but what part he played in the
trouble between his fellow officers of the militia company
is not remembered. As befitting military young men of high
temper, the difference, no matter how slight the reason
therefor, must necessarily be adjusted with bullets.

Dr. John M. Johnston acted as second for Davenport.
with Robert L. Mercer serving in that capacity for Lathrop.

The surgeons were Dr. Benjamin S. Purse for Davenport and Dr. John D. Fish for Lathrop. Dr. Read's place was selected as the meeting spot. This old Brampton plantation, originally the home of Jonathan Bryan, friend and co-laborer with Oglethorpe, had been for some years a favorite resort for Savannah duellists. Long before daybreak the seconds called for their principals and surgeons and all were on the ground by 5 a. m., there to await the dawn that would permit of the exchange of shots. The early start was made to prevent interference by the county officers, who, under the pressure of public opinion, had recently become quite vigilant in their efforts to enforce the laws against duelling.

As the parties gathered at the spot selected, Dr. Purse said to Dr. Fish:

"This matter ought to be adjusted; there is no sense in these boys shooting at each other. One of them may get hit."

Dr. Fish laughed. "Don't worry," said he. "I've been to ten duels, and I never saw any one hurt yet. You and I might as well have left our surgical instruments at home."

Dr. Fish's prediction, based on past experiences, proved well founded. Stationing the principals twenty paces apart, the usual preliminaries were carried out. At the signal to fire, Lathrop quickly pulled the trigger, sending the bullet over Davenport's head, and Davenport, appreciating this, aimed at the ground between him and his opponent.

Then the seconds performed their functions as arbitrators, the young men were, without reluctance, induced to shake hands and let bygones be bygones.

"They were a much relieved pair of boys," said Dr. Purse, forty-five years later, "and I was a much relieved surgeon, as I knew both families and disliked more than I can express it the idea of taking one or the other of the young men home wounded or dead. But Dr. Fish was right in his diagnosis. Duelling, generally speaking, had become rather a harmless sort of affair."

An amusing incident is told in connection with this duel. The sister of Davenport, afterwards Mrs. William Harden, was a teacher at the time. To her school room there came that morning a visitor, a Northern woman then investigating educational methods in Savannah. She had heard of the duel, but did not know the principals, and was eager to condemn the custom and the parties thereto.

"Have you heard that two young men are to fight a duel today?" asked she.

"Yes."

"It is a crime," said the Northern woman, with much heat. "They should both be imprisoned. Don't you think so?"

"Hardly, as one of them is my brother."

"Oh, what have I said? I beg your pardon a thousand times."

"Never mind. He came a few minutes ago to tell me that neither was wounded. They are friends now."

The visitor probably never understood the psychology of duelling, but thereafter she did understand that it was perhaps best to know the parties thereto before discussing them with acquaintances.

A little later trouble was that between Capt. Augustus P. Wetter, a well-known architect, and Capt. James H. Johnston, a gallant Confederate soldier, for many years superintendent of the Savannah street car lines. Both are well remembered by many Savannahians of today. R. Alexander Wayne, prominent merchant, was to act as second for Johnston, with Capt. Michael Cash, one of the city's leading contractors of that day, doing the honors for Wetter.

Dr. Purse was requested the day before the meeting to be in the vicinity of Causton Bluff the following day at noon, as "There might be a call for his services." Much secrecy was necessary, the sheriff being on the alert to arrest all parties concerned in the widely discussed prospective duel. At noon, Dr. Purse, surgical case in buggy, was maneuvering around the Bluff to find where his services were needed, when a buggy came dashing up and lawyers N. Calvin Collier and R. R. Richards alighted and began to question him. The first thought was that they had warrants to arrest all parties involved, but assurances were quickly given that they had come to act as friends of Capt. Johnston in place of Wayne. Collier fired a pistol in the air to attract the other parties to the spot, but some time elapsed before another buggy was seen coming along the weed-grown road as fast as a thoroughbred could bring it. Out of it jumped Wetter and Cash. After a long wait, with the other principal not appearing, the party separated, and made their way back to town by different routes, there to find that Capt. Johnston had been kept away from the Bluff by the sight of deputy sheriffs in that vicinity.

It was then necessary to get new seconds and surgeons to avoid detection and the next day and the day thereafter the principals, who had been under cover, got out of the city and to Wilmington Island. There their differences were considered at length by friends and finally a satisfactory adjustment was reached without the use of the firearms provided. The "Morning News" made but a brief mention of the affair, although the entire city had been discussing it for four or five days, and the sole question when men met was "Have you heard from the Johnston-Wetter duel?" Here is the published account of how the doves of peace figuratively perched on the duelling pistols and cooed affectionately to each other:

"The affair of honor which has been the subject of intense interest in the city for several days was satisfactorily settled yesterday. The challenged party went to Wilmington Island on Wednesday morning and the other party arrived on the ground late yesterday morning, the meeting having been delayed through the efforts of the officers of the law to arrest the principals. The amicable settlement of the affair has been a subject of congratulation among the friends of both parties."

At this time the laws of Georgia relative to duelling were specific and sufficiently severe, if enforced, to make participation in such an encounter fraught possibly with very unpleasant consequences to all involved, although as a matter of fact no one was ever punished. Under the State Code of 1873, sending or accepting a challenge made one liable to a fine of $500 and imprisonment in the county jail for not exceeding six months, or, if the jury so recommended, the imprisonment could be made in the penitentiary, with hard labor, for not less than one year nor longer than two years. The seconds were subject to the same penalties as the principals. If a duel were actually fought, the principals were guilty of "high misdemeanor" and on conviction were punishable by imprisonment with labor in the penitentiary for not less than four nor more than eight years. If death should ensue from a duel, "all parties, both principals and seconds," were held to be guilty of murder, and on conviction were to suffer the death penalty unless such sentence was commuted.

Any justice or other public peace officer, having knowledge of the intention to fight a duel, and who "should not use and exert his official authority to arrest the parties and prevent the duel," was punishable on conviction with dismissal from office. Any person sending or accepting a challenge, or aiding or abetting a duel, was to be disfranchised and debarred from voting or holding office, in addition to being subject to the other penalties imposed by law. The State Code also provided that any person who in a newspaper or handbill, written or printed, published any other person as a coward, or used any other opprobrious or abusive language for not accepting a challenge or fighting a duel, should be, on conviction, fined $1,000 and imprisoned not to exceed six months, to work on the chaingang not to exceed twelve months, any one or more in the discretion of the court. The printer or publisher was likewise made a witness in such cases, and if he refused to divulge the writer of the card, he was to be considered as the author and punished as such and also held in contempt of court.

Similar provisions are found in the Code of 1861, except that posting or publishing a man with opprobrious epithets brought a fine of $500 and a jail sentence not exceeding sixty days. As far back as the Code of 1817 penalties covering all these features of duelling are to be found. The legislators had done their best toward breaking up the practice, but the public sentiment to sustain the laws had not heretofore existed. The increasing disposition to enforce the statutes, and the greater likelihood of juries refusing to longer look indulgently on those resorting to the "Code Duello" explain the exertions, or apparent exertions, of the various public peace officers in Chatham to do their duty and the necessity for Savannah duellists and their companions covering their movements with the veil of secrecy.

In the years that followed the Civil War a tendency became apparent to ridicule duels which were the topic of widespread talk but failed to materialize into definite action, or where there were ludicrous features that lent themselves to the shafts of raillery. W. T. Thompson, author of "Major Jones' Courtship" and other stories of Georgia life, was editor of the "Morning News," with Joel Chandler Harris, of later "Uncle Remus" fame, as his associate. While they kept their humor within bounds, they occasionally made a duel that fell cold and flat the subject of ironical comments that perhaps pierced the hides of bellicose individuals, even if a mutual exchange of bullets did not. Here is one of the "News" thrusts at a still-born affair of honor in 1872:

"ANOTHER DUEL FIASCO: Late Thursday night, a certain young gentleman of this city, representing one of the First Families of Virginia, visited one of our leading hotels, became offended at one of the clerks, and threw him his card, at the same time asking if he knew what that meant. The clerk, without hesitation, replied that he did and would be ready to receive any communication which the Virginian might send through a third party. The consequence was that yesterday the second of the Virginian called on the second of the Canadian and assured him that he meant business—that his gentleman would exhibit no white feathers. The clerk's second responded very much in the same spirit and claimed the choice of weapons, when it was arranged that, in a quiet kind of place, the affair of honor would be settled this morning to the satisfaction of all parties. About half past two o'clock yesterday afternoon the friends of the Virginian apologized for their friend—and from the popping of pistols the sound was changed to the popping of corks."

Again, the same year, when two Liberty countyites fell out about politics and one slapped the other's face, Harris— or it may have been Thompson—made subsequent developments the occasion for a picture that must have intensely amused the people of Liberty, at least. The political attitude of the challenger had doubtless put him outside the pale of public sympathy and invited the satirical pen.

After some persiflage describing the entry of the armed and irate colonel from Liberty into Savannah, the "News" treated the incident with more levity than would have been tolerated a decade or two before. The writer evidently enjoyed what he was penning:

"Some time ago a controversy sprang up between Mr. Walter A. Way, of Tebeauville, Liberty County, and Colonel Wm. B. Gaulden, sometimes known as the 'Roaring Lion of Liberty,' in regard to the expulsion of the latter from the Democratic committee in consequence of his announcement as an independent candidate for Senator, in opposition to the regular nominee of the party. Several communications were published in one of the city papers, in which they handled each other without gloves. It was supposed that the offensive remarks would result in a difficulty, but nothing was heard of it until a few days since, when it is reported that Mr. Way met Colonel Gaulden in Hinesville and slapped his face.

"The gallant colonel, who, it seems, possessed wonderful control over his temper, did not resent the insult at the time, but intimated his intention to appeal to the code of honor. In pursuance of this determination, he endeavored to obtain a second, but was unsuccessful, and was compelled to send a challenge to Mr. Way by a particular friend of the latter, who only carried it as a favor and with the understanding that he had nothing to do with the affair. Mr. Way, it is stated, read the challenge, filed it away, and took no further notice of it. The colonel, it seems, concluded, or expressed the belief, that the challenged party would meet him at the appointed place, Screven Ferry, on the South Carolina side of the river.

"During Saturday morning he hunted round Savannah for a second and asked two gentlemen to act in that capacity for him, but both declined the honor. The colonel, who had his spirit up, gave out the impression that Mr. Way was in town and that he was hunting for him. The gentleman was not here, it seems, and after spending a fruitless

day on the war path, with his rifle as company, Colonel
Gaulden left with an acquaintance for Screven Ferry in the
afternoon, concluding that as his enemy was not in the city
he had gone over to the Ferry and was awaiting him. On
his arrival at the grounds the savagerous colonel hunted
around, but no game worthy of his mammoth rifle offered,
and disappointed he returned to the city. The report that
Mr. Way had sent a challenge to Colonel Gaulden, we are
informed, is untrue; that face slapping proceeding was the
extent of his code. The colonel with his trusty rifle left
for home on the 7 o'clock train. We learn that, in a brief
conversation with the party who checked his rifle, he stated
that he had been over to Screven Ferry to meet a man but
that he was not there. The colonel expressed gratification
at his absence, saying 'If he had been there, I would have
killed him, and I am glad he kept out of the way.' So this
wild hunt for gore resulted in a grand fiasco, and the colonel
will probably live to fight many more such duels."

In this incident, even though the "Colonel" had made
himself a legitimate butt for ridicule, there is an intimation
that the code duello was falling from its former high estate,
that a change in the tone and standards of life in this section was doing for it what Cervantes did for a ludicrously
degenerated chivalry in his Don Quixote, making it the
target of satire and jeering laughter when occasion offered,
against which no custom, no matter how time-honored, could
long continue to exist.

Tradition throws a somewhat different light on this
incident. Many a better man than "Colonel" Gaulden has
been forgotten by Liberty countyites, but reminiscences of
that obstreperous and somewhat picturesque character sur-
vive. The living who still recall him describe the "Roaring
Lion" as fully seven feet tall, straight as an Indian, of a
dark, swarthy complexion, with high cheek bones. Overbearing and dictatorial to those whom he thought he could
insult with impunity, he persistently resorted to bulldozing
tactics in his court practice. Without finished culture, or refinement either of feeling or in conduct, he was nevertheless
a born lawyer. Wrote a former prominent Liberty County
attorney to me:

"He was powerful as an advocate and it was rarely he lost a case before a jury. His success was due entirely to his strong natural abilities in cross-examination and as a pleader and to his unscrupulous use of them. He lived about three miles from Hinesville for years and had considerable practice in the courts there. On the trial of a case there he crossed swords with Way, who had bitterly attacked his desertion of the Democratic party and claims of old allegiance in sentiment to the Republicans. During the argument Gaulden used language personally offensive to Way, who, without hesitation, vigorously slapped his face in open court.

"The court habitues expected a personal difficulty immediately after adjournment, but Gaulden appeared to avoid it. Later he challenged Way, who accepted it, the duel to be fought in South Carolina. Way, though, was soon after arrested on a warrant issued, it was reported, at the instance of Gaulden through a friend, and in this way deprived of the opportunity to meet Gaulden. It was then that the 'Roaring Lion,' 'armed like an arsenal,' traveled to Savannah and across to the Ferry, and returning boasted of 'having backed Way down'."

The war records of the two men illuminated their varying types. Way volunteered at the beginning in the famous old Liberty Independent Troop and served throughout the war, mostly in Virginia. During part of the war he was in the command under Colonel Pierce M. B. Young, afterwards brigadier-general, and took part in a famous charge under that gallant officer. On that occasion Young volunteered to charge with his command across a bridge, heavily protected by Federals, and take the enemy's guns which were playing havoc with the Confederates. The charge was lead by Young, it is said, with the exclamation, "Follow me, boys. Here's to hell or a brigadier-generalship." The guns were captured and Young was promoted. At this and other times Way displayed cool courage to such an extent as to win the admiration of his comrades. Gaulden, on the other hand, is stated never to have smelled powder except at a Savannah review. Soon after hostilities began he secured permission from Governor Brown to organize a regiment, of which he was to be colonel, and advertised in the "Morning News" and other papers for "patriotic Georgians" to enlist in it. The responses were evidently not flattering to Gaulden's pride. Three years later, when Sherman was marching on Savannah, he made a further abortive effort, it is stated, and perhaps got together a semblance of an organization and assumed the title of "Colonel." "If any one under Gaulden ever fired a gun at the enemy, no Liberty County citizen recalls it," is the emphatic declaration of one acquainted with Liberty's history. His war record and his duelling record appear to have been along parallel lines.

Gaulden, as did some others, became a vociferous "Loyal Citizen" as soon as the war was over. He had been a member of the Baltimore convention and had supported Douglass there. In a speech at Savannah, in May, 1865, he declared that when secession was advocated he had sought to "bring the people to their senses out of their frenzy and madness," and denounced the organizers of the secession movement as "traitors to constitutional liberty," and laid at their doors the "responsibility of the widows' tears and the orphans' cries." He hoped the Georgia Union Club would "succeed in keeping down the leading traitors, but still guard themselves against malignant feeling." He is a striking illustration of those who, born and reared in the South and professing devotion and adherence to the Confederacy, quickly veered and won for themselves the title by which they will always be known—"scalawags."

The number of duels actually fought does not indicate or approach the number of local difficulties of a grave nature which arose during the last years in which the code was recognized and followed in Savannah, but which were happily disposed of by wise and cool counsellors. On many occasions, without publicity, differences which might otherwise have progressed to an impasse, only to be broken by recourse to pistols, were quickly and satisfactorily handled by committees or courts of friends. At other times the correspondence and ruling of the "Court of Honor" were published for the protection of the principals who regarded themselves as standing before the bar of public opinion and public judgment.

"Commodore" William Hone is still remembered by many Savannahians. Few recall, though, that fifty-two years ago he was challenged by William M. Davidson, another well-known citizen of that period, as a result of an unpleasant personal allusion Hone had made at a public sale at the custom house.

Both were wholesalers of liquors, jealous as to business supremacy in their line. The trouble grew out of an importation of fine French brandy Hone had made. Until Bimini and the swamps of Bryan County became the chief sources of its supplies, Savannah prided itself on the quality of liquors it imbibed. "Commodore" Hone selected his importations with the greatest care and entering them directly through the custom house took no chances of substitutions en route.

In this particular instance a barrel of extra-quality brandy was found sadly depleted in contents when Hone called for it. Either it had leaked out on its way across the Atlantic or the "Carpetbag" collector had looked elsewhere while his "Black Republican" minions in the granite building on the Bay sucked twenty-six gallons through a crack in the bung. Hone properly refused to pay duty on fifty gallons and the government ordered the barrel and its contents confiscated and sold.

When the deputy called for bids Hone made a public statement of the facts, from his standpoint, and bid $1 a gallon. Much to his disgust and anger, his rival, Davidson, bid $4 and the brandy was knocked down to him. It was then that the "Commodore" indulged in language more heated than polite.

The inevitable demand for a retraction came. Hone declined to give it. Under the circumstances, he maintained, "No proper thinking person would have bid against me without intending to show a marked hostility to me." Davidson disclaimed any intention to injure Hone by his action at the sale and authorized his friend, Major A. Bonaud, to make all the necessary arrangements for a meeting under the code.

Before plans could be perfected, Henry Brigham and Edward J. Harden intervened and suggested General Robert H. Anderson, General W. W. Kirkland and G. B. Lamar, Jr., as referees. These gentlemen wrote the principals: "Before accepting so delicate a responsibility we beg to know if you are willing to bind yourselves to abide our decision."

Both agreed to this, the challenge was withdrawn, and the correspondence and statements of facts were turned over to the committee. The referees ruled:

"In our opinion the act complained of by Mr. Hone did not warrant his insulting language. It was at best only ungenerous. Our decision is that Mr. Hone should retract his offensive language and Mr. Davidson express his regrets at the unintentional injury complained of by Mr. Hone."

In this case, as in others, the referees found a way of appeasing the wrath of both principals. No matter how apparently unfavorable the prospects when they began their labors of love, they inevitably found some "Balm in Gilead" to apply to the rasped feelings of honor. No principal ever seems to have been entirely in the right or hopelessly in the wrong.

The committee of conciliation, or Court of Honor, of which glimpses are seen in the proceedings of the Anti-Duelling Association, came very much into evidence in the last years of duelling. Probably the most distinguished of these boards of referees that ever investigated and satisfactorily disposed of a serious trouble between Savannahians was that which, early in 1876, intervened between Robert R. Dancy and George W. Owens. The procedure in this instance was similar to that in other cases not so well remembered, or the details of which have not been preserved. It illuminates the manner in which friends interposed their good offices and exerted themselves to avoid duels—or, what was worse, street encounters with pistols.

The original source of the trouble in this instance lead to Mr. Dancy applying opprobrious language to Mr. Owens on the street, resulting in the latter striking Dancy, followed by a physical struggle between the two. Mr. Dancy immediately challenged Mr. Owens, who replied under date of January 27:

"I am in receipt of your communication of this date, through the hand of your friend, Mr. Steele McA. White, in which you say: 'After our meeting of yesterday I suppose you are prepared to give me the satisfaction due any gentleman.' In reply, I will say that I always hold myself as a gentleman ready to exact reparation for an affront offered to me, and to accord proper and due satisfaction for one extended by me. But under the circumstances, I am convinced that, after mature reflection, you will consider the occurrence of yesterday no more than might have been expected by you as a result of the insulting and opprobrious language used toward me. Having promptly resented it, as any gentleman would have done, I do not consider that I am called upon in this matter to answer any presumed claim for satisfaction which you might entertain. This will be handed you by my friend, Mr. W. H. Daniel."

News of the difficulty between the two men soon became widespread and aroused a feeling that efforts should be made to bring about a restoration of amity. To that end Colonel George A. Mercer, Colonel Charles H. Olmstead and General Henry R. Jackson intervened as pacificators. In a letter to Messrs. White and Daniel, they said: "We do not think that the quarrel is of such a nature as to require mortal combat, but that it is capable of honorable adjustment. As disinterested parties, and with friendly sentiments to both principals, we take the liberty of requesting a submission of the matter to such mutual friends as you may select, and that a reasonable delay be allowed in the premises."

The following day Dancy wrote to Owens: "Your note is unsatisfactory. Amongst gentlemen, Wilson's code of honor, in this community, has long been considered authority. I refer you to chapter 8, paragraph 2, and I again peremptorily demand satisfaction at your hands, feeling that you have deeply aggrieved me. I hope you may prove a generous foe, and not stand upon technicalities or push me to the final requirements of the code to procure the satisfaction that is clearly due."

The rule of the code referred to read: "When words are used and a blow given in return, the insult is avenged, and if redress be sought it must be from the person receiving the blow."

Back came the immediate answer from Owens: "I peremptorily decline to accede to your presumed claim for satisfaction, fully impressed with the conviction that my action in doing so is correct and proper under the circumstances."

Four days had passed since the altercation on the street between the principals and the situation was regarded as exceedingly grave. At this juncture, Mr. Robert N. Gourdin, General J. F. Gilmer and General Henry R. Jackson intervened. A letter signed by them was sent to the representatives of the principals, Messrs. White and Daniel:

"Understanding that the unhappy difference between Messrs. R. R. Dancy and George W. Owens remains unadjusted, and apprehending that it may lead to consequences which this community would deeply deplore, we respectfully request that you will submit the same to a committee of gentlemen in whom you have confidence, that it may, if possible, be settled peaceably and amicably, consistently with the honor of both. Should you consent to make this reference, we suggest that the cartel be suspended for forty-eight hours, and the correspondence, with the matters in controversy, be submitted to the gentlemen who may be chosen."

This letter was handed to the friends of the principals by Dr. J. T. MacFarland.

W. H. Daniel, in reply, pointed out that the "peremptory challenge of Mr. Dancy having been renewed, and in the latter instance accompanied also with a threatened course of action on his part, reassures me in the correctness of the position assumed. As long as the challenge and accompanying threat of Mr. Dancy continue in force, Mr. Owens must continue to reserve an affirmative or negative response to your request."

Steele McA. White wrote to the voluntary conciliators that he would "suspend the proceedings I proposed to take for the vindication of my friend, R. R. Dancy, until 8 o'clock p. m. on Tuesday night, February 1. I regret I cannot comply with your further request for the suspension of the cartel. It is not in my power to do so. Mr. Owens having declined it, I hold that none exists."

The following day Chairman Gourdin wrote to White suggesting that further proceedings be suspended until the benefit of the counsel of General Joseph E. Johnston could be had. White accepted this suggestion.

In this connection it is recalled that General Johnston had been successful in adjusting several difficulties between gentlemen of Savannah, his patience, tact, high standing as a soldier and as a Christian gentleman, contributing to his influence in that direction.

In one instance, it is told, the principals were unusually hot-headed and obstinate and the other members of the committee were inclined to throw up their hands in despair and allow them to settle the trouble on the field.

General Johnston refused to consent to this.

"Gentlemen," said he, "remember the Master's words: 'Blessed are the peacemakers.' Let us persevere."

The committee continued its work and in the end smoothed out the trouble and brought a lasting peace between the principals.

General Johnston accepted the delicate task again in this Dancy-Owens affair, uniting with General Gilmer, General Jackson and Mr. Gourdin. It was soon decided that an "obstacle still existed to the committee taking the matter up, in the threat of posting indulged in by Mr. Dancy in his second challenge. The non-existence of the challenge because declined is held not to have removed with it the threat," it was pointed out to White, and it was urged that it be withdrawn.

"We ask only what is usual and held to be proper in such cases and feel confident that you will not hesitate to make the withdrawal."

White replied that "it was not intended as a threat, but merely indicating what course we would be compelled to pursue, deprecating, as we did, a street encounter, and preferring a fair and square fight upon the field." The implied threat was then formally withdrawn and the suggested reference of the trouble to the committee of four was accepted by both principals.

Gen. Joseph E. Johnston, Who Composed Many Savannah Differences
and Prevented Duels.
"Remember the Master's Words, 'Blessed Are the Peacemakers,'"
Said He.

The next day the committee made its award, holding that Mr. Dancy had no sufficient cause of quarrel and erred in seeking redress in such a manner as to cause a street encounter with Mr. Owens.

"Nevertheless," held the committee, "in view of all the circumstances, his honor as a gentleman has been fully vindicated by his course of action and nothing further upon his part is required by any code of honor."

The course of Mr. Owens "commanded the full approbation" of the committee, who "saw nothing to prevent the existence of friendly relations between these gentlemen."

The award was signed by the entire committee, Robert N. Gourdin, J. F. Gilmer, Henry R. Jackson, Joseph E. Johnston, four of the most prominent men in Georgia at that period, and published for the information of the public that had been for nearly two weeks discussing the matter and awaiting the final issue.

Seven months before this, in June, 1875, a committee on which two of the same former Confederate generals— Johnston and Gilmer—served together with a third, Gen. A. R. Lawton, brought to a peaceful settlement the difficulty between two well-known young commission merchants, C. C. Hardwick and Robert Wayne.

This grew out of a quarrel at the sale of pools on the races of the Regatta Association of Georgia. Blows were struck, a physician and a lawyer were secured as seconds, and events rapidly drew toward a hostile meeting. News spread abroad and came to Magistrate Elsinger, who, mindful of the law which made him removable from office if he failed to attempt to stop a duel, issued warrants for principals and seconds. One principal got across the river, the other and the seconds were taken into custody. At the hearing Solicitor General Law represented the majesty of the State, while William U. Garrard represented the principal under arrest and R. R. Richards the seconds. The defendants were all discharged and arrangements for a duel proceeded. It was then that the committee came into being and succeeded in conciliating the principals and adjusting the matter in accordance with the code.

Those in position to know say that probably in no other community did the old leaders of the hosts of the Confederacy do such magnificently effective work in restoring peaceful relations between men intent on duelling as was accomplished by those who for many years after the war were the most honored and beloved of Savannahians. Men naturally turned to them for the settlement of the grave questions of personal honor and courage involved in such disputes, and apparently they never failed to hold the headstrong in check until, by careful hearing of the facts and a conscientious consideration of the positions of the principals, they could speak without bias or prejudice, do justice to each, and, by awards that were manifestly based on truth and justice and friendship for both, persuade them to lay aside the duelling pistols and re-establish amicable, if not cordial, relations.

Out of the yellow fever epidemic of 1876 there developed trouble between Dr. James J. Waring and Mayor Edward C. Anderson, which culminated in a challenge from the Mayor's son to the physician to give him "the satisfaction due a gentleman."

Dr. Waring was unsparing in his criticism of what he openly denounced as "The indifference or incapacity of the Mayor of Savannah to alleviate or arrest the epidemic." The doctor criticised verbally, at meetings of the physicians, and in the public prints. Finally he attacked Mayor Anderson for "supineness and indifference" in handling the situation and referred to him as a "professional office holder and politician." This was in October, when the fever was at its height.

E. M. Anderson, son of the Mayor, resented what he considered "venemous and insulting insinuations," which, he declared, his "father, in view of his official position, could not resent," and through his friend, T. S. Wayne, Jr., demanded an unmistakable apology over Dr. Waring's signature.

As Colonel Cuthbert had done in 1788 in his dispute with Major McIntosh, Dr. Waring declined to recognize young Anderson's right to interfere in the matter. He had never met the Mayor's son, he declared, and did not know him. Young Anderson reiterated his demand for a "correction of misstatements and a disavowal of insulting insinuations." Back came the doctor's reply: "I cannot recognize your right to make the demand," and the next day Anderson wrote: "I demand of you the personal satisfaction customary among gentlemen." "My friend, Mr. T. S. Wayne, Jr., will deliver this to you and he will represent me in the arrangements of the preliminaries of a meeting between us."

Dr. Waring in a card to the people of Savannah said: "In spite of a spirit of forbearance, which must manifest itself to you in this correspondence, and in spite of the determination that a young man, untrammeled by responsibilities of business or of family, should not interfere in a difference between men of mature years, the young gentleman has persistently forced upon me the alternative of a violation of the moral law and the laws of the State of Georgia, or of maintaining in a quiet, and I trust dignified, manner the cause I advocate, which is the cause of all the people, the right of free speech, and the right of criticism and censure, if deserved, of public men. I shall not yield this right. Any misstatements of mine I would most cheerfully correct, and if I have made any unfair deductions from the facts I should always be most happy to withdraw them, but not at the threat or menace of a party whose right to interfere I do not recognize. I have placed this young gentleman under bond for good behavior, and if driven to the necessity I will prosecute criminally in the courts of law the offender."

A few days later young Anderson withdrew his challenge through his friend, T. B. Chisholm, claiming that Dr. Waring had forfeited the recognition due a gentleman under the code by his procedure in issuing a peace warrant against him. In a final bitter card to the public, Anderson pointed out that Dr. Waring himself, on April 28, 1868, had made a demand "on one of our most estimable citizens for the satisfaction customary amongst gentlemen," and claimed that the disparity in his age and that of the doctor was no greater than that between the Mayor's and the doctor's ages. Here the matter was permitted to stand, although the feeling remained acute for some time between the Andersons and the physician, who continued his criticisms of the mayor's policies during the epidemic, but in a more decorous and professional language. The next year Dr. Waring was again elected an alderman, he having previously served in the City Council in 1866-69.

Anderson was correct in his contention that the doctor eight years before had been involved in a dispute with a prominent citizen and had sent him a challenge. Old citizens still dimly recall this as the Waring-Levy affair, the other party to it being Capt. S. Yates Levy, then the editor of the Savannah "Advertiser."

Levy's connection with Savannah journalism was brief but spirited. Brilliant as a lawyer and literateur, with polished dramas to his credit, one of which, "Venetia, or the Italian Bride," was presented in New York, Boston and other cities by Miss Eliza Logan, one of the popular lights of the American stage of that period, who had achieved her first success in Savannah, Capt. Levy carried his fearlessness and forcefulness into the newspaper arena at a time when Savannah still lay under the domination of the Federal troops. As Agnew said of him:

"On January 1, 1868, S. Yates Levy, Esq., engaged as editor-in-chief of the 'Advertiser.' Under his able management the paper at once took rank with the leading journals of the State. Mr. Levy was a vigorous and fearless writer, pointing out and condemning abuses wherever discovered. So keen were some of his remarks upon the tyrannical actions of the military that an order was sent from General Meade to either suppress the paper or moderate the tone of its editorials. Soon after Mr. Levy was obliged by military pressure to retire from the editorial chair."

Levy's editorship was but four months old when the trouble came with Dr. Waring. Differences of political views and judgments were at the bottom of it. An editorial appeared in the "Advertiser," in which there was no name used and no direct reference to the physician. Apparently some of the doctor's friends aggravated him by intimations that it was meant for him. Aroused and indignant, he wrote to the editor, pointing out that a paragraph in the editorial reflecting upon the "personal character of an educated and professional man," "whose name you withhold for reasons of your own," was construed as pointing to him, and demanding to know if he were the party intended.

Editor Levy's answer was to the point. "I am constrained to say that such a question is extraordinary and unprecedented in journalism, and I cannot recognize your right to require an answer to it, any more than any and every other member of society."

With his sensibilities ruffled and wounded in all likelihood by the further remarks of associates, Dr. Waring repeated his demand:

"In the opinion and belief of various friends," declared he, "I was the person referred to in your editorial. Doubtless you did not intend to commit yourself in the article alluded to, but you went far enough to lead others to infer that I was the person. Any communication that does not admit or deny the fact will be regarded as an admission that I am the party referred to. This will be handed you by my friend, Capt. David Waldhauer, who will receive your reply."

The editor again refused to reconsider his position and the physician formally demanded a "retraction of the offensive language contained in that article." But he obtained no satisfaction from Levy. "As a member of the editorial fraternity," answered he, "I will not, at your solicitation, violate the established rules which govern it upon such a subject. I do not recognize your right to make of me any of the demands contained in your several notes."

The doctor insisted that the editor was seeking to shield himself from giving redress by hiding behind the "established rules of the editorial fraternity," that he had afforded Levy an opportunity to make amende for the article that aggrieved him, "and it is now only left for me to demand the satisfaction customary amongst gentlemen. My friend, Capt. Waldhauer, will confer with any friend whom you may name, and arrange all preliminaries for a meeting."

Capt. Levy was a brave soldier and courageous editor. When this crisis came in the correspondence he did not hesitate. His reply was immediate, brief and unmistakable:

"I shall grant you the satisfaction you demand. My friend, Henry Williams, Esq., has kindly consented to perform on my part all that is necessary in the premises."

On Friday, May 1, Capt. Waldhauer and Mr. Williams, as duly selected seconds for the prospective duel, met for the purpose of arranging the terms to be observed at the meeting between the doctor and the editor. But before coming to an agreement as to time, place and weapons, a note came, signed by H. W. Mercer, Henry Brigham and Henry R. Jackson, suggesting that the matters in controversy be submitted to gentlemen of the seconds' selection, "with a view to a settlement which shall be in accordance with the laws of honor and which will avoid the necessity of a hostile meeting."

There was a prompt acquiescence. Capt. Waldhauer accepted the proposal for his principal and asked the three gentlemen to "undertake the proposed mediatorial office." Williams insisted that the challenge from Dr. Waring be first withdrawn, which was done, and then accepted mediation. The volunteer committee declined to act as arbitrators, however, and William Hunter, John Screven, Robert H. Anderson and George S. Owens, among the most prominent Savannahians of their day, were chosen.

Fourteen days after the beginning of the bellicose correspondence this "Committee of Honor" announced that it had been "unable to discover anything in the editorial which particularizes any individual specially," and that there "was not sufficient reason for the assumption by Dr. Waring that he was the person alluded to." The committee further held that "whilst we recognize fully the equal responsibility of an editor of a public journal and a private citizen for abusive or insulting language, yet we cannot admit the right of everyone who pleases to consider himself the subject of remarks couched in general terms to compel the editor by this self application either to withdraw the article or render satisfaction. Such a course would be productive of endless difficulties and injure the usefulness of the press as censors of public conduct. We feel constrained, however, to express our disapprobation of the imputation of improper 'motives' to any one to whom the article in question may be conceived to apply."

This last sentence may be looked upon in the light of an emollient to the offended physician or any other Savannahians who were constrained to believe that Capt. Levy's impersonal editorial strictures had concealed personal allusions to themselves. It took some of the sting out of the award so far as the doctor was concerned.

The Waring-Anderson affair was not the only one that was disposed of by the swearing out of warrants. In 1872 a difficulty arose between William C. Hayes and James Hunter. Hayes alleged that when he called at the offices of Bryan & Hunter, brokers, on business, Hunter became abusive and used insulting language to him and refused to retract. Representing Hayes, Major Charles Macmurdo, a well-known insurance agent of a half century ago, handed Hunter a note demanding satisfaction. Hunter sent it back and refused to receive any further communications, informing Hayes' friend that he would not accept a challenge.

According to a published statement by T. L. Robertson, a kinsman of Hayes, "before any further action could be taken Mr. Hayes and Major Macmurdo were arrested on warrants issued at the instance of Major Henry Bryan," Hunter's partner. It was claimed that this "evinced a malicious intention to have these gentlemen indicted, tried, and if possible imprisoned for violation of a law repugnant to every man who, finding his dignity assailed and his honor outraged, is determined at all hazards to protect the one and redress the other," and that Hunter was "sheltered from the consequences of his conduct by this appeal to the law."

The intimation was made that there was collusion between Hunter and his partner in the issuing of the warrants. Major Bryan indignantly denied this. Hearing of the trouble between the men, he said, and ascertaining that "personal interference would be useless," he had gone on his own volition "to Judge Chisholm's house at night and presented two warrants for his signature, sending them when signed to the sheriff for service." "I simply set in motion that legal machinery which every member of society may use in such cases. I did not push the law. I am not seeking to aggravate the quarrel or maliciously pursue any individual." "My conviction and my sense of social duty impel me to check, if possible, or mitigate a quarrel occurring within the sphere of my personal association. I acted on my sole individual judgment and called in the summary interposition of the law of Georgia to arrest what I presumed might prove to be a bloody, if not fatal, termination of the pending difficulty."

Hunter declared that Major Bryan had acted without his knowledge or approval and that he had expressed his decided disapprobation of the course his partner had taken. He declared that Hayes' note challenging him had been so discourteous in tone that it had been returned to the writer through a friend. If this were so, he was acting in accordance with the dictates of Wilson's Code, which prescribed, "If the note received be in abusive terms, object to its reception and return it for that reason," and which further specifically insisted that the note must be "in the language of a gentleman."

The warrants against Hayes and Macmurdo were changed so as to avoid a prosecution under the anti-duelling laws and they were simply placed under bonds to keep the peace. The atmosphere was soon after cleared and a hostile meeting avoided in that way. This and other incidents showed how recourse to the law was apt to be misconstrued and complicate a trouble by provoking an insinuation of cowardice.

The feeling that duels were private matters that did not concern the general public still lingered in many minds. Major Charles S. Hardee, now and for so many years Savannah's city treasurer, was at this time the editor of the "Daily Republican," and in that capacity he gave voice to this long cherished sentiment as to the right of gentlemen to arrange for the settlement of their private differences without the public interfering. Wrote he as to this particular affair:

"Rumor hath it that the code has been called upon to settle a personal difficulty between two well-known gentlemen of the city of Savannah. We have been made acquainted with the facts, which, it is thought, warrant this resort; but while we are non-committal on the question of the duello, we regard these matters as entirely private, and not the subject of local paragraphs. The least said (in such cases) the sooner end it."

While the would-be duellists of this period were sometimes compelled to remain under cover during the making of the arrangements for their meetings, this may not have been due to any fear in their minds of unpleasant results under the law in the event that the duels actually occurred. Truth to tell, the judge on the bench and the solicitor-general charged with the prosecution of such cases, had themselves resorted to the code and could not be regarded as having very pronounced sentiments against it or its devotees. Many prominent citizens, some of whom were apt to be on the grand jury, had likewise imperilled their lives and the lives of others in similar fashion. The tendency to defy the state statutes as to duelling, while less pronounced than before the war, was still sufficiently in evidence to show a reasonable assurance of safety from vigorous prosecution. In fact, during the whole duelling period no Savannahian seems to have been haled into court and forced to face a jury for participation in an affair of honor.

Judge Henry B. Tompkins, who presided over the Savannah circuit at this time, had before his elevation to the bench traveled across the river and faced another attorney with the usual code formalities. He and T. W. Rucker, so well known here and throughout the state as "Tinie" Rucker, had a falling out in a magistrate's court in 1872 over a case in which they were opposing counsel. A sharp exchange of unpleasantries was followed by a quick resort to the code, and before any committee could adjust the trouble the two young lawyers met with their duelling pistols at hand ready for use. On the field, however, cooler heads succeeded in averting a tragedy and they returned to Savannah with the cases carrying exactly the same number of bullets with which they had been taken from the city.

As usual, the "Morning News" withheld names in its reference to this affair, which follows:

"Yesterday our citizens down town were on the qui vive in regard to an affair of honor which was pending between two lawyers of this city. It appears from what we can learn that the difficulty grew out of a case in Justice Elsinger's court, in which one of them impugned the veracity of the other. A written request was made for a retraction, which was met with a refusal, and the result was a challenge and an acceptance. The place selected was the well-known duelling ground at Screven Ferry, and the weapons chosen were pistols—distance ten paces—and yesterday at five o'clock the appointed time for the hostile meeting. As the parties were about to be placed in position, the friends of the challenged party stated that they could submit a proposition which would lead to an honorable adjustment of the difficulty. After some parley the matter was amicably arranged by a disclaimer of the offensive language which was the cause of the affair. The parties returned to the city about seven o'clock."

Judge Tompkins was an Alabamian who had fought bravely through the war, and when nineteen years of age, after valiant service on the field, commanded a company. He was wounded in the head at Chickamauga and shot through the body at Atlanta. His opponent was equally brave, and without the intervention of friends at the duelling ground a fatal result would probably have ensued from their meeting. Tompkins is described as a man of fine personal appearance, large, tall, with an air of dignity but devoid of arrogance, affable in manner, pleasant in conversation, fond of society, just and generous and an able attorney. Appointed by Governor Smith in 1875 to fill the unexpired term of Judge William Schley, he remained on the bench here five years, 1875-79, during which time the noted Telfair will case, and the remarkable efforts of English descendants of the Boltons to lay claim to a large part of Savannah, were argued before him. From Savannah the judge removed to Atlanta, where he became a prominent member of the bar. It was during his life there that he took part in a minor way in the last duel fought in Georgia, the unique Calhoun-Williamson affair in 1889.

The principals and seconds in this duel are recalled by many Savannahians. Patrick Calhoun, grandson of the famous John C., was at one time general counsel of the Richmond Terminal Co., and J. R. Williamson was one of North Georgia's railroad magnates of that period. Before a legislative investigating committee Calhoun made a remark which was construed as deliberately reflecting on the integrity of Williamson. A sharp denunciation of the statement as a falsehood lead to a demand from Calhoun for an apology, which was refused, and Calhoun sent a challenge which was accepted. Capt. Harry Jackson, son of General Henry R. Jackson, of Savannah, became Calhoun's second, with Capt. Jack King acting for Williamson, with Judge Tompkins acting also as a friend and in an advisory capacity for the challengee.

Gordon N. Hurtel, of the Atlanta "Constitution," has told of the duel in detail. By different rail routes the parties sought a meeting place in Alabama. There were amusing incidents with country sheriffs seeking to arrest them before they finally succeeded in facing each other at a secluded spot, whether in this State or Alabama no one knows. For some reason Calhoun objected to Judge Tompkins leaving the train and going on the field as a witness of the meeting. Hammerless Smith & Wesson pistols were used, each carrying five bullets, the arrangement being that five shots were to be exchanged, if necessary. Williamson interpreted this that each principal could fire the five shots as quickly and as continuously as he might desire. When the signal to fire was given he proceeded to unload his pistol in the direction of Calhoun, but the five bullets whizzed by without reaching the target. Calhoun had fired one shot and paused. Williamson was at his mercy, with the right in Calhoun to take deliberate aim four successive times, if he wished to do so.

"Capt. Williamson," said Calhoun, "I have four bullets left and I demand that you retract the insult you offered me."

"I have no shot left and you have four," was the reply. "You will have to fire them."

Calhoun hesitated a moment and then fired the four shots in the air.

"It was not my intention to reflect upon you in my comments before the legislative committee," said he.

Capt. Williamson then withdrew his words which had given such offense, and, a reconciliation effected, the parties returned to Atlanta.

As Savannahians were connected with the first duel ever fought on Georgia soil, so former Savannahians, in the persons of Jackson and Tompkins, played their part in this last duel between Georgians.

CHAPTER XX

THE LAST DUEL BETWEEN SAVANNAHIANS.

A HARMLESS MEETING BETWEEN YOUNG ATTORNEYS—HOW
SURVIVORS OF THE OLD SCHOOL OF THOUGHT RE-
GARD DUELLING THROUGH THE MELLOWED MEM-
ORIES OF A HALF CENTURY OR MORE—THE STIRRING
SPEECH OF THE PROGENITOR OF SAVANNAHIANS OF
TO-DAY THAT LEAD NORTH CAROLINA TO ANTI-DUEL-
LING LEGISLATION—THE STORY OF OLD SAVANNAH
INCOMPLETE WITHOUT THE CODE DUELLO.

ONE hundred and thirty-eight years after the first recorded duel in Georgia, two young Savannahians exchanged shots as the shades of night were falling and thereby satisfied the demands of honor as the code prescribes.
This was the last duel between Savannahians and occurred
in the summer of 1877, a few weeks after the Johnston-
Wetter affair.

The principals were two lawyers who were destined to
win and hold recognition for many years among leaders of
the bar. Their hostile meeting grew out of a law suit in
which, in later years, one admitted he had been unduly aggressive toward his brother barrister. Under the code, the
trouble should have been amicably adjusted, but the representative of the aggrieved attorney violated the spirit of
the code itself by a letter of an offensive tone, which precluded the withdrawal of the objectionable words that otherwise might have been forthcoming. The challenged party
was seconded by an attorney who early in life became and
is yet one of the prominent figures of Savannah life.

Brampton was the scene of this closing episode in Savannah's duelling history of nearly a century and a half.
It was late in the evening when the parties met. The delay
was due to the challenger and his friends losing their way in
trying to find the place agreed upon. After the first harmless exchange of shots the seconds drew apart to consider
the matter of an adjustment which would avoid the necessity of the principals firing at one another again.

Dusk was rapidly drawing on and the attending surgeon for the challenged party, was manifestly disturbed. Impatient over the delay, the physician impetuously remarked: "This must be settled, or we must have another shot promptly. It is getting dark and my man is nearsighted. It is not fair to him to further delay."

Whether this hastened the conclusion is not known, but the seconds speedily announced a settlement which proved agreeable to all concerned. The surgeons, whose instruments of steel were carelessly exposed to the glances of the principals, gathered the keen edged tools of their profession, closed their cases, and all returned to town, with cordial relations renewed between the principals, that were not broken in the forty-six years that passed before one of them a few months ago passed to the "great majority."

The principals and one second in this affair subsequently took high rank among the recognized leaders of the Savannah bar, honored by all. This last meeting under the code gave living illustrations, almost a half century later, of the fact that an unfortunately well aimed bullet might have deprived Savannah of a citizen of the highest type of character and usefulness.

In common with many others, the gentleman who accepted the challenge for this meeting has always insisted that the code in some ways had, at the time when it was resorted to, been a benefit to the South, that it had prevented much unseemly brawling, had discouraged private vengeance, given opportunity for reflection and the mediation of friends, and had lead to the peaceful adjustment of many difficulties which but for its regulations might have terminated in personal encounters on the public thoroughfares. In fact, he and the other older citizens of Savannah who passed through part of the era of duelling believe that the code acted as a check on the use of offensive remarks, prevented the dissemination and magnifying of scandal, and had been in that way an agent for positive good.

"The fatalities are recalled," remarked this Savannahian of the old school, "but it is not remembered that had it not been for the code the participants in many duels, in the first heat of anger, might, in all probability would, have resorted to weapons without the intervening endeavors of friends to pacify, nor is it credited to the code that where one man was slain many doubtless were saved by the interposition of its rules. The spirit of the times has changed and duelling has forever passed away, but one may well doubt whether the atmosphere of the present is as free from slanderous innuendoes, whether the honesty of men and the virtue of women are as free from the sullying tongues as they were when it could be invoked."

But as an offset to this mellowed aspect, and to give a fully rounded picture, I will reproduce an extract from the speech of the twenty-two year old Nash which bowled over the opposition to the anti-duelling law in the North Carolina legislature one hundred and twenty years ago and placed that state in the vanguard of those putting the stern ban of legal disapproval and condign punishment on the devotees of the custom. In a somewhat puritanical spirit, not characteristic of the South of that day or later, with all the fires of emotion awakened by the recent slaying of an honored citizen of his home county, he pictured duelling as "cherishing our evil passions and destructive of the happiness of others." Said he:

"Few and feeble are the arguments upon which the practice of duelling is defended, while, on the contrary, those against it are numerous and weighty. Nor is it a little remarkable that the former are drawn from the weaknesses and vices of human nature, while the latter have their foundation in its virtues.

"We are told that the lofty spirit which leads the duellist to the field is one essential to the well-being of society—placing the weak upon a level with the strong, and redressing injuries which lie beyond the reach of the law—that if you could succeed in entirely abolishing the practice, you would introduce in its place assassination.

"Is this true, Sir? Do, indeed, the courtesies of life depend on the base principle of fear? And is this lawless practice a potent agent to correct the morals of society? Is it, indeed, true, that we depend for any part of our comfort upon a practice condemned alike by the word of God and by the dictates of reason?

"No, Sir, the idea is not to be harbored. Duelling fosters those feelings and principles which are at war with our happiness here and hereafter. What is that 'lofty spirit' but the spirit of revenge and pride? That deadly and vindictive principle, smothering every gentle and benign feeling of the heart, bids the duellist wash away the fancied insult in the blood of the offender.

"Every virtuous feeling of the heart withers, every endearment is crushed and subdued. The desolating ruin the duellist is about to pour on others who have never injured him cannot arrest his progress—he presses forward to his object regardless of every tie, social and divine, and glories in his laurels, though steeped in blood and bedewed with the tears of the widow and fatherless."

And realizing that there, as in Georgia and other states, many of the combats originated in the stress of political differences and conflict of political ambitions, he pointed out that exclusion of duellists from public honors would be the strongest medium for the suppression of such meetings. His graphic portraiture is well worth preserving as presenting concisely the argument which lead many states to compel public officials to take a solemn oath that they had not been concerned in any duel after a certain date.

"Ours is a country in which from its happy Constitution the offices of government are open to the genius of every grade. Our young men of talent no sooner enter busy scenes of life than they perceive a glittering prize before them. Pressing forward, they encounter spirits equally ambitious, restless and sanguine. And it is by such that most of these duels are fought. Once convince them that this act of folly and madness consigns them to the shades of private life, and many a one who now laughs to scorn the denunciations of religion as the cloak of cowards, will pause and hesitate, and many a dispute that now is incapable of adjustment will be amicably settled."

Instances came after 1877 of personal difficulties with talk of challenges, almost precipitating duels, but none in which the parties actually resorted to the field to exchange shots. The inclination to condemn duelling grew stronger and stronger, and it is doubtful if at any time in the last thirty-five years there has been any real likelihood of two Savannahians resorting to the code.

When Governor Wilson wrote the introduction to his "Code of Honor: Its Rationale and Uses," he spoke in the most positive of words:

"So long as the gentleman is not eliminated from existence—until the advent of the millenium—the Code of Honor will be used."

No one will contend that the gentleman has been eliminated from Savannah, or that the millenium has come here any more than it has elsewhere—but the compiler of the code under which many men fought, and under which many men were saved from fighting, simply erred in his foresight and judgment. Copies of his "Code" are preserved in Savannah and elsewhere as relics of a bygone day. The rules and regulations so carefully prepared by him have long ceased to have value or interest save as they throw light on the obsolete custom of duelling in the South. Duelling seems almost as remote from the life of the present as the feudal age out of which it sprung. It was a last, long-lingering remnant of the customs of chivalry and found its grave in the new conditions of life that came after the South's war for separate nationality.

It is all academic now. But no picture of the Savannah of the past can be complete without including the code duello within its scope, and no study of its political and social life would be quite the truth that excluded it from its purview. And if history is but a pageant, as Birrell says, then the unrolling of its varied scenes reveals no local incidents of more dramatic interest than those in which Savannah's most virile men, feeling that "honor is not to be sported with," calmly met to exchange shots, with utter disdain of results:

"Set honor in one eye, and death in the other,
    And I will look on both indifferently:
    For, let the gods so speed me as I love
    The name of honor more than I fear death."

INDEX

G

Gadsden-Howe duel, 19.

Ganahl, Dr. Charles, duel with T. S. Daniell, 254.

Garrard, William U., attorney for duellists, 286.

Gaulden, Wm. B. trouble with Walter A. Way, 276-79.

Gentlemen, obligation of not altered by challenge, 220-21.

Georgia Gazette, references to, 9, 11, 59, 96, 132.

Georgia laws relating to duelling, 113, 188, 273-75.

Georgia Steamboat Company, monopoly of, 66.

Georgian, attacks of editor on Republican editor, 229, 232, 235; references to, 66, 67, 119, 160, 192, 194, 228, 238, 240.

Gibbons, Thomas, charged with corruption in congressional election, 41-42; methods alleged, 41; Jackson's attack on, 42; character of, 44; earning powers as a lawyer, 44; services as mayor and alderman, 44; takes oath allegiance to King George, 57; attainted by legislature, 57; petition for restoration to citizenship granted, 59; revolutionary patriots protest, 59; readmitted to full rights, 60; appeal to Gen. Lincoln to disprove slanders, 60; becomes interested in steamboat navigation, 61; associated with Aaron Ogden, 61; New Jersey Historian's view of character, 62; relations with Ogden severed, 62; Restrained by New York courts appeals to Federal courts, 63; famous case of Gibbons vs. Ogden, and Marshall's epochal opinion, 63-66; posts Ogden at latter's home, 68; challenge ignored and damage suit by Ogden, 68; Gibbons attack on Stockton, 70; hatred to son-in-law Trumbull, 71; paragraph from will, 71. (See corrections page vii.)

Gibson, Judge R. T., on Cohen-Aiken duel, 268.

Gilmer, Gen. J. F., as a conciliator, 283, 286.

Gonzales, Editor, on Tillman and duelling, 248; killing of, 248.

Gordon, Ambrose, removed from U. S. Marshalship, 105; presides at dinner of Chatham Troop, 108.

Gordon, William W., elected to legislature, 229; verse on, 230.

Gourdin, Robert N., as a conciliator, 283-86.

Grand jury presentments against duelling, 134, 135.

Grant, Peter, first Savannahian killed in duel, 1, 2.

Gresham, Capt., trouble with Maj. Johnson, 106-08.

Griffin, John A., duel with R. Wayne Russell, 213.

Gue, Frances L., trouble with E. L. Guerard, 218-19; sketch of, 219.

Guerard, trouble with James Kerr, 192.

Guerard, Edgar L., posts F. L. Gue, 219; sketch of, 220.

G. Guerard, trouble with Charles Rossignol, 198.

Gunn, James, in revolution, 73; origin of trouble with Gen. Greene, 73; two challenges to Greene declined, 74; threatens personal violence to Greene, 76; Greene's reply to, 76; character and record of, 78; connection with Yazoo land grants, 78; death and funeral, 79; attacks on memory of, 79-81; trouble with Capt. Welscher, 91-93.

Gwinnett, Burton, sketch of, 11; duel with McIntosh, 11-16; military aspirations of, 13; burial place, 23.

H

Habersham, Col., urges Madison administration to pause in war policies, 87.

Habersham, Richard W., toast to Georgia, 179; connection with Anti-duelling Association, 187.

Habersham, Robert, as a conciliator, 232.

Hall, Dr. Lyman, on Gwinnett-McIntosh duel, 15.

Jenkins, E. E., duel with E. M. Whaley, 211.

Jewish burial ground used for duelling, 112, 114, 117.

Johnson, Capt. R. P., kills James Wilde, 150-51; army career, vii.

Johnson, Dr. Samuel, dinner with Oglethorpe, 4; views on duelling, 5-7.

Johnson, Maj., Thomas De Maltos, appointed collector of port, 105; duel with Capt. Gresham, 106.

Johnston, James H., trouble with A. G. Wetter, 272-73.

Johnston, Dr. John M., as a second, 270.

Johnston, Gen. Joseph E., as a conciliator, 284-86.

Jones, A. Maybank, part in Hart-McConnell trouble, 223-27; challenges McConnell, 223; correspondence, 223-25.

Jones-Baker meeting near Midway, 16-18.

Jones, Dr. George, connection with Anti-duelling Association 183-86; sketch of, 186-87.

Jones, Henry Hart, in Jones-McConnell affair, 224.

Jones, Rev. J. L., 190.

Jones, Maj. John, sketch of 17-18.

Jones, John Paul, battle of Bon Homme Richard with Serapis, 25-27.

Jones, Seaborn, acts as friend for Waldburger, 56.

Jones, Seaborn, 194.

K

Kerr, James, trouble with Guerard, 192.

Kimbrough, O. S., kills Jacob E. Hendricks, 256.

King, Capt. Jack, as a second, 296.

King, William, trouble with Dr. Wayne, 234.

Kirk, Dr. killed by Lieut. Chaplin, 211.

Kirkland, Gen. W. W., as a conciliator, 281.

Know Nothing Party, 222.

Kollock, Rev. Dr. Henry, 69.

L

Lamar, G. B. Jr., as a conciliator, 281.

Landais, Capt. of Alliance, treachery of, 26, 27; challenges John Paul Jones, 30; wounds Capt. Cottineau in duel, 30; burial place of, 31.

Last duel between Savannahians, 298-99.

Lathrop, James W., duel with Davenport, 270-71.

Law, Judge William, connection with Anti-duelling Association, 185-89; disqualified at Minis trial, 195; grand jury on his selection as judge, 201; resents insult and challenges attorney, 202; speech in favor of secession, 203-04; resists test oath, 204-05.

Laws of Georgia, relative to duelling, 113, 188, 273-75.

Lawton, Gen. A. R., as a conciliator, 286.

Leake, Richard Henry, trouble with John Miller, 99, 100; disappearance of, 101.

Lee, Frank D., challenges Editor Hayes, 241.

Lee, Gen. "Light Horse" Harry, injured by Republican mob, 89.

Legislation against duelling in South, 131; New York refuses to act, 135.

Leman, Ensign, wounded in duel, 2.

Levy, Capt. S. Yates, 270; editorial experiences, 289; trouble with Dr. Waring, 289-91.

Lewis, Robert, as a second, 213.

Liberty County, troubles in, 222-27; "Roaring Lion" of, 276-79.

Mc

McAllister, Mathew Hall, connection with Anti-duelling Association, 187; sketch of, 189; elected to State Senate, 229; verse on, 230; Democratic candidate for Governor, 235; called "War Horse of Chatham," 236.

McConnell, James D., troubles with Dr. Hart and A. Maybank Jones, 222-27.

O

O'Driscoll, Dennis, killed by John Edwards, 154.

Ogden, Aaron, sketch of, 61, 62; association with Thomas Gibbons, in steamboat navigation, 62; famous litigation with Gibbons in Federal courts, 63-66; declines to challenge Gibbons and sues for damages, 68; secures verdict for $5,000, 68; thrown into prison for debt, 69; Congress acts in his behalf, 69.

Oglethorpe's views on duelling, 4-7; clash with Prince of Wirtemberg, 7.

Olmstead, Col. Charles H., as a conciliator, 282.

Owens, George S., as a conciliator, 291.

Owens, George W., elected to Congress, 229; verse on, 230.

Owens, George W. (2nd), trouble with R. R. Dancy, 281-86.

P

Patterson, William, kills John Barnard, 216.

Penalties for duelling never inflicted, 207, 294.

Pendleton, Nathaniel, in revolution, 124; Chief Justice of Georgia, 125; appointed United States Judge, 126; considered by Hamilton for Secretary of State, 126; second for Hamilton in duel with Burr, 127; political careers of his son and grandson, 129, 135.

Pettigru, James L., 195.

Philbrick, S., as a second, 191.

Physicians as mayors, 235.

Pickering, Timothy, toast to by Chatham troop, 108.

Pierson, Midshipman, kills Midshipman Cottineau, 33-35.

Pinckney, Midshipman Richard, duel with English naval officer, 177-78.

Pitman, Henry, appointed commander of Revenue cutter, 105.

Ploudon, William, advertised, 132.

Political banners, 236.

Political party headquarters and parades, 234.

Political parties in Georgia in early 19th century, 83; party passions, 108-09.

Pooler, Robert W., trouble with George Millen. 190-91.

Ponsonby, George, in Gresham-Johnson trouble, 106-08.

Posting at vendue house, 96, 97, 133, at postoffice, 219.

Powell, James, removed as Collector, 105; resolutions of business men thereon, 106.

Pratt, Charles M., troubles as editor American Patriot, 84-88.

Pritchard, W. R., trouble with Stoney, 197; in affair of McConnell, 226-27; in Sneed-Hamilton affair. 239.

Purse, Dr. B. S., as surgeon, 271, 272.

Putnam, Henry, trouble with Lieut. John Wood, 96.

Q

Quarterman, A. S., trouble with A. M. Jones, 225-26.

Quoit or Coit, club, 192.

R

Randolph, John, duel with Henry Clay, 172-76.

Read, Dr. J. B., 185.

Recall amendment to national constitution suggested by Georgia legislature, 84.

Republican, difficulties of editor with Georgian editor, 229, 232, 235.

Republican mob violence to Federalist editors, 84-89.

Republicans secure control of city council, 115, 119; appeal to, 119.

Rhett, Edward, Jr., in Magrath. Taber affair, 244-46.

Rhett, U. S. Senator Barnwell, on duelling, 246.

Richards, R. R., as a second, 272.

Robertson, Capt. James, acts for Jacob Walburger, 54.

Roberts, Dwight, in Cohen-Aiken duel, 263.